THE PURSUIT OF SPORTING EXCELLENCE

A STUDY OF SPORT'S HIGHEST ACHIEVERS

THE PURSUIT OF SPORTING EXCELLENCE

A STUDY OF SPORT'S HIGHEST ACHIEVERS

DAVID HEMERY

WILLOW BOOKS
Collins
8 Grafton Street, London W1
1986

Willow Books
William Collins Sons & Co. Ltd
London · Glasgow · Sydney · Auckland
Toronto · Johannesburg

First published 1986

British Library Cataloguing In Publication Data
Hemery, David
The pursuit of sporting excellence.
1. sports
I. Title
796 GV697.A1

ISBN 0 00 218145 2

Set in Monophoto Times by Vision Typesetting, Manchester
Printed and bound in Great Britain by William Collins Sons & Co. Ltd, Glasgow

Contents

INTRODUCTION

Eight athletes are being held in a caged area, waiting to be led into the arena for their Olympic final. Physically there is little to choose between them. They are strong, lean, supple and gifted. All have spent years getting to this point. The problem facing their bodies and minds is that only one can be crowned the winner.

The scene may change and the level of media attention will differ, but almost everyone who has been involved in competitive sport will be able to identify with the feelings of these finalists. Regardless of the levels of personal achievement, the sensations will be similar: anticipation and excitement mount, apprehension increases. What will my opponents do? Will I be able to perform up to my own and others' expectations?

What did these achieving athletes do to hold together so well under immense competitive stress? Was it something in their background or personality? Was it something they thought or did? Did it come naturally or can it be learned?

The question is, what makes a winner? This study has addressed the question by interviewing some of sport's highest achievers. The criteria for the interviewees was that they had to have been consistent winners and to have proven themselves under the most intense competitive pressure. All are, or have been, world or Olympic champions, or the winners of tournaments, or end-of-season championships; they are from a dozen different countries, and from twenty-two different sports.

Almost everyone will have experienced the exhilaration of success. That sweet feeling of effortlessness when the ball strikes the centre of the bat, the racket or the club; or perhaps it is a perfectly thrown ball or a kick or shot which landed exactly where it was intended. We know the feeling when it happens but it would be so much nicer if that could happen more often. We watch, often in awe, but certainly with respect and pleasure, those who consistently produce winning performances. Many achievers have wondered themselves as to what has made their achievement so consistently successful.

It would be easy to say, 'Oh, they're just naturals, they were born with the genetic gifts to do it'. However, that is not the whole story: it cannot be. If you attend Wimbledon and watch the players on the practice courts, almost any of them strike the ball equally well; physically there is little to choose between them. Billie Jean King provides a good illustration. She is remembered for having won more than her share of Wimbledon singles and doubles titles. She was neither the most powerful, nor the fastest, nor the best server, but she won consistently. What was it that enabled her, and others like her, to handle that challenge and to keep control while under pressure? What makes a winner? What does human achievement entail?

These were questions which I wrestled with in October 1968 after I had won a gold medal and set a new world record. I wondered what the contributing factors were that put me on the winner's rostrum. These questions were more acute because I was still painfully aware of having been the smallest in my school year at fourteen years old. In retrospect, I felt that physically, there had to be many others with more natural talent. It made me wonder, if there was a desire to succeed and a commitment to working towards a goal, could any individual become a high achiever? That does not mean that everyone has been born with the physical characteristics to become an Olympic winner, but along the lines of the parable of the talents, each of us has talent in some area. If there were common factors among sport's highest achievers, were they things which could be applied by anyone who aspired to fulfil their talent? Were there also aspects that could be gleaned from parents, coaches or others, who assisted or inspired the development of this talent? Almost everyone who has worked with youngsters knows that the possession of talent does not necessarily make that individual a high achiever.

I decided to try to find out more by interviewing those who were recognizably the best in their sport. I limited my interviewees to sport for three main reasons. Firstly, I felt that because of my experiences in sport, my questions would be better related to sports people. Secondly, the definition of ultimate and consistent sporting achievement could be quite clearly defined. It was not a question of making too many value judgements. Thirdly, if the field had been broadened to include the arts or business, the complexity and enormity of the task would have been beyond the time and finances of a single individual. Nevertheless, although the interviews are limited to sport, it is my belief – and one that is backed up by recent research – that many aspects of the route to achievement are true for all fields of human endeavour.

One common experience in competition is pressure. Many people can produce a great solo effort in practice, only to have the percentage slip rather disastrously under the pressure of competition; or they have one great performance and can never quite recapture it. This is referred to as either 'choking', the 'yips' or 'losing one's bottle'. The importance of the coming event works in the competitor's mind and tension mounts. One wants to avoid the embarrassment of letting oneself and other people down. This intense desire to succeed leads too often to the athlete trying so hard that the natural flow and ease evaporates into a struggling effort. The muscles become tight and the performance falls short. However, the best sports people do not seem to crack under stress; often, they actually perform better!

What makes an individual behave in a certain way is an extremely complex issue. We are born with a genetic blueprint but we are also a product of our environment and of our past experiences. Added to this, we also have the power of self-determination, which means that we are a product of our thoughts, hopes, dreams and visions of the future. Under the belief that human beings are a combination of body, mind and spirit, the questionnaire which was developed touched on aspects of the achiever's physical, social, mental and moral development and behaviour. Questions were asked in any area which *might* have affected their sporting progression and performance. At the time that this study started, I was coaching and studying for my final degree at Boston University. This environment gave me access to some helpful individuals. The questions were compiled through discussions with several athletes, coaches and my own academic advisors, John Cheffers and Len Zaichkowsky. They all reflected on what they thought might be factors which could influence the athletes' development and final performance. They also interviewed me in order to see what sort of questions elicited the responses I would be seeking from the athletes whom I hoped to interview. These discussions and interviews, together with extensive personal reflection, produced about two hundred questions; that number had to be drastically reduced. Andy Ronay, a friend and colleague who had reached an international level in track athletics, kindly acted as a foil for an initial interview, to help sort out any overlapping questions. The total was brought down to under one hundred questions. Following the first couple of serious interviews, the total was again readjusted and fixed at eighty-eight questions. These can be found in Appendix III at the back of the book. Where the exact wording of the question is considered relevant, this is given in full in the main body of the text.

Considering the length of interview time, and the busy lives led by most of the high achievers interviewed, the athletes were exceptionally generous and cooperative. I am most grateful and indebted to each of them for their time and the openness of their answers. For many, their diaries are extremely full, and often appointments had to be made months in advance. For example, Jackie Stewart has his life booked up six months ahead of time. He fitted me in around a couple of commitments during a flying visit to London: part of the interview took place in a car en route to his next appointment. Wayne Gretzky receives hundreds of fan letters and requests every day: his press interviews are usually ten-minute slots. It was helpful that my career was known to his Edmonton press liaison man, who arranged an interview for me and had us photographed during our session.

I met Torvill and Dean while they were performing in Australia and we set a time and date for when they were back in Great Britain. O.J. Simpson was off to cover the Superbowl when I met him. He suggested that I return a couple of days later and to see both himself and Arnold Palmer during the making of their Hertz commercial at Los Angeles International Airport. I had three weeks on a cheap rate, unlimited US travel ticket, and so I flew back across America that night for the appointments with Rod Laver in Philadelphia, Pete Rose in Cincinnatti, and on the same day, Billie Jean King in New York – prior to the return trip to Los Angeles! Billie Jean's agent had forgotten to let her know about our appointment. She arrived for a practice session at her club and to her great credit, cancelled a dinner engagement so as to honour the commitment which had been made to me.

Almost all of these athletes have agents or managers who act as buffers and go-betweens. Prior to the US tour, I had written to them but received no responses, so on landing in America, I found myself living on the telephone. I reviewed briefly what I had written, and explained to them my background and the idea behind the project, saying that I was prepared to meet their athlete at any time and anywhere. I could buy them a meal and give them a copy of the book on completion but that was the limit of my budget. Over 85 per cent agreed to be interviewed, many not even taking up the invitation to a meal!

The minimum time taken for interview was with Herb Elliott and Steve Ovett, both around fifty minutes. Jonah Barrington and Gareth Edwards topped the time chart at around four hours each. It had been my intention to interview each athlete's coach as well as their parents. Early on, I covered Carl Lewis's, Steve Cram's and my own coach and parents; Mary Twomey's coach and mother; and Lynn Davies's and Steve Ovett's coaches. However, when interviewing Al Oerter on Long Island, New York, I asked whether it would be possible to interview his coach and father. 'Sure,' he said, 'my coach is living in Kansas and my Dad's in Florida.' Time and cost loomed to make an already daunting task quite impracticable.

I would like to have included many more sports as well as a wider cross-cultural spectrum. The Australian visit was made possible by fortunate timing and generous assistance. Dr John Cheffers, my doctoral advisor at Boston University, had become the director of the Australian Institute of

Sport. Jean Roberts, who had beeen coaching at the University of New Hampshire, had also returned to Australia as national director of track and field coaching. Both of them combined to assist greatly my interview tour. In exchange, I sang for my supper, giving sprint and hurdle clinics in cities across the country, culminating in a week at the magnificent Institute of Sport in Canberra. My cousin Bob Hemery was the Australian team manager for the Olympics. He assisted me in contacting some athletes in his area around Perth, including driving me 200-miles south into the bush to interview Shane Innes.

Eleven requests for interview were turned down. US golfer Jack Nicklaus and Australian fast bowler Dennis Lillee were both involved in biographies and declined because participation might detract from sales of their own books. The agent who had agreed a date with me to interview the boxer Marvin Hagler was no longer in his employ. Marvin was a few weeks away from his fight with Thomas Hearns and had become saturated and fed up with media attention. Australian cricketer Sir Donald Bradman has been a recluse for many years and made no exception for my project. US basketball players Dr Julius Erving and Larry Bird were heading towards their play-offs and, after several days' deliberation, turned down interviews. Canadian ice hockey man Bobby Orr was too busy with business commitments and Swedish tennis star Bjorn Borg was going through a separation from his wife. John McEnroe's father refused on John's behalf, saying that John never gets involved with such interviews.

Just getting to the individuals was sometimes a major task. I arranged a trip to the Soviet Union to interview Valeriy Borzov and his wife Ludmila Tourischeva. Having confirmed the appointment, only on arrival was I informed that Ludmila was away! My flight was delayed and I discovered that telephone communication in the USSR was even more difficult than it was from outside, and you have to book well in advance. I had no home number for Valeriy, so began asking Intourist for alternative flight options or for the number of Aeroflot airlines. Each time I was greeted with the same response, 'It is not possible'. The interview with Valeriy finally took place in Kiev, between 10 p.m. and midnight. He was very helpful and cooperative.

As I left each interview, I wondered, 'How am I ever going to do justice to all that these athletes have contributed?' Their sporting records are often staggering and they were prepared to join in the search for the keys to their successes. They shared their experiences and gave an insight into their pursuit of sporting excellence.

PART 1

PHYSICAL FACTORS

CHAPTER 1

SPECIALIZATION

'Line up please! Okay, let's see what time you all take to get once around this field. Set! Go!' The natural movement of some of the runners will be apparent to anyone who has an eye for rhythm and flow; the variety of styles and forms has to be seen to be believed. Some are simply better suited to running faster than others. It does not mean that they are any better people, but their physiological blueprint enables them to start out with a physical advantage in that particular movement. All the people in this book started out with a blueprint which enabled them to compete in their sport at top level. But there was considerable difference of opinion as to how much their natural physique made them winners. Double Olympic sprint champion Valeriy Borzov said that his innate speed was the biggest single factor in his success, whereas baseball star Pete Rose said that the only physical advantage he had was that he was not born with a handicapped body.

The age old question as to which is more important, nature or nurture, will not be answered fully here but there is evidence to support both points of view. One cannot underestimate the substantial abilities born into these very high achievers. However, it is apparent that a great deal more than physical gifts goes into the making of a champion. The title of Part I is therefore slightly misleading. No physiological tests were carried out on these top sports stars. There is little point in finding the maximum oxygen uptake capacity of a yachtsman or snooker player, or to discover the hand–eye coordination of a marathon runner. All that can be said is that they all met the normal physical requirements for performing their sport well.

At what age did you start any type of competitive sport? Most athletes started competitive sports while at school; generally this was between the ages of six and thirteen with the average starting age being at around nine. The ages at which the athletes 'specialized' are given in their respective biographies. Taking out Barry John and J.P.R. Williams of rugby union, Bob Tisdall, Olympic 400m hurdle champion, and Ian Botham, the all-round cricketer, who have never, in their opinion, specialized in one sport or at least not for more than a few months in any one year, the average age is still over sixteen. Most of those interviewed were very happy that they had not specialized until quite late on in their sporting life. They had fun in a variety of sports and had only started to make a push when they decided that they wanted to exclude the other options in order to see just how far they could go in their chosen speciality.

Certain sports had a definite bias towards a younger starting age. Duncan Goodhew led the swimmers in at seven years old, Chris Evert Lloyd the tennis players at nine years old. (Gymnasts would also fall into this early specialization category.) The majority of achievers seem to have delayed their decision until the end of school days; for some this meant they were fifteen or sixteen years old, and for others seventeen or eighteen. Those pressing the top end were squash champion Jonah Barrington and racing driver Jackie Stewart,both not starting until they were twenty-three, although it should be pointed out that Jackie won international recognition in shooting before getting behind the wheel of a car. At the extreme end is John Gilmour who started his long and still continuing track athletics career after the Second World War at the age of twenty-six, and at the same age Pat O'Callaghan who decided to specialize after he had won his second Olympic hammer title in 1932. His aim was the 1936 Games but unfortunately Ireland did not compete!

Were you always good at sport? It seems that several of these athletes were, or could have been, highly successful in other areas of sport. The rugby men Gareth Edwards and Barry John were offered trials with good football clubs, and J.P.R. Williams won junior Wimbledon when he was nineteen. With almost no exception, these achievers played a variety of sports. Olympic track athlete Peter Snell recalled that at school, he played in the top rugby and cricket teams. 'I was tennis champion. I was a 12-handicap at golf. I had a good background at field hockey, and played badminton and table tennis. I did gymnastics and, when running schools steeplechase, I usually won.' Peter, like American football Hall of Fame member O.J. Simpson, was a winner in International Superstars. 'O.J.' was also on a world record sprint relay team while at the University of Southern California and John Havlicek, basketball star with the Boston Celtics, was, during his high school days, an All-State football, basketball and baseball player. Marathon runner Joan Benoit Samuelson was a state skier, and ice hockey scoring star Wayne Gretzky was the Ontario schools champion at eleven years old in 800m, 1500m and cross-country. Heather McKay, multiple world squash champion, started out as the local tennis champion and a member of the local softball team, and was twice named to the All-Australian hockey team; and she became world racketball champion following her exceptional squash career.

Obviously these are extreme examples. However, most of those in the study were above average in all the sports in which they participated. Many who are now at the top in individual sports enjoyed team sport at a reasonably high level. Track athletes Carl Lewis, Lynn Davies, Daley Thompson, Seb Coe, Steve Cram and Steve Ovett were all good at soccer. The list could be very much more extensive, pointing out the variety of sports in which everyone has competed, but the main point of interest is that there was opportunity for a diversity of sports. One hopes that the recent trend in government thinking in Great Britain and the United States to allow sport and physical education to receive less funding will not result in a loss of opportunity for the young; not just for sport's sake, but for reasons of personal growth and as an educational tool.

A definite pattern emerged in the development phase of sport in the lives of these high achievers. The first step was that they were introduced to sport as fun and that it was enjoyed for its own sake. Often the games were created to suit the environment. For example, Gareth Edwards talked of using a local lane for his own England v West Indies cricket match, where the placement of the ball over walls and past certain trees had special scoring significance. Lynn Davies and his friends had challenges as to who could jump the stream furthest down the valley where it gradually became wider. The games usually had a competitive element whether they were soccer, basketball or whatever, but they were informal teams and the children enjoyed themselves so much that they would stay out until darkness forced them home.

The second step in their development was the introduction of fundamental skills. Quite often these fundamentals were introduced by their father or a school teacher, but it was done in a clear-cut manner without pressure. The basics of good sound technique were invaluable because, under pressure, people tend to revert to what is their own natural, fundamental way of doing things.

The third and final step was the introduction of 'pushing'. More will be said about this later, but in almost all cases, the push did not come from the parents; it came from within the individual and in several cases it was assisted by a coach *after the individual* had made the commitment.

CHAPTER 2

TRAINING

In many cases, the time spent in training did not alter significantly from the start of specialization right up to top level. The rugby players rarely practised more than three times per week from club to international level unless they were on tour. Olympic swimmer Shane Innes was training seriously from the age of thirteen with nine or ten sessions per week. The aspect which changed with most athletes over the years was the level of intensity. There was a gradual recognition of the requirements to make it to the top. It was like stepping stones with the athlete taking the first step, and doing what was needed to reach the next one.

The total time commitment varied considerably in each sport. For a distance runner, an hour at either end of the day may well mean covering over twenty miles, and if more miles are then thrown in, the body simply will not recover in time to do the same distance on the following day. It seems astonishing, but often the time commitment did not change whether the individual was working, studying or playing sport full-time. Obviously there were extensive hardships endured by those such as the swimmers, who had to get up in the middle of the night to start swimming in order to get the required practice hours in before school or work. In the case of ice dance champions Torvill and Dean, it was the restriction of the available time on ice in Great Britain which inhibited the hours put in. They were limited to a maximum of six hours per week and those were either after 11 p.m. or before 6 a.m.! On these limited hours, the duo reached fourth in the world and came fifth at the Olympics. They were subsequently granted the opportunity to train overseas which enabled them to spend six hours on the ice every day – perfect scores of 6.0, gold medals and a new standard of excellence were the ultimate result.

Another athlete whose training commitment was changed dramatically through sponsorship was world pursuit cycling champion Steele Bishop. Between the ages of fifteen and nineteen, he trained for thirty to forty-five minutes every day of the week. On the same seven-day schedule, he increased his workouts to more than six hours. The days went as follows: 'Two hours on the road in the morning just taking it easy, rolling along at 20 m.p.h., which is training pace, then on to the track at the velodrome for starts and sprints – two hours solid and really hard work. Ride back to the hotel, twenty minutes and shower; a bite to eat for lunch and put my feet up for twenty minutes if I was lucky. Then two more hours on the track behind a motorbike, followed by a full body massage. That was the daily routine.' A similar devotion can be seen from Daley Thompson in his decathlon training, and Jonah Barrington in his squash practice.

How often do you give 100 per cent in training? Jonah's response to this was that he gave it too often. 'Training was pretty haphazard. I didn't know about half-effort and three-quarters effort. I was putting in too many long sessions back-to-back. I called them total reduction sessions. I would start again far too close to eating, and feel ill and get a cold sweat which would disappear after forty-five minutes. I would crawl through day after day and was terribly lucky not to have more injury. So little knowledge was available. Nobody stretched or warmed up before they played.'

More than half of those interviewed felt that they gave 100 per cent every time they went out. Sometimes the effort was in terms of mental concentration, more often it meant that at some point, if not in the whole session, they were giving their all both physically and mentally. Heather McKay said that she would rather do one hour at 100 per cent and be finished than stay on court for an hour and a half and give only 75 per cent. The old adage 'as you train so will you compete' seems to be borne out here. Additionally, the volume of training always exceeded the competition time. After very intense training, Heather often said if she ever felt like that in a match, she would give up the sport. But once in the match, she would say to herself, 'Come on, if you are tired, the other person has to be just as tired and that is when I would push and that extra little bit of training would pay off.'

The notion that it takes hard work to improve one's standard was accepted by all athletes. Rugby league's Peter Sterling said, 'The only thing that makes you successful is hard work as there are always going to be others with similar ability. The only thing that is going to make you more successful is the amount of work you put in.' Twice Grand Slam winner Rod Laver believed that the reason he was able to go successfully through any five-set tennis match was the intensity of his practice. He would go full out for three to four hours on court, enjoying the effort, and not just playing sets but rallying two-against-one. Another reason for giving 100 per cent to their sport came from Gene Upshaw in American football, Ian Botham and Clive Lloyd in cricket, and Billy Beaumont in rugby union. Each felt that their role as captain demanded setting an example. Clive had turned around the thinking in the West Indies team and with it came a new determination to succeed. 'In the old days, when under pressure, we were seen to be unable to fight our way out of it. I saw that if you were physically fit, it helped you to think straighter. It meant that your mind and body were alert and that to me was the most important thing in being a top class sportman.'

It is interesting to find that some of today's top runners do not train to 100 per cent. Sprint-king and long jumper Carl Lewis said that he would give 100 per cent on starts and jumping but not running. Middle-distance star Seb Coe would give it his all in conditioning sessions, but again, not in running. The same was echoed by world 1500m champion Steve Cram. Steve Ovett, 800m Olympic champion, world marathon champion Rob de Castella and Ed Moses, Olympic 400m hurdles champion, said that they hardly ever gave 100 per cent in their training sessions. Peter Snell, another Olympic middle-distance winner, pointed out that it was not always appropriate: with multiple repetitions and steady long hard runs, the work load could be enormous and it was important not to get to a state of complete depletion with the resulting risk of injury or sickness.

There were several exceptions to this track rule. Herb Elliott, unbeaten over a mile, pushed himself to the limit on four to six days each week. Joan Benoit Samuelson pushes herself to the limit on one of her two daily sessions. Long jumper Lynn Davies, sprinter/hurdler Shirley de la Hunty and 800m champion Ralph Doubell were part of the majority who replied 'most of the time'. Obviously, those who did not push themselves to 100 per cent in training did not see this factor as being necessary. Steve Ovett's view was that consistency was better than quality. On a long run, feeling a bit tired, there would be the option to stay on the flat or go up a hill. He would go up the hill, 'and it would hurt but it wouldn't be 100 per cent flat out. You have to endure a bit of pain in training for our sport. It's not the name of the game, but to a certain extent it's an acceptance of pain. It doesn't have to be severe, it can be gradual.' This is not masochism where one is seeking pain, rather it is an understanding that it is productive pain. The body is being positively modified in its strength and efficiency.

Intensity

How much do you think that your training intensity made a difference to your level of success? The words differed but the answer was virtually unanimous. 'All the difference'; 'totally'; 'enormously'; 'terribly'; 'vital'; 'tremendously important'; 'it was the root of everything'. Lynn Davies pointed out that the mind has a significant part in setting sights and tolerating the level of training and stress. He recalled the story of the woman who lifted the side of a car when her child was trapped underneath. Many of our limits are self-imposed.

Duncan Goodhew believed that an athlete was only as good as his worst day. Two to three days each week he would not be feeling up to par and those were the days that he would push himself. 'I found that 95 per cent of the time it was psychological. I would get in and forty-five minutes or an hour later, I was knocking out amazing times. I was doing broken competition distance, with five seconds' rest every 50m. I would come in with uncontrollable shakes and still maintain the times on each 50m. My body was actually shuddering with the strain and I used to take it to that point two to three times each week.'

Heather McKay summed up the overall view by pointing out that to succeed, anyone would have to go out and make the commitment whether it was in sport, work, school or marriage. If you only give 40 per cent, then you cannot expect a 100 per cent return.

I talked to the athletes about the type of sessions which would take them to their hands and knees, and their level of acceptable pain tolerance. Billy Beaumont's immediate response was, 'Ah! Hanging over the rail! I think you have to do that.'

Herb Elliott explained, 'In retrospect my training wasn't to improve my physical strength or stamina; those came along as a secondary result, but the primary purpose of every training session was to toughen up mentally. A training session was totally useless until it started to hurt. That was the point when it started to be worthwhile.'

This reminded me of a line from *The Thornbirds*: 'The best is only bought at the cost of great pain.' While training, Steele Bishop's thought was, 'If I don't suffer I'm not going to win'. Ralph Doubell did not like the term pain. He saw it more as a willingness to push oneself and that was both a mental and a physical exercise. He referred to the classic comment of the Oxford University coach who spoke to an athlete who was sweating while running round the track, 'Don't worry, it's only pain'. It reminded him of his coach Franz Stampfl. Half-way through a session, Ralph would say, 'My legs are killing me', and Franz would reply, 'Well that's fine as long as your chest is okay'. He would try the next time and say, 'My chest's caving in'. Franz would reply, 'How are the legs, fine?' This was strongly reminiscent of a session I had with my coach Billy Smith. My legs were painfully tired and I told Billy that they hurt. Billy put his hand on his own leg and said, 'I can't feel a thing, let's get on with the next repetition'.

Gareth Edwards pointed out that in a physical game like rugby, a player may be carrying an injury or may have been hit and be dazed, feeling physically and emotionally drained. This is the time when you have to be emotionally stronger-willed, to maintain and hang on when it's hurting. One key is not to be afraid of pain. O.J. Simpson would get hit during a game and say, 'That's going to hurt tonight', then it was dismissed from his mind. Also from American football, Gene Upshaw said, 'If you don't push yourself that way, you're never ever going to move higher than you are.' Ian Botham believes that one can or cannot deal with pain, but being able to cope with it distinguishes the *top* sportsman from the *good* sportsman.

In many cases, it was the blood, sweat and tears given by these top athletes which made them individual record breakers; they chose to make such efforts and it was done once they had reached maturity. Peter Snell reckoned that a top athlete could only push hard at the international level for about six years. It would be a waste if a youngster was encouraged to push like this and left sport with a feeling of distaste rather than a sense of accomplishment.

In spite of the need for intensity, it must be remembered that these athletes are still enjoying what they are doing. It is their choice to push themselves. A memorable illustration of this came from four-time Olympic discus winner Al Oerter who sees training as an integral part of enjoying his life. 'I make sure that I work out every day. Anything else good that happens, that's gravy.'

Duration

The question of the natural process of the ageing of the body was raised by soccer captain Bryan Robson. He said that he had always had the will to train hard and was a glutton for punishment. He had never been one to pack it in when it started to hurt. Most of these athletes were prepared to stick it out and, in a sense, discover that the discomfort was not quite as bad as they had first feared or thought, or at least that it was quite possible to learn how to cope with it. Bryan went on to relate that at the end of a practice session when they were quite tired, they sometimes had a timed run, twice around the field. He would try to see if he could beat the times he had done when younger. When others pointed out that as you get older the legs go, Bryan enjoyed proving that with age one can improve strength and endurance.

One of the classic examples of durability is Al Oerter who was challenging for another Olympic discus place in 1984, having won the first of his four successive Olympic titles in 1956. At fifty years old, Reg Harris came out of retirement and won yet another world sprint cycle title. Pete Rose is still playing successfully in major league baseball at forty-three. Billie Jean King said that she was still not sure whether it was because women's tennis standards were not that high, allowing her to be ranked sixth at thirty-seven, or whether she should reassess the fact that one still can play well longer than was thought possible a few years ago. It is probably the latter. The peak of our physical achievements seems to be related quite substantially to environmental and social factors, such as getting a job and starting a family. With greater sponsorship of amateur and professional sportsmen and sportswomen, it will be interesting to see whether the average age increases. Certainly in track and field athletics, the world records established by Jamila Kratochvilova in 400m and 800m at thirty-one, and the marathon world best by Carlos Lopes at thirty-eight, suggest that the college and university representatives of the last generation were several years short of their ultimate best performances. It underlines the need to allow youngsters to enjoy a variety of sports for as long as possible, having the fundamentals of several sports given them when young with continuing opportunities to play and compete after school days.

CHAPTER 3

FITNESS AND DIET

Another area which has changed considerably during the last decade is the awareness that what you eat can seriously affect performance. Six of those interviewed were now on the 'Pridican' diet – a high carbohydrate diet with no red meat.

Quite surprisingly, most said that they never gave their diet much thought, it was just 'Mum's home cooking'. When asked if they thought it was a balanced diet, they said yes. In most cases it included meat and/or fish and/or poultry, green vegetables and potatoes, and fruit. Several of the track athletes claimed to be junk food addicts. Daley Thompson said that he gave up so much in so many other areas that he could not face giving up his McDonald's diet, which he really enjoys. Similarly, Steve Cram is addicted to fish and chips.

Ed Moses believes that we all eat far too much food and, on several occasions, has continued training hard while fasting. Although it is a sad extreme, John Gilmour virtually lost his eyesight as a result of malnutrition while a POW for three and a half years with the Japanese during World War Two. His diet was rice, occasionally seaweed as a vegetable, pickled horseradish and sometimes the tops of sweet potatoes boiled into a type of soup. Surviving on this diet, with a very heavy manual workload, made him aware of the infinite powers of the body when there is a will to live and a will to win. That learning has, in no small way, contributed to his phenomenal succession of world records and wins in veteran track athletics.

Many laymen have been made aware of the difficulty the body has in digesting meat, and that for endurance events which last for a couple of hours, pasta and other high carbohydrate foods are the best answer. Rob de Castella said that he had moved away from the commercial interest areas of high fat, high sugar, high salt, and low fibre, and was back on fresh fruit, fresh vegetables and no red meat. This is the enlightened view but it was surprising just how many referred to the fact that as training increased, so did their apparent need for chocolate or similar sugary items. Obviously there is a need for a fast-burning energy source and the quick fix of chocolate or sugary items was a popular remedy. However, the problem with this solution is that it produces a roller-coaster effect as the blood sugar level rises quickly then drops, with the result that there is once more a craving for another sugar fix! Carbohydrates break down more slowly in the body, providing a constant natural source of glycogen which the body needs for energy.

Twenty-five years ago, Herb Elliott was in the media's spotlight for living on nuts and raisins. In fact, he was on a balanced diet but breakfast was a mixture of nuts, raisins and rolled oats, which today is commonly known as muesli!

Not many athletes were taking multi-vitamins pills, but one person who did say he occasionally took them was Lester Piggott. As a large-framed jockey, he had to limit himself to one main meal a day. He did not go very long without food but never ate much. When I asked him whether his sport had forced him to lead an imbalanced life, he replied, 'Well, it has really, yes. The biggest thing is not eating; I've had to be careful for so long.' I did some mental arithmetic and realized for just how long: Lester has not allowed himself to eat a proper meal for thirty-four years. I think he may enjoy his life as a trainer!

Reaction to injury

How did these top performers 'read' their bodies? Five per cent had given it no thought. Billy Beaumont said, 'I'm not bothered, I just get stuck in.' Basketball's Bob Cousy had the same reaction, 'I never thought about it, I was so healthy.' Another 5 per cent felt that their assessment was better further on in their careers. Downhill skier Ken Read, 'I overdid it when I was young.' Tennis star Margaret Court, 'Better years later.' And Seb Coe, 'I do now.' A further 8 per cent did not feel that they were very good at assessing themselves. Duncan Goodhew found it difficult, as did fellow swimmer Mike Wenden, while J.P.R. Williams added, 'I competed too often. The day after an international I'd be out playing flat out in a fun game, in a different position, but that's just me.'

The other 82 per cent said that they could read their bodies very well. Steve Ovett said, 'I didn't in L.A. [during the 1984 Olympics], but normally I do perfectly. It's part of the tools of the trade, of being honest with yourself and respecting your body.' Snooker champion Steve Davis referred to his high degree of sensitivity. 'I do a lot of practice on my own and I can detect a fault in myself quicker that way . I'm one of the few players who can detect a fault without having anyone to tell them.' Soccer legend Bobby Charlton commented, 'If I ate too much pre-match or if I hadn't slept well on the night before or maybe gone to bed an hour later than I should have done, I could sense it.'

Tennis player John Newcombe gave an illustration of body awareness during a Wimbledon final against Stan Smith in 1971. 'I won the first set and it was four all in the second, when I dived for a ball at the net, landed on my gut and blew the wind right out of myself. We went on to five all, then he beat me 7–5. At 4–2 to him in the third, I suddenly realized that my energy level was very low. My first thought was panic. Then I realized that after the fall, I hadn't spent any time recovering, so I thought to myself, "I've got about ten minutes before I've lost this set so I've got about ten minutes to get myself back again." So I just spent ten minutes trying to get inside myself, taking deep breaths and relaxing and summoning the adrenalin to go again. I lost the third set 6–2. I didn't lose a point on my serve in the fourth until I was serving for the set.' John went on to win in the fifth and final set. He said, 'It's funny hearing the other guy's story. Stan thought at two sets to one, he lost concentration because he started thinking of his victory speech, while on my side of the net I'd recharged my batteries and came out in the fourth changed up a gear and had another gear ready for the fifth set when we got into it.' Many a champion knows that a game is never lost until the last point is decided, the last ball bowled or pitched, or the final whistle blown.

Being in tune with one's body is vital to remaining healthy. One of the most difficult aspects to judge for both the athlete and the coach is when a stress-induced injury starts hurting. It is very difficult to distinguish the normal aches and pains associated with improving the condition of your body from the pain which might be signalling potential damage to the body's structure. Often it seems that the right thing to do is to press ahead and the discomfort disappears during the training session. However, Mary Decker Slaney is an example of an athlete who was not correctly diagnosed and the result was years of pain. She was continually told that she had shin splints, but in later years a bone scan showed that she had had a series of stress fractures. Most paediatricians are now strongly advocating that children are not introduced to either heavy weightlifting or long-distance running until they are fully mature and the bones have stopped growing.

Another aspect of reading one's body involves a sense of its position in space. Certainly some people have a more advanced sense than others. Gareth Edwards, for example, could simply see someone doing back somersaults and, with little practice, could duplicate the action. As a personal illustration, I found myself completely disorientated while attempting to tumble-turn in a pool yet when hurdling, there were times that I was so aware of my movements, I felt as though I was outside of myself and able to see the action and simultaneously correct any slight imbalance. Jayne Torvill and Christopher Dean have increased their body awareness through ballet classes and by skating in an area surrounded by mirrors. The visual picture enabled them to define a mood in bodily art form. Billie Jean King took this one stage further than physical awareness; she felt that self-awareness was probably the most important thing in fulfilling yourself because then you can set proper goals. 'Champions have an unbelievable level of self-awareness. The talent is conception. Some are born with talent and either don't do anything with it or don't even recognize it, but those who develop their potential, they are really talented.'

An interesting reflection on being ill came from swimmer John Konrads. 'Our coach was pretty brutal. There were no excuses. You just weren't allowed to get sick or feel off and maybe as a consequence we weren't crook all that much.'

A concise response on injury came from Joan Benoit Samuelson. She said that injuries were frustrating but when she recovered from them, she felt stronger and hungrier than ever for success. As I shared an office with Joan while coaching at Boston University I know a little more of the awesome determination and courage which she exemplifies. Those who follow track athletics will know that only seventeen days before the US Olympic marathon trials, Joan underwent surgery on her knee. The next day she was swimming and 'pedalling' the exercise bike with her arms! She progressed to pedalling the bike and twelve days before the qualifying race, started easy running. She won that trial and Athletics West coach Bob Sevene said he thought she was probably the toughest athlete he had ever known. The emotional effort of running while unfit and competing on will-power alone was similarly demonstrated by Daley Thompson when he won the decathlon at the World Championships in 1983. In both cases the effort left them physically and emotionally spent. Both won their speciality event in Los Angeles in 1984.

Several of the top athletes have had the good fortune of not being injured, but those who were often competed with it if they could, or else worked around the problem. At thirteen, Bob Cousy fell out of a tree and broke his right arm. 'I had it in a cast but I was soon out practising, shooting with the other hand and within the year, I could shoot left-handed almost as well as I could right-handed.'

Pete Rose echoed Ian Botham's comment that at times you continue to play with 'the odd broken finger'. Pat O'Callaghan had a late case of measles at twenty-one. He still went ahead and competed in a contest of throwing a weight over a bar for height. 'I could see two bars when I was throwing the weight into the air, but that was over in a week!' Gene Upshaw, involved in one of the most punishingly physical sports, American football, never missed a game, playing in 217 consecutive matches. To an extent, playing on in a somewhat battered condition is all part of the battle in other games such as rugby union and horse racing.

Barry John was very badly injured in a motorbike crash in his mid-teens. During his international playing career, he would go to the hospital for back therapy and when he saw what some of the children were coping with, he said it put his forthcoming match into perspective. 'The therapy was more in the mind. I could say to the youngsters, "I'll kick a goal for you".'

Lester Piggott accepted the possible prospect of injury. 'Well, we all get injured, that's inevitable.' This attitude exemplifies the acceptance of injury or sickness as a slight inconvenience, not as something which would stop work or the individual's desire for progress or achievement. In their eyes, it is merely a frustration and an interruption to plans. There is certainly a worry, even concern, about whether it will be possible to make a come-back and to be as good, if not better, than before. The intention to try is never questioned.

Naturally with some forms of illness or injury, it is unwise to try to come back into sport too quickly. Nevertheless, the feeling was that most could not wait to get back and start again. Billie Jean King had five knee operations which not only shortened her playing career but forced her to set targets, such as learning how to walk again, rather than an unrealistic immediate goal of winning another Wimbledon.

Injury in only his second year as a professional caused O.J. Simpson to realize that he would have a tough time adjusting to not being a sportsman. 'At that time I resolved to do something that interested me when I got away from sport.' Unlike those who are prepared for retirement in their sixties, many youngsters are unprepared for the feeling of loss when their playing days are over. Injury is one possible cause but even those with lengthy playing careers, unless they have a masters' or veterans' level to enter, are faced with a serious personal challenge to find an activity which will provide equal inner rewards. It may sound strange but at the very top level, the integration of mind, body and spirit in pursuit of excellence cannot be matched in any other facet of life. There may be individual tasks which pose a specific challenge, such as climbing Everest without oxygen or studying for an advanced degree, but the fusion of a healthy, fully-fit body and an alert, concentrated mind, coupled with a will to reach new levels of achievement, produces feelings which only the sportsperson can fully understand.

CHAPTER 4

PHYSICAL ATTRIBUTES

Dr Roger Bannister, the world's first four-minute miler, acted for a few years as chairman of the British Sports Council. During that time he launched a campaign entitled 'Sport for All' – in my view, a laudable one because for each individual there is a sport through which they can develop themselves. There are well over a hundred different sports which all require various skills and body types. Just within the sample of twenty-two sports in this study, the attribute requirements vary immensely. Bob Cousy at 6 ft 2 in was considered a very short basketball player. He described his style of play as 'going in amongst the "big trees"' when he drove for the basket. (Several of 'the trees' to which he refers are in excess of 7 ft tall.) On the other hand, Lester Piggott at 5 ft 9 in was considered very tall for a flat race jockey. Within track and field athletics, there is quite a spectrum of sizes. Marathon runners are usually quite slight and not very tall, the men generally 5 ft 5 in to 5 ft 8 in, and the women 5 ft 2 in to 5 ft 4 in. Sprinters are usually well muscled. They vary in height from 5 ft 6 in to 6 ft 2 in, but rarely above that as it takes taller people longer to unwind from the blocks. Middle-distance runners have a similar height variance to sprinters, but their physiology and temperament differ considerably. Sprinters tend to be more highly strung, rather like race-horses. They also appear to be more extroverted. A general rule of thumb is, the further up the distance scale, the more introverted the runner, but as in all generalizations there are exceptions.

It has been my observation that one finds in humans a similar spectrum of attributes as are found in nature. The physiology of athletes such as sprinters, American football linesmen and throwers is such that they are capable of explosive effort. As with jet fuel, they ignite and burn up their energy sources very rapidly. After a few seconds effort, a sprinter often needs to put his hands on his knees to recover from the rapid depletion of oxygen from his system. The middle-distance runners are the wood-burners; they are exciting to watch as they flame for several minutes. At the far end of this spectrum are the coal- and coke-burning endurance athletes who glow for two hours or so. Even with a flame-thrower, one cannot hope to make coal react like jet fuel. The system may be modified to some extent, but the general percentage of fast- and slow-twitch fibre types is born in the athlete. A simple test of fibre types is through the 'sargent' jump. Standing beside a wall, with heels to the ground, the athlete stretches a hand straight up, making a mark on the wall with chalk dust to indicate the height reached. Then the athlete, with no run up, crouches and springs straight up in the air, touching as high on the wall as possible. The endurance runners, having little explosive capacity, usually get 12 to 18 in off the ground. Some exceptional sprinters, jumpers and basketball players have sargent jumps measuring over 40 in!

The well-trained endurance event athlete will have a greater cardio-vascular efficiency than the average athlete or the untrained individual. This means that the athlete is able to breathe more efficiently by absorbing more oxygen per breath. During 1969 at Salford University, England, twenty road-racing cyclists were tested physiologically and given some mental-state variable tests. The conclusion was, quite predictably, that the more genetically-gifted and physically-conditioned athlete will produce the better result. Without a fair amount of natural attributes, the competitor will not be vying for the very top. The fundamental question is, given adequate physiology to be in with a chance, what are the factors which will determine the winners? The Salford findings on the mental state of the competitor showed that during intense effort, the threshold level of discomfort varied between individual riders. This difference, they believed, could be accounted for by what their researchers referred to as 'selective attention'. (Further mention is made to this in Chapter 14 under 'focus of attention'.)

Various physical attributes can assist performance; for example, large hands and long fingers help the basketball player, as does wide peripheral vision. Throwers with long arms have an advantage because this allows them to exert force over a longer time on whatever is being thrown. Bulk helps some players as they need solid force behind the effort which helps them to throw further. Most top-class male discus throwers and shot putters would be 6 ft 3 in to 6 ft 6 in, and between 200 and 300 lb. The confining element on speed and size for both these throwers is the requirement of staying within the relatively small circle. Speed is a common factor in most physical sports. Team games require the application of speed many times over a short distance. In spite of their massive size, the American football linesmen or the international rugby forwards have such great power-to-weight ratios that they can exert enormous force and move quickly over short distances.

Some of the questions in this study have been geared towards physical effort. However, several sports require a greater percentage of mental effort and concentration. In the case of a yachtsman, it may take five minutes to inch past another vessel, gaining perhaps a foot each wave. A sudden burst of adrenalin and physical effort will not necessarily be helpful. The calm control of the yachtsman can be paralleled in the worlds of motor racing, equestrian events, bowls, shooting, darts and snooker. The requirement is to lower the heart rate and where possible bring down the excitement level. Later on in Part Three under 'athletic intelligence', there is discussion of the mental attributes and what part the mind plays in enhancing sporting performance.

Another obvious physical requirement is the need for good hand–eye coordination in ball sports. The brain calculates rapidly the speed and direction of the ball, puck or whatever is the target object; then instructions are sent to the muscles via the brain to place the body, hands or racket in the right position, and at the right time, to intercept and make perfect contact. If we did calculations to work out how this is achieved, it would fill pages. Most of us take this sort of skill for granted and simply focus our eye on the object and the subconscious mind does the rest. (The following pages show that those who are left-handed or cross-dominant may have an advantage in this respect.)

Yet another variable between the different sports is the degree of body contact. In sports such as rugby, American football and ice hockey, the confrontation is not only highly physical but mental as well. In some sports, there is a moderate level of body contact, basketball and soccer being examples. In most sports, direct physical contact is rare. For some, the opponents are on opposite sides of a net as in tennis, volleyball and badminton. Many sports require competitors to share space and the athletes react to the moves of the other competitors. In addition to the contact sports, other examples are squash, bowls, baseball, cricket, yachting, snooker, middle and long-distance running, and horse and motor racing. In golf and sprint events, the competitors will usually be aware of each other but rarely impede another's progress. Swimming is probably the closest to the isolated effort which exists in downhill skiing, shooting and archery.

Left-handedness and cross-dominance

This phenomenon is being raised because there are a disproportionate number of highly successful athletes who are left-handed or cross-dominant. When you consider that approximately one in ten of the population is left-handed, then this area should not be left out of the discussion.

In February 1985, Robin Brightwell of the BBC produced a Horizon programme based on the research of the recently deceased Norman Geschwind, head of the Neurology Unit at Beth Israel Hospital in Boston and a professor at Harvard. In 1968 Geschwind had shown that the two hemispheres of the brain are physically different. The left hemisphere, for most people, controls language, writing and calculations; for right-handers, it controls the dominant hand. The right hemisphere is more spacial and comprehension-orientated. For the left-handers, this right side of the brain controls their dominant hand. Geschwind showed a strong connection between dyslexia, handedness and language. Dyslexia occurs ten times more frequently in left-handed people. He identified that if testosterone, the male hormone, had seeped into the embryo before birth, growth of the left hemisphere slowed, allowing the right hemisphere to take control. This hormone is produced by the mother as a by-product in making female hormones. The negative result for these individuals is that they often have allergies and because of their left-eye dominance, they frequently have learning difficulties. On the other side, the advantage gained by these individuals is that they have a greater three-dimensional skill level. Several gifted individuals including Thomas Edison, Einstein and Woodrow Wilson have had great difficulty in learning to read.

Within this study of sports personalities, both Jackie Stewart and Duncan Goodhew have severe dyslexia. Both have learned to compensate and have become exceptionally articulate. The advantage for the ball players, and in Jackie Stewart's case shooting and driving, is clear. The better the spacial awareness, the clearer the perspective. Several top tennis players are left-handed including Martina Navratilova, John McEnroe, Jimmy Connors and Rod Laver. Many of those interviewed were either left-handed or cross-dominant. Of significance is that several have taught themselves to be ambidextrous – basketball players Bob Cousy and John Havlicek, and baseball player Pete Rose can all play equally well with either hand. Rugby players Barry John and Gareth Edwards can kick with either foot. Soccer player Bryan Robson is left-handed, but kicks well with either foot, plays snooker left-handed and cricket right-handed.

Fellow coach and doctoral student at Boston University, Bill Thierfelder, has been carrying out research in this field. His interest is in reproducing peak performances through a psycho-physiological approach. He has made the assessment that the left and right sides of the brain, although serving different primary functions, are not totally separate. His view is that a certain amount of skill transfer can be learned and should be encouraged, the object being to enhance and integrate the whole brain. For example, if a youngster is right-handed and is primarily a logical, linear-thinking person, then he or she could benefit from doing something to enhance their creativity. In the case of the sportsperson, encouragement should be extended to spend at least some time and effort practising with the other hand or foot. Apart from some transfer of learning, there is also the advantage of building up a more balanced musculature system. In several sports, the option of striking the ball with either foot or shooting with either hand provides a double threat to the opposition and enhances the player's chances of success.

Physical Development

Do you consider that you were early, late or average in physical development? It may have been imagined that most of these high sporting achievers matured early and gained adult size soon after puberty, but research showed this was not the case. Exactly two-thirds of the athletes were late developers! Both rugby league's Des Drummond and Ian Botham said that they had achieved strength early on, but that they did not fill out and grow until after their school days. Lynn Davies represented another segment of this group. 'I was skilled at ball games but didn't start to grow until I was sixteen.' Not only the lateness but the magnitude of growth was illustrated by Bob Tisdall and Gene Upshaw. When fourteen years old, Bob was only 5 ft 2 in and weighed 84 lb . He grew to 6 ft 2 in and 170 lb. When Gene Upshaw left school at eighteen, he was 5 ft 10 in and between 175 and 180 lb. Yet he grew to 6 ft 6 in and 260 lb during his college days. Bobby Charlton and J.P.R. Williams gave some credit to weight-training, the latter saying, 'Lynn Davies started me on weights when I was about fifteen and I grew five or six inches in one year'. By contrast, 22 per cent classed themselves as early developers. This meant that nearly 90 per cent of those interviewed perceived themselves to be different from their peers. One has to wonder, therefore, whether this had any subconscious effect on their need to achieve. If one is larger than average during childhood, then often there may be an added expectation of responsibility and performance; for those who are smaller than average, then there may be a personal need to prove oneself.

A clear illustration of successful handling of early talent development is the case of Chris Evert Lloyd. Although she was good enough to embark on the circuit when she was fourteen years old, her father held her tournament play down to a minimum until she had completed high school. A section of the early developers achieved astonishing levels of performance very early on in their lives. Shane Innes started breaking world swimming records at thirteen and only a month after her fifteenth birthday, she held every freestyle record from 100m to 1500m. Her time of 17 min 06 sec for the 1500m in 1970 would have beaten the men in both the 1960 and 1964 Olympics! Her schedule in Munich was fifteen races in eight days, four of them on one day. She came away with three golds, a silver and a bronze, all in individual events, and the media was disappointed! Shane's career ended when she was fifteen. A similar phenomenon was Wayne Gretzky, who was so good at ice hockey that expectations and pressure from the media and supporters caused him to start again in a new environment. When he was fourteen years old, his parents moved him from his home in the west of Canada to Toronto so that he could become 'just another kid'. That move probably saved a great talent. Fans, Press, parents and coaches all have a great responsibility in the protection of young talent. Exaggerated expectations will often cause the athlete disappointment, not to mention the supporters. It seems that many people involved with young talent are too often seeking the effects of a time-lapse camera in the opening of a rose. The real appreciation only comes when the flower can be seen in all its glory as it gradually blossoms.

Statistics can be misleading especially with such a small sample in several different sports. However, it is worth noting a few of the sports where early developers were common: swimming had 75 per cent (three out of four); cricket 50 per cent (two out of four); and tennis 40 per cent (two out of five). Alternatively, of the twenty-one track and field athletes interviewed, 71.5 per cent classed themselves as late developers, 19 per cent average and only 9.5 per cent as early developers. Also all four rugby union and both rugby league men classed themselves as late developers physically.

The fact that so many high achievers are late developers should underline the need to allow young athletes the alternative of specializing as late as possible. This should encourage those who are not winning constantly to, as the Americans say, 'hang in there'. Examples are numerous but to name just a few, Steve Cram was fourth in the 1500m, aged fourteen, in the English Schools track and field athletics Championships and fifth in the 3000m at fifteen. Billy Beaumont started playing rugby for Fylde RFC in 1968, aged sixteen, playing full-back for the sixth team. He said that when he left school, he would have been quite happy to have made the first team at his local rugby club. At a higher level, neither Gene Upshaw nor Ed Moses entered university with the intention of doing anything other than getting an education.

CHAPTER 5

COURAGE AND RISK-TAKING

It is a point for debate whether courage and risk-taking is an inherent part of one's physical make-up or something that one has to adjust to psychologically. The following examples are taken from what can be termed 'contact' sports. These sports lend themselves to the vision of courage and risk-taking through their speed or physical contact. Several sports can endanger limbs and, at times, life itself. Examples of these sports are motor racing, downhill skiing, boxing, ice hockey, American football, rugby, and horse racing.

There is also a more subtle element of courage and risk-taking that involves choices which often determine the outcome of a contest. Individuals need courage to take chances in life. For example, should you give up a secure but boring job to try and make it in your own business? In sport, a certain amount of courage is needed from the start, trying out for a place on the team, competing for the first time in front of family, friends and public and within the event itself, the courage to take a risk and make a decision to go for it, to leave the pack and make a break on your own. Many individuals do not have the courage to become the front runner or the highest goal-scorer because they fear being different. They may also fear public failure. The question was whether the high achievers ever saw this as a threat or only as an opportunity to challenge and to prove themselves.

Do you consider that either courage or risk-taking played any part in your sport? 22 per cent saw no risk involved. Even Bryan Robson who is known for diving to head a ball at boot-kicking height said, 'No, it's just a natural part of the game'. A very similar response came from Pete Rose. 'A lot of people think I take a risk because I slide into base head first, but I don't. I just think it's the fastest and safest way to survive.' More than three-quarters of the athletes interviewed (78 per cent) were aware of the courage and risk-taking involved in their sport, but for these athletes it was not a source of concern; in their minds, they had already dealt with these factors.

American football provides an obvious example of visible violence. Gene Upshaw said, 'You have to have courage to take the risk, because you're only one play away from ending your career at any point in time, but you can't worry about it either.' In the same sport and as his team's primary ball carrier, O.J. Simpson was a certain target. 'It's simply the nature of the game, in my position carrying the ball, and the men on the opposing side are mostly bigger than me and most have a lot more aggressive dispositions, which is the nature of a defensive player, all wanting to get me because of my status in the game. They would like to injure me and put me out of the football game – not just stop me on the play but to get me out of the game. I never really focussed on it because I've always approached the game as a game and I've always enjoyed it as a game. I've had conversations with the defensive players during the course of the game, but I do realize that at the core of one's personality, there must be a certain courage to play the game with passion.'

John Havlicek referred to his playing the part of the hero in high school and learning a lesson. He said that he had pulled a muscle and was persuaded to have a shot of novocaine. 'It was probably the worst thing I ever did because after the football game, I could barely walk and for the next week, movement was severely limited.' Even though John allowed this to happen, the onus seems to be even more on those who used John as a scoring threat, placing the outcome of the game as a higher priority than the well-being of the player.

Rugby union and rugby league are also physically demanding contact sports. Peter Sterling commented on the latter: 'Yes, you have to have a bit of courage to dive on a loose ball when there are boots flying around. It's a physical sport and you just can't survive if you aren't courageous to a fair degree.' As with most of these athletes, the risk-taking was a calculated factor. Peter continued, 'Our game is getting very disciplined with less and less risk-taking. The game is becoming one of controlling the football and not trying to get in the extra pass, which might be a risk. That is the point where you have to weigh up quickly whether the risk is worth it and a try could be on.'

A bad neck injury was the reason for Billy Beaumont's decision to stop playing rugby, but in spite of his awareness of the risks, he said, 'If you don't fall on the ball someone has to. As captain you have to do it because you could never ask them to do anything you wouldn't do. I'd never chicken out of anything – even if I knew I hadn't a chance, I'd give it a go.' Bill epitomized the blind overpowering element in the make-up of forwards. A more cautious, less risk-taking approach was held by Gareth Edwards, whose job it was to get the ball from the forwards to the backs. He said that he was told, 'Never be a hero for anyone. Never go down on a ball in a position that you can't get back up.' He said, 'I never forgot that but I never thought about it. It's a case of putting ability above recklessness.'

Also from the sport of rugby is J.P.R. Williams who spoke of the risks being calculated and learning how to avoid injury. 'You know what you can get away with. In a contact sport it's very important to know how to fall. Fall the wrong way and you get injured. You learn to fall as you would from a judo throw. I suffered a few injuries and was involved in tremendous collisions. I think the harder you go in the less likely you are to get injured.'

Des Drummond liked to get involved in the most physical play. 'If you don't take risks you've had it. Trying to get through gaps between players, they try to knock you out of the way. More often than not they're the ones that get knocked back. A lot of wingers don't have the aggression that's needed. I want to get involved. I like tackling bigger blokes.' On the subject of racial discrimination, Des showed a special type of courage in letting his actions speak louder than words. 'There is racial discrimination until you prove yourself. From your own players, "black this and black that" and when they realize that there's a black chap there, they try to retract what they've said, but the damage is done. I never let them know how I'm feeling. If I get it from the opposition, I know that they're trying to rile me up. I just carry on my own game and show them – I just keep performing and they can't say anything. I've gained a lot of respect from players because I don't get fired up . . . I used to when I was younger.'

Ice hockey is another sport renowned for violence. Wayne Gretzky said of the sport: 'It's rough. It's physical. But if you think about it when you're playing, then you're in trouble. I would say the faster you're moving and the more you're moving, the harder it is to get hit. When you're standing around thinking about it you're in trouble. There are some big boys out there!'

Jackie Stewart made the point that even in potentially lethal sports, courage involved self-mastery. 'Courage does play a part but risk-taking doesn't. I think there's a difference between courage and bravery. Bravery is usually a blind instinctive reaction, which is sometimes more dangerous, whereas courage is the control of fear and being able to channel and manipulate it, still with the full knowledge of the calculated risk. There has to be a very clear analytical evaluation of risk.'

Ken Read is another travelling at awesome speed. He said that courage was definitely needed. 'To press yourself when travelling up to 90 m.p.h. on skis, you have to handle the risks mentally within yourself. You are exposing yourself to danger. You realize the course is safe but there are very high risks there. You have to be able to take a realistic view and deal with your emotions and channel them because they're right there on the surface. You have to know your limits, what you've trained yourself to do but you must be prepared to take risks. You have to know when it's worth taking a risk to win a race . . . In the middle of the downhill at Kitzbühel, there's a section which they don't show on live television. It comes off the flat and is a long side-hill pitch, that's very, very rough. You can hold a tuck all the way across it but it's really tough physically and mentally. You can do it but you get rattled around and it's a question of locking yourself in there and just holding it. You're coming across at 70 m.p.h. and many times you feel you've got to move an arm out to keep stable, but if you do you're losing one-tenth of a second. It took me five years running the downhill there to realize that if I came across there and just stayed locked in and could gut it out all the way across no matter what, I could win, and sure enough it was the big difference in 1980. Five guys can do it and five others will pop out of their tuck, but once you've realized that you can, you've taken the risk, you've extended your limit; you realize there's no more risk there!'

Lester Piggott was involved in another sport which results in many accidents. Lester's reaction was, 'Most jockeys have courage and have to take risks all the time; in every race you've got to decide whether to go between two horses or go on the inside, here or there; it's all calculated risk, especially today where you have to be so careful with all these young colts.'

West Indies cricket captain Viv Richards laughed as he said, 'I do treasure my teeth a lot!' He went on to explain that he does not wear a helmet while playing cricket – it takes some courage to face fast bowlers sending down four bouncers in an over. Former Australian captain Greg Chappell said that he was never frightened of getting hit during a cricket match; any fear was caused by the fact that they might get him out!

Although it is a non-contact sport, Steele Bishop referred to the risk of cycling at 55 to 60 m.p.h. downhill on his way to training every morning. 'I don't wear a helmet and if a tyre blew on the bottom bend – I'd be gone!' In the other non-contact sports, courage and risk-taking were still seen as part of what makes achievement. US golf legend Arnold Palmer wrote a book called *Go For Broke*.[48] 'People used to say that I took chances and went for broke every time. I never really felt that that was the case. I always thought the winners had to play aggressively and that they had to go and get it. It's an inner thought as much as anything. But gambling and not laying up was one of the things that I was known for and I suppose it was just a natural part of my game.'

Mike Wenden referred to the risk to one's ego. 'Every time you compete you are putting your ego and your reputation on the line.' Sprinter Marjorie Nelson said, 'It took courage to get out in front of people. At the Olympic Games in the tunnel leading to the track before the 100m final, my heart and legs felt like jelly. I didn't think I'd be able to walk let alone run. I wondered whether the Christians felt like that when they were about to be fed to the lions, because that's exactly how I felt.'

Herb Elliott referred to the psychological barrier of fear. 'If courage is beating your own fears and your uncertainties, then there was a lot of courage.' Heather McKay pointed out that it took courage to push yourself past your previous limit, giving yourself that extra push when you thought you could not do it.

Duncan Goodhew did not consider that courage or risk-taking were a part of his competitive experience, but he thought that courage related far more to his training. 'It comes to reaching down for something you didn't know you had. My hardest sessions were done when I felt my worst.' He laughed, and said, 'It's easier to do it on the worst day, you feel lousy so you're not ruining a good day anyway!' John Konrads also saw courage relating to training. 'It takes courage to be willing to hurt yourself, the ability to train hard, put up with the tiredness and come back for more.'

PART 2

SOCIAL FACTORS

CHAPTER 6

CHILDHOOD AND GROWING UP

There are such negative associations in class distinction that I felt some reluctance in asking the question of class background. Nevertheless, it was important to try to see whether or not class had any bearing on sporting achievement. Many journalists have referred to the athlete's need to be 'hungry' in order to win, and have implied that many have used sport to 'get out of the ghetto'. There were no extremely affluent families represented in this study; one rarely hears of millionaire's children stepping onto the Olympic podium. American decathlete Bill Twomey was reported to be in this category and it became news-worthy copy at the time of the 1968 Olympic Games only because it was so unusual.

In this study only 3 per cent classed themselves as upper-middle class, with a further 44 per cent placing themselves in the middle-class category. This type of class definition is difficult across various cultures, because class distinction is based on different factors, for example in the US it is largely based on money, whereas in Britain money is not necessarily a determining factor.

It was amusing to hear how Carl Lewis defined the poor. He is from a well-educated, professional family and defining his middle-class status, he said, 'There were some rich folks who drove new Cadillacs and there were some poor folks who only had one car.' Only in America could a definition of 'poor' include the owning of a car!

Slightly more than half classed themselves as either poor, working class or lower-middle class. Nevertheless, it would not be accurate to say that there was a desperate desire to 'get out of the ghetto'. The spartan conditions were accepted and in most cases it brought the community together. Gareth Edwards spoke of the typical attitude of the Welsh mining communities: 'The backing from parents was absolute. Things were tight but we never wanted for anything. The only thing you missed were the luxuries, but what you never had you never missed.'

Significantly, in each category, regardless of how they had defined their social background, it was stated that in retrospect they realized that their parents had made sacrifices in order to allow them to pursue their sporting interest. Whether it was purchasing the necessary equipment or providing the bus fares to away games, somehow the backing was found. Additionally, it was never made obvious to these future high achievers that they were placing a strain on the family resources. They may have been aware that it was being found, but they were never in any way made to feel awkward or uncomfortable.

Many of the creature comforts of today, including television, were not important to most in this study. The entertainment was often self-created and in many cases bore a striking resemblance to some future training endeavours. In track and field athlete Ann Brightwell's childhood, her entertainment was to run and walk her dog all day on the Berkshire Downs. For Herb Elliott in Australia, the castles being captured were sand-hills, while roaming in the outback with her family was the game for both Shirley de la Hunty and Heather McKay when they were not involved in hard physical chores on their parents' farms. In one of New York's ghettos, Bob Cousy learned street sense and played basketball inner-city style. After school in the mining communities where Lynn Davies, Barry John and Gareth Edwards lived, they would join other village lads and play soccer until it was too dark to see the ball. There were no facilities for technical event practices, but the activities were fun and the stamina, coordination and individual flair were allowed to develop naturally.

Parental provision

In a recent study on high achievers in business,[25] the researchers found that a high proportion had some kind of trauma in their early life: the death of a parent, abandonment, left in care and so on. The question was whether the same would be true of sports achievers. Quite the opposite seems to be the case. This survey found that only 6 per cent had either a parent die or parents who were divorced. Even in the latter cases, the difficulty it caused had been less than traumatic. O.J. Simpson said, 'My father lived on the other side of town after the split and we visited during the holidays. He still gave us presents on our birthdays and at Christmas.'

Rather an overwhelming statistic is that 98 per cent felt that their home life was stable, and 100 per cent felt that their parents had been consistent in their behaviour. With the increased divorce rate throughout the western world, one has to appreciate just how fortunate this group of athletes has been.

The responses in general were exceptionally consistent in the following areas. Most athletes, 94.5 per cent, felt that their parents had provided a secure home, while 93.5 per cent described their childhood as happy, with many adding the word 'very' to their answers. Crops grow better in good soil, and this seems to show that the athletes benefited from happy, stable and supportive homes. 92 per cent said that their parents were both supportive and encouraging, but 95 per cent firmly believed that they were not pushed by their parents. Illustrations were often given as to what was meant by support and encouragement without pushing. For example, in many cases, it was the parents of these achievers who were the ones to drive team members to an away game. Where work did not interfere, one or both parents would be watching. In most cases it was the 'full-time Mum'. Greg Chappell recalled: 'Dad instilled in us that every game was important. You played fairly but you always played to win. We had cricket practice in the backyard and he would come out and throw balls to us. Mum was very supportive in everything we did. She was always there. I remember on one particular day she was the only parent at the game and I felt annoyed that she was there, and wished I could be like the other kids who didn't have a parent there and we could go down the back and have a smoke or whatever else the blokes were doing. On reflection in later life, I realized how lucky I was to have that sort of support. She wasn't there to keep an eye on us. She was really interested in what we were doing.'

Once a father's interest in sport almost disrupted a happy home. Pete Rose told me the story. 'Our family was poor but the home was very stable. I only saw my parents have an argument once. My older sister needed a pair of shoes. Instead of using the money that week for my sister's shoes, my father bought me a pair of boxing gloves. He said, "She doesn't need no shoes, it's summer time!"'

Christopher Dean thought that it was important that parents were there as a sort or rock, 'to support you when you needed it'. Jayne Torvill remarked, 'They can advise you but they don't push you. There's quite a difference.' Support can come in all forms. For Olympic yachtsman Rodney Pattisson, it was his father setting a trend by building him a boat suitable for children, and not setting him against adults too early. Rodney's view was that parents usually pushed the wrong guys: 'The guys with ability don't need to be pushed.'

Third Force theory

It would be helpful at this stage to put briefly into context the findings relating an athlete's upbringing to a theory of personal development and motivation. Many will be familiar with the psychologist Abraham Maslow. During the 1950s, he was a professor at Brandeis University in the United States and was responsible for identifying the Third Force psychology.[22] At a time when the height of inner-understanding did not go beyond Sigmund Freud, Maslow introduced the advancement that, if a man is trying to discover how to run a mile faster than anyone else has done before, he does not look at the sick; instead he must look at the best that has gone before and attempt to see how he can improve upon that. Similarly, in looking at personal development, one cannot discover the positive capabilities of the human being if the main source of investigation is the psychologically unwell. Maslow formed his positive view of Man following his research on the great people of history and interviews with the outstanding individuals of his time. He proposed a now famous theory based on the hierarchy of human needs and outlined that in order for human beings to fulfil their potential, they had first to have certain needs fulfilled. In his view, there were five levels and the key factor was that the needs at one level had to be fulfilled before there could be development or advancement to the next level. It is relevant to note how well the information gathered in this survey endorses his theory.

The first two levels have a physiological base. The basic stage for the perpetuation of the human race is the need for air, food, water, sleep and sex. Procreation, nurturing and tending are the providing elements here. The next level is the need for safety and security. In these first two levels, the families of these achievers have, in most cases, provided the stability (98 per cent), safety and security (94 per cent) and sustenance for them all to be able to move on to the third level. It is at this level that Maslow believed that psychological factors came into play. The third level is the need for love and the sense of belonging. This is an area which may be fulfilled from several different sources. Certainly in addition to close family ties, athletes can also gain a real sense of belonging from both a good coach–athlete relationship and being part of a team or training group. The fourth level is the need for self-esteem and esteem by others; being able to feel that what you are and what you do are recognized as worthwhile by yourself and by others. Sport holds an unusual position here. The public at large follows sport in some depth in every part of the globe. If someone finishes a marathon, the personal feeling of accomplishment and the recognition from others is established, regardless of whether the individual took just over two hours or just over ten to complete the course. Sport holds a unique position in this regard and has been opened to almost everyone from tiny tots to geriatrics, whether mentally or physically handicapped, gifted or not. The recognition and interest shown by parents will go a long way towards giving the youngster the sense of self-worth which he or she needs. The fifth and final area Maslow called the need for self-actualization; in other words, becoming what you are capable of becoming. This has also been called self-realization[66] and it is an open-ended and never-ending quest. At some stage in the lives of these highest achievers, they fulfilled a small part of their human potential.

Parent-child relationship

Just over 70 per cent of the athletes interviewed characterized the relationship with their parents as either close or good; an additional 9 per cent had a good relationship with their mothers. Another 7 per cent said that their relationship with their parents was one of respect. The remaining 14 per cent reflected on it as being neither warm nor close, because their parents were either too busy or too old, or that there was friction or strife in the family.

Several family differences can be attributed to the way in which the offspring were treated. They were certainly not all treated the same. Four went away to school which made any meaningful relationship difficult. In the case of Bob Tisdall, his parents were in Ceylon and he was sent back to England at the age of six. From the start of his school days until he was eighteen, Bob 'had to get to know them again in the holidays, then forget them'. In the other cases, separation was later: one at twelve years old, and two at fourteen. For Valeriy Borzov, it was a case of being selected for a sports school. In the Soviet Union, the choice is left to the child and his parents to decide, but it is rarely refused as it is seen as a privilege and an opportunity, just as a scholarship offer is seen a few years later at American colleges. The biggest difference seems to be that the State and those who organize the different schools, provide the care and socialization. Family support and encouragement was 'nothing special', said Borzov. The family is not the most influential factor. One of the reasons for this is that there has been full employment for thirty years in the Soviet Union: either university or technical training with a guaranteed job is part of this. The result is that children are dropped off at school at 7.30 a.m. and picked up at 6.30 p.m. from three years old; indeed, they can be there from the age of one. Many do not pick their children up during the week but have them live in at school. At fourteen, Valeriy was selected to attend a 'special' school where he could receive specialist coaching alongside his academic lessons. 'In school the best care is given to each child, but they are not pushed.' The route was similar to that found in the West with the child being introduced to sport as fun. Later came the careful introduction of skills, and at university the intellectual understanding and serious training.

In order to reach the top level in world sport, there is a requirement for self-discipline and obviously there is a limitless number of ways in which one may learn. However, as the parents are a significant early influence, three topics were examined which might have had bearing on the achievers' values and behaviour. The subjects were asked whether they thought that religious values were important to their parents, whether they stressed fair play and keeping within the rules, and what form of discipline was employed, verbal or physical:

1. RELIGION. The majority (55 per cent) said that religious belief was important to their parents. Several who said that it was not referred to the fact that the code of living was based on Christian principles but without going to church. Billy Beaumont said that the code of living would have been by the Ten Commandments. Nine of the achievers volunteered that they had been regular attenders of Sunday school and even if they did not attend church regularly now, the influence was still there.

2. FAIR PLAY AND RULES. Once one moved to values upheld by the parents in terms of whether or not they had stressed fair play and keeping within the rules, the positive percentage soared with 93 per cent saying yes, they had always been told to play fair and abide by the rules. The sentiment was so strong, in fact, that it elicited responses such as 'totally', 'very much so', 'no question', 'always' and 'no lying or cheating'. Billie Jean King had been told by her father: 'If you cheat you'll never have won. You may walk off the court and everyone else may think that you won, but you didn't win at all.'

Several athletes recalled incidents where their parents had made a direct intervention to alter their behaviour. John Newcombe was playing a junior final and was losing. 'I was dropping my racket and all that and my mother was sitting at the court side, and usually said nothing during my matches. But on this occasion as I passed her, she sort of hissed, "Why don't you start playing tennis and stop feeling sorry for yourself?" Within three paces I realized that she was right, so I started playing tennis, stopped feeling sorry for myself and won the match.'

For Arnold Palmer, it was his father. He spoke of a match when he was about sixteen years old. He had just missed a short putt: 'I wheeled and threw the putter fifty or sixty feet over a row of poplar trees. I went on to win the match with a sizeable putt on the last hole. I was elated about my success but when I got into the car, it was total silence. I expected "nice going" or "congratulations" – there was nothing. The first thing that came out of my father was said in no uncertain terms: "If I ever see you do that again, in competition or otherwise, you will not play golf and live in my house at the same time." He meant it and I knew he meant it.'

A story was related about Bjorn Borg, how early in his playing days, he had displayed a bout of bad temper on court; afterwards his parents locked his racket in a cupboard for several weeks.

O.J. Simpson reflected on the guidelines taken from his mother together with a sense of fair play learnt on the field. 'My mother taught us a strong religious sense of right and wrong, but through team sports, I established a strong foundation in a "do unto others" type of system. You give to the whole and you take back what you need.'

Gene Upshaw saw the significance of the simple disciplines implemented by his parents in the home. 'Clean the yard, wash the dishes, straighten up the house, discipline. I believe that you learn discipline at a very young age and there are certain things you do in the rest of your life that reinforces what that discipline was. Some people never know what discipline is so when it hits them smack in the face, what do they do? They rebel.'

Lynn Davies spoke about the ethics that can come from a whole community. 'My father was very critical of bad sportsmanship. You find that coal miners generally have a tremendous code of ethics, a tremendous sense of fair play. '

3. DISCIPLINE. The most direct area of parental intervention in a child's behaviour is discipline. The question was asked in order to find out whether or not there was any bias in the form of that early discipline. For the majority of 66 per cent, it was entirely verbal. Several emphasized the fact with statements such as, 'Oh, we were never hit!'; 'I can never remember being hit'; and 'We were just told why it was wrong'. A further 20 per cent said that they received both verbal and physical punishment. Comments varied from, 'We got what we deserved' to 'Both, but no beatings, just a short clip'. Only 8 per cent said that it was primarily physical. The other 6 per cent had received neither physical punishment nor verbal berating. This was either because expectations within the family were such that it was unnecessary or that the parents were not concerned with their discipline. Within this group was Bob Tisdall who had been sent to a boarding school. He recalled being one of those who was often beaten unjustly by school prefects. The memory was obviously vivid and the lack of opportunity to talk or explain the circumstances was resented.

It was interesting to see how the different forms of discipline seemed to affect the relationship with their parents. As the total number interviewed was not large, it would be wrong to draw too many conclusions; however, the following analysis does give a great deal of food for thought. For those who had been verbally disciplined, 97 per cent had a good relationship with their parents. For those who were both physically and verbally disciplined, 55 per cent were close to their parents and another 27 per cent had respect for them. The other 18 per cent were not close to their parents.

A percentage turn around came with those who received primarily physical discipline. In this instance, 75 per cent said that they were not close or they had strife with their parents! Some parents believed in the Old Testament mentality of 'spare the rod and spoil the child'. They may have established control, but in these cases, it certainly did not add up to what could be considered a good or close relationship from the achievers' point of view. It appears that the New Testament teaching of love and understanding, taking time to listen and talk, at least in this group of athletes interviewed, produced a closer family unit.

The athletes were asked which attributes would best characterize their parents. The follow-up question was whether any attributes taken from their parents had helped their sporting performance. The attributes give a reasonably comprehensive list of what the athletes needed in order to reach their goals. They are as follows: patience, fairness, hardness, control, discipline, conscientiousness, dedication, sincerity, courage, honesty, enthusiasm, pride, reserve, humour, determination, humility, and last but not least, diligence.

Some felt that their parents provided a balance. Where one was intense the other was controlled, and the athletes often felt that they had taken the best from each parent. Both Steve Davis and J.P.R. Williams referred to taking their love for sport from their fathers and the mental toughness and hardness from their mothers. In several other cases, parents were seen as very similar types. It would be fair to say that the parents in general were greatly valued, many achievers saying that they could not have wished for better parents.

Whatever guidelines for behaviour that were not given verbally were more than made up for by example. One attribute which was consistently agreed on was that their parents were extremely hard working. Phrases such as this one came from John Havlicek: 'They portrayed an attitude of work and a respect for work.' Ed Moses referred to it as 'the work ethic'. Whether it was on a farm, in the mines, driving a cab, teaching, running their own business or running a home, their dedication, effort, commitment and reliability was evident to their offspring. This diligence was an example followed by all.

Parental competitiveness and expectations

Did you consider your parents to have been competitive people? One might have expected a positive response but in fact less than half (45 per cent) of the athletes considered their parents to have been competitive. It is interesting that this is an attribute not acquired by example.

A less overt form of parental pushing comes through expectations. Following the question, *Did you feel that your parents had high expectations for you and if so in what areas?*, more than half (53 per cent) felt that there were no high expectations expressed or felt from their parents. Another 3 per cent said that they had had a little pressure. Almost one-third (27 per cent) said that the pressure was unrelated to sport, but that their parents had expressed a strong desire that their children should get a good education. Lynn Davies, for example, was encouraged by his mother to have the option not to go down the mines. Education was seen worldwide as a strong tool for upward mobility.

The other 17 per cent felt expectations in all areas. Ken Read said, 'There was expectation for each of us in the family to realize our potential in everything.' Billie Jean King: 'Every area. I once came home with a school report showing all A's and one A– and my Dad asked why there was one A–! I said "Daaad!" and he said, "Oh, I was only wondering what it was for".' For both Heather McKay and J.P.R. Williams, the sport expectation was tennis, which was not the sport of their ultimate success. But with them, as with Al Oerter and Peter Snell, the reference was also made to the importance of scholastic achievement.

Half of the parents who were not competitive themselves still held high expectations for their children. Two-thirds of these expectations were in the area of education with a further 20 per cent including education in their high expectations of all areas. The majority (67 per cent) of competitive parents were the ones who expressed high expectations, either in academic or in all areas. The remaining one-third of the parents who were competitive themselves did not verbally attempt to transmit high expectations to their children.

With the parents who did have high expectations, there was no mistaking the belief expressed in their offspring. Steele Bishop said that his parents told him, no matter what he put his hand to, he could become the best in the world. Steve Cram, in his interview, which incidentally was prior to his multiple world records in 1985, said that he thought his parents at times tended to over-estimate what he could do. Perhaps now he will have to agree with them!

The parents of these achievers may not have been deceiving themselves in expressing their belief and faith in the youngsters who they knew could reach the very top if they fulfilled their potential. A problem arises with parents who are working with a child who doesn't have the talent or personal ambition to make the top. Often, neither parent nor child understands the number of levels which there are to climb and subsequently sets unrealistic or unattainable targets. An illustration of this is where the father is a successful businessman and he expects perfection and performance from the young child, who just cannot match up to the parent's expectations. The result is that the child starts to feel insecure or inadequate because he or she can never match up to their successful parents' expectations. The key is to allow the youngster to be the one to accept the challenge, and the parent must, at that stage, give support, and only *if* it is requested, assist in the setting of realistic, challenging but enjoyable goals. More often, however, this goal-setting is either done by the individual or in concert with the coach.

Over-ambitious parents

John Newcombe had an early problem with his father. 'If I'd won, it would be a really nice ride home. If I hadn't, by the time we got ten minutes from the house, we'd be having an argument. Finally, I said to my mother, if he didn't cut it out he just couldn't come to matches and if he insisted on coming I wouldn't play . . . so he cut it out and it was fine.' This statement makes one wonder how many youngsters have stopped playing because their parents have become too involved, demanding victory. Their children's success in many cases has become an extension of their own ambitions, perhaps linked to feelings of frustration at their own lack of achievement.

Only Lester Piggott said that he was pushed by his father, but added that he thought he needed to be. Lester was trained by his father and started riding for him at the age of fourteen. 'I think that for anyone to be good at anything they need some help and they've got to be pushed a bit. Nobody's a natural really. They've got it there but they've still got to be put right at the beginning.' Lester felt that he was lucky to have a father who shared an interest. As with Seb Coe and Steve Davis, each was coached by his father. Seb remarked that he was the one who pushed himself and that there had been occasions when both his parents had told him to back off.

Billie Jean King's parents went out of their way to get her to tournaments but did not ask, 'Did you win or lose?' but rather 'Are you happy playing? Are you sure this is what you want to do?' One might well have expected that Shane Innes was pushed by her parents to produce such fantastic times whilst still so young, but not so. 'My parents were always very supportive and encouraging, never pushing. My Dad would sometimes turn off the alarm clock so I wouldn't go swimming in the morning because he thought I was too tired to go.' In fact there was conflict between her parents and her coach because they believed that Shane was too young to be doing so much training. They felt she was being worn out and might get tired of it mentally, so they were trying to hold her back. Most other parents also showed their concern. Three-Day Eventer Lucinda Green's parents told her to give up riding if she did not enjoy it.

As the volume of interviews increased, so did the indications that parents of high achievers had not pushed them; but in addition, I was confronted with disturbing stories about those who had. Here are a few illustrations from three continents. In little athletics in Australia, a young lad of eight, running in a national championships, was passed in the last few yards of a quarter-mile race. At the finish, he fell to the track exhausted, crying because he had lost the race. His father came over and whacked him about the head, shouting at him for losing. I related this story to an Australian coach who said that he had watched a similar scene where a girl was told to swim the last repetition in 60 seconds and she finished, obviously in distress, having swum it in 62 seconds. Before she was even told her time, her mother slapped her across the face, saying that she could have tried harder! Ed Moses talked about those parents involved with their children's track athletics practice in the United States. 'I've seen six, seven, eight, nine year olds doing five or six back-to-back 400m. I'm against pushing. The person is usually going to motivate themselves if they're going to be a champion, even with a good coach. The worst thing I'm aware of is that some parents are putting their kids onto anabolic steroids!' Arnold Palmer commented, 'I've seen pushy parents in every sport and the results are generally bad. The kids that are pressured to play sport usually get sick of it and are disgusted with it for that reason. They decide to do something else.'

When Gareth Edwards was at a New Zealand school which boasted having trained some of the greatest All Blacks players, the headmaster pointed out a boy who he believed could have been the best of the lot but had stopped playing. Gareth went and spoke to the lad who said that he had started playing competitive rugby at the age of five and so by seventeen, he had already played intensive rugby for twelve years and had had enough. Gareth's opinion is that, 'Currently in Great Britain, we have many do-gooders in mini-rugby, and too often the only things being taught are how to stop the opponents and how to set up certain moves. They neglect the basic skills – how to pass and how to kick.' Billy Beaumont saw mini-rugby as being all right in most aspects such as teaching children the rules of the game and how to enjoy themselves. 'But don't get them organized into competition at the age of eight because you're taking the whole fun aspect out of the game. You see little lads crying because they've lost the game . . . so what?'

Heather McKay in Canada said, 'Part of the problem with sport today is that the parents want the kids to be what they weren't and are trying to live through them. There's a difference between encouraging and standing behind versus pushing, and when the kid gets old enough to make a choice, they give it away because they've been pushed so hard.'

The obsession with winning as well as pushing children at such a young age has not only forced youngsters to drop out of sport, but in an extreme example in tennis, has produced a resentment towards a father to the point of being willing to kill him! There is nothing wrong with introducing children to sport at an early age, but the whole affair has to be kept light-hearted and made to be fun. The important aspects to be stressed here are taking part, making an honest effort and being pleased with the feeling of movement; the thrill of scoring if you can; the gaining of knowledge about how to play; experimenting with different styles and techniques; discovering that with practice one gets better; and hopefully one is encouraged and recognized for effort and improvement even if one is still in last place. This is where it helps to keep a note of performances. No matter how slow one runs or how few points are scored, if it is possible to judge improvement, then it is a marvellous source of reward. Pete Rose said something with which I strongly agree: 'Encouragement rather than putdowns. Cutting someone down doesn't bring the best out of them.'

Some parents are better than others at reading situations. Duncan Goodhew remembers one scene. 'My mother was brushing her hair, I was about fifteen or sixteen years old and I walked in and said, "I'm giving up swimming". My mother stopped brushing her hair and then carrying on said, "Well, whatever you want to do", and that really took the wind out of my sails because I'm sure that if she had said, "Don't you dare give up now", I would actually have done the opposite. I was a bit anti-establishment and took the opposite view to everybody else.' It was his decision to continue and not anyone else's. Wayne Gretzky felt he was shown the difference between being pushed and having a responsibility. 'I wasn't forced into any sport but I had agreed to play for a local baseball team and half-way through the season, I wanted to quit. My Dad said, "You finish the year, then you can quit."'

Rod Laver also had some balanced views on the subject. 'There are a lot of reasons why you would want a child to be encouraged and pushed. It's nice to have the financial opportunity for success that there is today. When we played it was purely an amateur game; the only glory was trophies and to try to represent Australia. Now the financial incentives are great, but if pressure outweighs enjoyment, parents' pushing goes for nought. You have to enjoy it – the thrill of winning and being there. You don't have to have the agony of defeat, it's just that you're disappointed and you've learned something.'

This now prompts the question as to whether or not the sport played by the parents influenced their child's choice. On the basis of the current study, it seems to have had little bearing. In exactly half the cases, only the father played sport. It should be noted that several of those interviewed had parents who lived in an era when sporting opportunities for women were far less open than they are today. Nevertheless in 5.5 per cent of families, only the mother played, while 32 per cent said that both parents played. Rather surprisingly, in the case of the remaining 12.5 per cent, neither parent participated at all. One might have imagined that the parents who played sport would have been involved in the sport in which their children had their ultimate success. However, this does not appear to be so. Less than one-third (31.7 per cent) of those who had parents who played sport, chose a sport played by their parents.

Within the group who did follow in their parents' footsteps, one-third of them had both parents involved in the same sport. They were Billie Jean King and Chris Evert Lloyd from tennis, Carl Lewis in track and field athletics, David Bryant in bowls, Clive Lloyd in cricket and Lester Piggott from horse racing. The remaining two-thirds had fathers who had played the same sport and in several cases, the father was a very significant figure for these achievers. Arnold Palmer's father was a golf professional. 'I'd watch my father and I suppose I admired him and what he did.' For Pete Rose, it was almost hero worship. Pete greatly admired his father and believes that his Dad was the best athlete to come out of Cincinnati. Pete had followed him each season, acting as water boy, ball boy or bat boy for his father's teams. His father played until he was forty. Pete is still playing at forty-three and now says, 'I'm just a chip off the old block'.

Competitiveness with siblings

Fifty-five per cent of the survey said that they were not in a competitive situation with their siblings. The three who referred to their relationship as close and non-competitive were males who had sisters both older and younger than themselves. John Konrads and John Newcombe were both the second child of three; Peter Sterling was third child of four, the other three being sisters. In several instances, the lack of competitiveness was attributed to the fact that there was too great an age gap between them. Three years was often the break-even point. Any greater age difference and the individuals often referred to their brothers and/or sisters as much older or much younger.

Of the 45 per cent who said that their relationship was competitive with their siblings, the majority were born about two years apart. Shirley de la Hunty said that with her four brothers it was competitive but it was also very friendly. Many referred to fighting, particularly between the years of nine and fourteen but becoming closer later on. This is a fairly natural pattern in many families.

Mike Wenden, brought up in a pretty tough environment, illustrated this fact through one childhood recollection: 'My elder brother was a very strong muscular bloke and he had some rough mates who he'd bring home and line them up against me to see who'd come out on top. This was when I was about eight and nine years old and he would have been about eleven and twelve. You had to watch what you did, several had been in and out of boys homes. You had to be competitive to survive. You strive to be as good as some who are better than you and my brother was older and stronger, but I didn't think I wasn't capable of keeping up.'

From the list in Appendix I, it can be seen that the second born of three children is the largest group. Within that group, Ed Moses, Pat O'Callaghan, Mike Wenden and Greg Chappell were all second born of three boys, and Marjorie Nelson was second of three girls. Also it can be seen that the largest proportional representation from the families of two, three or four children, is one up from the bottom, i.e. number one of two, number two of three or number three of four.

The findings in this section raise more questions than answers. It is logical that the first child has the most attention from parents and they are the ones to whom the parents look to set an example. The eldest child often takes some responsibility for the younger siblings.

Previous studies on business achievers have indicated that the largest proportion of those who reached the top in that sphere were the first born. This is not the case for sports achievers. The baffling point here is why there is a disproportionate number of second born as high sporting achievers. It might be thought that the children after the first born have had to be progressively more self-reliant, but this is not the case as the percentage of achievers does not increase. Does the first child order the second around and create a mental state which allows an individual to accept instructions from a coach? In many cases, this is not the role of the coach and again, the further down the family one goes, the more they would tend to be told what to do. At birth, the second child is on average slightly larger than the first, but that would not necessarily equip them any better for a role in sport. Perhaps there is some assistance from the role model of number one and an unconscious striving to keep up while there are only two around. No clear explanation is readily apparent.

CHAPTER 7

PERSONAL ATTRIBUTES

As all the achievers interviewed have been watched by millions on TV, and generally could be considered performers, one might be forgiven for assuming that they are all extroverts. In fact, the opposite seems to be true. A remarkably distinguishing feature is that a large proportion, 89 per cent of these sports achievers, classed themselves as introverts. It may be of interest to know that a parallel study was carried out on double achievers,[24] that is those who had reached international level in their sport and had gone on to achieve notably in another field. The main difference between this group and the highest achievers in sport was that the double achievers were on the whole extroverts. The requirements for success in business certainly differ from sport because at least in some areas, there is a need for an outgoing personality in unfamiliar social surroundings. Only 6 per cent of the sports achievers felt that they were extroverts and the remaining 5 per cent felt that they were 'middle of the road'.

Reference is often made to the loneliness of the long distance runner, and when one comes to think about the number of hours of single-minded effort and inward reflection required to reach the top in many sports, it is not surprising to find that the vast majority of these athletes started as introverts. Steve Davis said that he did not mind either being alone or with just a few people practising because he would rather have been there than at a party.

Obviously, many of these achievers have been thrust into the public eye and have had to adapt. Barry John put it that he was a 'trained' extrovert. Billie Jean King referred to it as an 'adopted front'. Steve Cram along with several others said that sport was the tool which had brought him out. The general consensus was that their sport had helped them to become more outgoing, and had assisted in the promotion of self-confidence.

It was surprising to learn from so many interviewees that in their youth they had been painfully shy. The Press termed Marjorie Nelson as 'the shyest champion in Australia'. David Forbes, the yachtsman, referred to introversion as a possible motivating factor: 'Deep down you believe you're as good as anyone else, and you're trying to prove that by pursuing a sport to a top level.'

As was mentioned in the Third Force theory, sport can assist greatly in allowing an individual's needs to be fulfilled. The following examples illustrate the gaining of self-esteem and the esteem of others, which in turn establishes a sense of belonging.

Duncan Goodhew was an introvert who had continually been made to feel self-conscious, even inferior, because he had been diagnosed as dyslexic. Jackie Stewart has the same disability and both men are classic examples of people who have that difficulty and who have compensated by becoming exceptionally articulate. Nevertheless, the disappointments were very real and painful. (Duncan suffered an additional hardship when he fell out of a tree at the age of eight, damaging a nerve in his upper lip causing all his hair to fall out.) For both men, sport was a developmental ladder. Their achievements allowed them and others to realize that they had a special ability.

Peter Snell pointed out one benefit derived from sport – the gaining of social acceptability among one's peers. 'When my family moved, sport was a means of deriving social acceptability in any new group situation; for example, if I went away to YMCA camp, I would have immediate acceptability on the basis of my athletic skills, being able to play cricket, being able to run reasonably well, and so on. So I learned at an early stage that there was value in being physically competent.'

Assertiveness and aggressiveness

Do you consider that you were either assertive or aggressive off the field of play? A certain degree of assertiveness and aggressiveness is obviously needed on the field. To test the distinction between the two, individuals were given an illustration of assertiveness: they were asked whether they would send food back in a restaurant if it was not cooked properly. On this basis, over one-third (35 per cent) considered that they were neither aggressive nor assertive off the field of play. Bryan Robson said that he was happy to give instructions and take command on the field, but off the field he was quite the opposite. He added, 'I walk away from people in pubs or restaurants who are making uncalled-for remarks, trying to set me up for a fight.' John Gilmour pointed out that 'a lot of people who know me, don't even know that I run'.

The majority (55 per cent) said that they were definitely not aggressive but were assertive. Rodney Pattisson said that he stood up for his own rights and the rights of others. 'If someone makes a questionable move in a yachting race, many will say, "Who cares?", but I will get a ruling on principle.' Duncan Goodhew and Steve Cram pointed out that they had become more assertive since winning.

In some cases, injustice provoked action. Bob Tisdall said, 'Only if I see someone being cruel to an animal . . . then I could see red and become very violent.'

Others defined themselves in relation to this question. For example, Herb Elliott said that he was persistent; Billie Jean King referred to her actions as 'manipulative' and Peter Sterling said, 'I'm not a follower'.

The remaining 10 per cent felt that they were at times both assertive and aggressive. For Bob Cousy, it varied. In his book *Killer Instinct*,[12] he outlined the dilemma of the 'must win' philosophy. As a player and as a coach, he had wound himself up to perform and could at those times very easily have lost his temper if anyone even looked at him the wrong way. Pete Rose went even further. 'My way of life is aggressive and assertive. I'm going to be an aggressive manager, you have to!' Daley Thompson was a little more tempered. 'I can be both but I don't like to be.' Carl Lewis added a serious but rather light-hearted note. He said that he was extremely aggressive when shopping!

It is recognized that in most sports there is a need for an assertive and/or aggressive action. Steve Ovett sees the track as a place where you take the rough with the smooth and you give as good as you get. If that means an exchange of elbows, so be it. Having said that, Steve does not see himself as an aggressive person.

Many of these achievers did not perceive their actions as aggressive against others, rather that they were directing the energy inwards. In some individuals, this produced a creative tension which was a vital source of usable energy. There is a philosophy behind this. One can climb the ladder of success by putting others down. It is an aggressive action if you step on someone else in order to win or take the next step up the ladder. On the other hand, it is possible to see a race as two or more people going in pursuit of the same goal and the efforts of one enhances the efforts of the other. In this light, each person's best effort raises the standard of the whole. It can therefore be looked at as constructive rather than destructive behaviour and the pursuit of excellence as individually and collectively elevating.

Earlier in this Chapter, there was reference to the large percentage of introverts found in this study coupled with the fact that they were at home in their sporting environment. In this bounded area, assertiveness, and in some situations aggressiveness, can be acceptable behaviour. For the shy person, it is a perfect arena through which to channel these instincts. Nevertheless, sport will survive in a healthy state only if assertive and aggressive behaviour is coupled with the ideals outlined in the paragraph above. The philosophy must be understood by players, coaches, media and fans alike. The aim may be winning but there must be respect for effort whether that results in a win or not.

Emotional and social development

Do you consider that you were an early, late or average developer? It is refreshing that at forty-eight years old, Al Oerter continues to say most things with a laugh. He followed his statement about being a late physical developer by saying, 'Emotionally I'm just coming together!' 56 per cent felt that they were late developers emotionally, while 25 per cent thought they were early and 18 per cent said that they thought that they were about average.

Bob Cousy felt that it was to be expected that many would be late developers. He said, 'Emotionally I was a late developer. I'm not sure that all athletes aren't somewhat late because we were so into our own thing, we were into sports emotionally, but in terms of inter-relationships with other people, I think it retards a bit.' Certainly if every free hour out of school time is spent playing sport, other social inter-action could be retarded. However, there are several aspects to emotional and social development and this question is too broad to give much more than an impression of the general development of these athletes.

Ian Botham's response represents another aspect of the same subject. He thought he was naive until about the age of fifteen. Many others put their age of reaching emotional maturity as much later. Seb Coe said he grew up quickly between twenty and twenty-one. Certainly few, if any, were prepared for the media pressure which hit them once a real level of success had been achieved. The aspect of naivety is worth a closer look. If a youngster at the beginning knew the degree of difficulty and the time and work required to reach the top, he or she might well be overawed and lose heart. Billie Jean King said that at eleven years old, she had set her sights on winning Wimbledon. Only later on did that become 'scary', when she realized the enormity of the task she had set herself. Ann Brightwell made reference to naivety, 'You don't realize all the external influences that can affect the eventual production of that sort of performance and, therefore, you're not inhibited by them.' It is that lack of inhibition and not having limits to one's aspirations imposed, personally or from outside, which can be vitally important to the level of success reached. It is through what might be termed naive thinking or just asking 'Why not?', that many new techniques and future records are subsequently created.

CHAPTER 8

Coach-Athlete Relationship

Eleven per cent of these athletes said that they never really had any coaching. The individuals who were given no significant help included the 1928 and 1932 Olympians, Pat O'Callaghan and Bob Tisdall. When asked about a coach, Bob said, 'I never saw one!' He had specialized for about three months before the Games. His world record time of 51.8 sec on a cinder track for 440yds hurdles is nothing short of staggering. He said that he thought he came from good stock as his father had once long jumped twenty-two and a half feet onto a tennis court in India! The athletes of today who have had no significant coaches, such as Ed Moses and Joan Benoit Samuelson, read a lot, experimented for themselves and then later on they had advisors with whom they sounded out their ideas.

The father as coach

Almost 20 per cent of those interviewed had some coaching involvement from their fathers. For five men, Ian Botham, Greg Chappell, Arnold Palmer, Pete Rose and David Bryant, their fathers were the ones who gave them the basics and apart from that, coaching was relatively minimal. For Wayne Gretzky and Viv Richards, their fathers introduced them to the fundamentals, and for Carl Lewis both parents were coaches. However, all three had other significant coaches who assisted in their development. Carl referred to the relationship with Tom Tellez, his long jump coach. There was a marriage of personalities and a mutual respect which is essential in any good coach–athlete relationship.

The introduction of the fundamentals by the father was mentioned during pre-game interviews before the 1985 Superbowl. Both quarter-backs, Joe Montana and Dan Marino, said that their fathers had taught and stressed upon them the fundamentals of play. Joe referred to family support as well as his father's dedication, and Dan made the point that he was not pushed by his father. 'But if I wanted to do it he'd be there to do it with me.'

Four other athletes had a more significant father–coach role in that they were the main coach. Lester Piggott and Steve Davis referred to the basics given to them in technique. Sebastian Coe and Chris Evert Lloyd were taken to the lift-off point by their fathers, after which they could cope for themselves but with their parent still retaining an advisory role. Seb's father was not involved in track and field athletics at all: he had cycled, but the main aspect he brought to the task was a clear logical brain. He applied his scientific and engineering training to the study of middle-distance running. To an extent, the success he has had with Seb is testament to this naive yet fresh approach. Peter Coe was not weighed down with tradition in his thinking. Seb said, 'I've got a great debt of gratitude for the amount of time and intellectual effort that my father applied.'

Thirty-four per cent of the achievers said that they had had more than one significant coach, many of the athletes saying that different individuals assisted them as and when it was required. Duncan Goodhew said, 'It's like a piece of string that makes the distance; you cut one bit out and it's not going to make the distance.'

Perhaps one would have thought that a significant coach–athlete relationship could only take place with one type of coach for each person; however, experience shows that that is not the case. One-third of the athletes had more than one coach and several of them demonstrated that they could be motivated by different people. It would be more accurate to say that these athletes were able to relate successfully with people of varying personalities and coaching styles. Duncan's experience with three coaches is a good illustration. 'Paddy Garrett of Millfield School was a friend with a sarcastic sense of humour which cut to the bone and was an effective way of dealing with teenagers. He played me like a salmon. Don Easterling at North Carolina State University had a financial and contractual hold over me. We used to have head-to-head confrontations as we were both extremely hot-headed; we were conflicting characters. And lastly Dave Haller, the British Olympic coach, was really a quiet person with a 'save it' type of attitude. His unique quality was being able to reduce the workload to make an athlete peak in competition. He knew what to say and when to say it, and during that pre-competition period, he was exceptional at bringing confidence into his swimmers.'

Forty per cent of the achievers had experienced a deep or intensely significant coach–athlete relationship which was non-family based. It is in this group where sometimes the name of the coach becomes as famous as that of the athletes. Here are some who have become legendary: Herb Elliott and Percy Cerutty; Peter Snell and Arthur Lydiard; Ralph

Doubell and Roger Bannister with Franz Stampfl; Welsh rugby and Carwyn James; Gene Upshaw and the L.A. Raiders with John Madden; Peter Sterling and Australian rugby league with Jack Gibson.

Coaching styles

Is it important for a coach to cultivate a particular style? Most people would advise that no one should try to be what they are not. There are horses for courses. As Olympic long jump champion Mary Twomey said, 'There's someone for everyone. John le Masurier was quiet and that suited me.' Wherever possible, the coach and athlete should try to establish early on whether they have a decent rapport and can work well together before committing themselves to a long and potentially disastrous relationship.

There are several types of coaching styles. A number have been given labels, which may be helpful as a model, but it should be understood that there are mixtures of each in every individual. It seems that most of the coaches had the capacity to be uncompromising at a certain level. They would not allow the gifted athlete to consider laziness as an option and most of them are from a generation where authority was not questioned. In some cases, their discipline produced an unnerving quality; if athletes stepped out of line, they would face great displeasure and that could jeopardize the relationship. It seems that the mature athletes who worked with these authoritarian coaches chose to adhere to the strict regime because they knew that it was the best way for them to fulfil their own ambitions and dreams. Bob Cousy referred to his high school coach as a traditionalist and a disciplinarian. Al Oerter referred to his high school coach as authoritarian. Jonah Barrington spoke of Nasrullah Khan as *very* authoritarian. 'He had an aura about him . . . an air of considerable authority.' Ralph Doubell spoke of Franz Stampfl as a Dr Doolittle, explaining the ways of the world but also teaching that there was only one way, his way. His style of motivation was 'propaganda – nothing but the best'. He would only drink the best French champagne and in turn expected the athletes to accept nothing less than aiming to be the best in the world. Peter Snell referred to Arthur Lydiard as 'an evangelist, dogmatic and a great motivator'. Herb Elliott spoke of Percy Cerutty as inspirational but also that his way was uncompromising. Lynn Davies spoke of Ron Pickering as quite authoritarian, quite dogmatic, but he also pointed out there are many aspects to each coach. Lynn also referred to Ron as 'very enthusiastic, a very good teacher, communicator, and motivator of people and a very strong outgoing personality that I responded to.' John Havlicek spoke of Al Bladnick, his high school coach: 'We had a 10 p.m. curfew, no smoking, no drinking and he required classroom effort. Failure in any of these areas and you were off the team.' Peter Sterling spoke of the exceptional rugby league coaching record of Jack Gibson. He also referred to the fact that he was an authoritarian and a good teacher. 'He spoke slowly and the words were carefully chosen.' He went on, 'He was very good at reading the game, the opponents and us but the best thing that I could possibly say about him was that he was more interested in you off the paddock than on. I think he must have a good feeling for psychology because he believes that if you're happy, then you'll come through; if you're having trouble at home, it'll affect your game.'

In most cases, the athletes reflected that there was a concern extended by the coaches off the field: they were not just interested in the results produced but had a concern for the athletes as individuals. This can be termed a 'humanistic' approach. It seems that this additional element is the binding ingredient which makes the authoritarian approach on the field understandable and therefore accepted by the athlete. Even though there was the appearance of heartlessness and intolerance in the authoritarian treatment on the practice field, out of the training context there was a genuine friendship and respect on both sides.

For a coach–athlete relationship to be successful, there has to be a matching of several different aspects, including aims, respect, commitment and communication.

What are the aims and why should they coincide? One difficulty in deciding the aims is that the coach and athlete may not know how far each is capable, or indeed prepared to go. Nevertheless, for each individual, whether a beginner or potential world champion, the aim must be personal improvement and the goal setting must be realistic. Obviously, the aims of the coach and athlete must coincide. If the coach would like the athlete to become a champion and the athlete is only interested in having some fun, then their relationship is probably not going to work. Likewise if the athlete wants to reach his full potential and the coach does not have the same interest for him and with him, then there is bound to be disappointment in the relationship.

Why is respect important? Without respect it is difficult to have confidence in the other person's efforts, and performance is tied closely to confidence. So there must be mutual respect between coach and athlete otherwise there will be a loss of faith and the strength of the relationship will diminish. Respect is generated in many areas – respect for knowledge or achievement – but most important of all is the respect for the individual. A personal illustration of commitment increasing respect occurred when I was a student at Boston University. I usually met Billy Smith, my US coach, at 3 p.m. but on this particular day there was a blizzard. I went to the door of the parking area at 3 p.m. not really expecting to see Billy, but instead bumped into him on his way in. I asked whether I should do some weight training or have a day off. He pushed the door open against the wind and driving snow, and said, 'Out there's the road to Mexico!' I thought he was joking – but he clearly wasn't! As I did a series of 800m runs, Billy just stood there with his coat collar up and his back to the wind and driving snow. I hoped that my efforts would raise his respect for me and certainly his presence during the session in those conditions raised mine for him. It is that sort of mutual endeavour, under intense conditions, which strengthens the coach–athlete relationship.

Must there be a long-term commitment by both coach and athlete? At the introductory level, the intensity is absent but the need for consistency is still vital. This is the time when the basics are continually repeated so that the correct form can become second nature.

When the athletes make their decision to commit themselves to the pursuit of excellence, then there is a requirement of time and effort needed from both athlete and coach. Gareth Edwards spoke of Bill Samuel as 'a man who cared and gave me time'. Few young athletes give much thought to the time commitment and effort required by the coach. Their thoughts are often very self-centred and to an extent they have to be, but it is only in retrospect that the wealth of knowledge which has been given can be fully appreciated.

Without knowledge an athlete can very easily be injured or burnt out, never to fulfil his or her promise. Initially the coach holds most of the cards, but it must be understood that no person knows all the answers. In addition, although the ingredients are known, the way they are put together produces very different results. A training regime which has worked for one individual will not work exactly the same way with someone else because the structure, chemistry and mentality are always different. This difference provides a challenge of creativity, for coach and athlete, to put the best package together for each person. For some, particularly the young swimmer, it often means following in blind faith, leaving the coach with added responsibility. Mike Wenden mentioned that as he grew older he felt resentful that his coach was trying to dominate him.

Many coaches, however, are in a sense trying to work their way out of a job. Their experience and knowledge is passed on to the athlete and at the same time, the coach is attempting to make the athlete more independent. Pat Clohessy has worked with Rob de Castella since he was a fourteen-year-old schoolboy. Rob still values his training with Pat, but at the same time he spoke of his own creative involvement, attempting to visualize what training would be like in twenty years. Another example of an evolved relationship is where Steve Cram was given the basics by Jimmy Hedley but determined his own track sessions from the age of eighteen.

'Jimmy's role has changed to being supportive, a motivator. It goes beyond a coach–athlete relationship. He's a friend of the family and another sort of father figure.'

It is necessary for coaches to be widely read in their field, but even more important is that they have experience and feelings. Elliott referred to Cerutty as 'inspirational'. He put together a nice blend of enthusiasm, confidence and intellect. He had a broad base of reading and knowledge on which to base his arguments and his directions, so that you felt there was some weight in them and his own personal life experience added to this and so the whole blend of his knowledge and experience gave enormous believability and credibility.'

Is it necessary to have played the sport in order to coach it well? Experience must be gained from somewhere. For the coach to have had personal experience of the sport is, without question, helpful, but it has been shown that it is not essential. Seb Coe's father demonstrated that a study of the sport and a knowledge of the individual are the key ingredients. However, participation can give the coach an appreciation of the elements required for success. The coach will also better appreciate what he is asking of his athletes.

The description given by Heather McKay of what she was taught by each of her coaches would lead us to believe that it would be difficult, if not impossible in some sports, to teach without experience. Heather said that she was taught the stroke play by Vin Napier. 'He was a teacher and perfectionist on strokes and footwork technique.' Keith Walker followed on from Napier and of him she said, 'He taught me how to get the relationship of wall angle, height, pace and spacial awareness – I started to think at twenty-two!' The assistance from Kevin Parker came next. 'He helped tactically by teaching me the best choice of shots.'

Ron Pickering, coach for Lynn Davies, gained some help from his wife Jean, who was European long jump champion. He had a physical education background and apart from his coaching experience, saw many athletes as he travelled in his capacity as England's team coach. He pointed out the significance of exposing the athlete to experience. Ron said, 'I was absolutely convinced Lynn had to rub shoulders with the Americans, and over there, Ralph Boston beat him by a foot. (Lynn beat Ralph by less than two inches in the Olympics.) I think he was the first British athlete to go into the American trials. We had to raise the money to sponsor that.'

Is it necessary, therefore, for the coach to set an example by attempting to lead and demonstrate? The problem here is one of ability. At some point in the coach's career, he or she may have been very competent. However, if they have not continued to practise their skills, then the demonstration may be less than helpful. In most cases, there is a happy medium where certain skills can be demonstrated by the coach, for example, how to hold the equipment, or what the finishing position should be for an effective follow-through. The athletes may have more natural talent but in several instances they said, 'I was never asked to do anything that my coach hadn't attempted first'. It is no longer rare to have the coach participating, albeit at a reduced level. One man who retained his intensity of effort alongside his athletes was Percy Cerutty, and a photograph from Portsea circled the globe showing Percy, then in his sixties, leading a group up the dunes. Herb Elliott recalled how on the morning of one of his races, Cerutty came back from a run and said to Herb, 'You may run faster today but you'll never run harder!' Percy lived out his example.

Another important factor is communication. Here are a couple of simple illustrations showing what can happen when communications break down. If an athlete is not completely open and does not tell the coach that he has a slight injury, the coach will not know that he needs to modify the training. On the other hand, if the coach fails to give clear instructions, then the athlete may start to practise an incorrect motion or do too much or too little training.

No matter how widely read and experienced a coach may be, if he cannot communicate effectively then his knowledge is worth very little. Communication is possibly the most important of all areas. It is an essential requirement for any effective relationship. Many is the time when a highly intelligent teacher or professor is criticized for being a poor teacher because of a failure in communicating with his or her students.

All the rugby union men spoke of the ability of Carwyn James to communicate effectively. He and John Madden, Los Angeles Raiders' coach, were cited as having the unique ability to deal with different types of people in varying ways. This is a very unusual gift and makes them ideally suited for coaching teams. J.P.R. Williams referred to Carwyn as someone who was able to treat everyone individually. 'Coaches today tend to treat the forwards and backs the same in training and it tends to make everyone average. Carwyn was not strict, instead he used gentle persuasion, but his force of personality was like a breath of fresh air. A lot of coaches place so much importance on winning; you don't need that, you need some positive coaching and you need to be relaxed to play a normal game. He would say, "It's okay to be nervous but try to be above the atmosphere. Get out there and express yourselves".' Barry John commented on Carwyn's attitude. 'He was in search of excellence and he got the best out of each one of us. It was man management. He had total authority, a counsellor, he would ask, cajole, talk, invite thoughts. He'd probably made up his mind anyway but he'd ask you and that made you feel important.'

Gene Upshaw spoke of John Madden as a players' coach. 'He had fifty individuals and made them pull as one. He would be authoritarian with some, would discuss and ask for suggestions from others. Each man was treated individually. You wanted to win for him.'

Elliott said that he and Percy had a tremendous rapport. 'We had a happy knack of being able to understand one another after about two words of a sentence. Percy might take half an hour to explain to a person something he was trying to get at, but within a couple of sentences, I would know exactly what he was talking about – there was a sort of empathy.'

Another aspect of communication involves the absence of conflict and for any relationship to work well this must be achieved. John Daly coaches Glynis Nunn, winner of the heptathlon in the Los Angeles Olympics. She referred to the need for a basic understanding, 'just as in a father–daughter relationship or in a marriage.'

The coach as motivator

Motivation is not an easy term to define as it can be initiated from so many sources. In practical terms, the coach may not need to have a very good understanding of the athlete's underlying motives. What he must be able to do, however, is attach importance to the athlete's drive and desire to demonstrate to himself and others that he has a talent which he is trying to fulfil. The coach does need an appreciation of the importance of psychology.

Exactly how the coach motivates is variable. It is really a misinterpretation that the coach motivates the athlete. A good coach brings out the best from the athlete. Jonah Barrington said of his coach, 'He was the catalyst in regard to my own ambitions'. The top athlete is usually very well motivated, all that is needed is for the coach to touch the stimulus which challenges and inspires him to reach for the height of his ability. No top athlete needs the type of crazed motivational stunt such as the American high school coach who charged into the locker room before the big game and bit the head off a frog, which he hoped would get his team fired up! Peter Sterling put it well when he said, 'If you look at the film *Rocky* and get all hyped-up before going on the field, it's going to be belted out of you in the first tackle. If you're not self-motivated, you're not going to make it.' Many athletes could not readily identify any action or word which was said or done by the coach in order to motivate them. There was just a mutual understanding that they were travelling down a road together and they both knew that the aim was to become the best. A few coaches are able to inspire by example, others may do so through words and for some it may simply be their presence. Often the coach is there prior to competition, simply expressing faith in the athlete's physical and mental preparation. What is important is that both coach and athlete desire the athlete's attainment to another higher level. This means that the athlete has inner-motivation and that the coach's ambitions for the athlete are on an even higher level than his own.

It is very rare when a coach has the knowledge and ability to inspire in the manner of Percy Cerutty. Herb Elliott eloquently summed it up: 'Percy wasn't standing there with a horsewhip flogging you up and down the sand-hills. His motivation would come in an indirect way. He seemed to sense what your own appetites and ambitions were. He would put the plate in front of you, he wouldn't shove it down your throat. You'd choose your own direction. An example would be a winter's night at Portsea, sitting around the fire and he'd start to talk about Beethoven, Jesus, St Francis, Leonardo da Vinci, anybody that he'd studied who was a great person, not in a sense of a passing thing like winning a gold medal or winning an Australian championship or anything like that, but in the sense of a person who is still spoken about two thousand or hundreds of years after they've died. Somehow or other he would excite a sense in me and I think in many others that each of us has our own greatness, we are all totally unique and we always will be, so that we have a tremendous opportunity for being great in our own sort of way. By talking about other people being great, he'd touch your own sense of yourself and freshen up your ambitions and almost challenge you in a way, though without saying it, not to waste your own greatness and that would sort of fire you up. He just had that ability – he did it with knowledge and careful planning, I think, of how he would speak but he never ever said, "Don't waste your greatness". He just let you make up your own conclusions so that the path you chose appeared to be self-chosen.'

Could you have reached the level you did without a coach? The question was asked to see whether those athletes who had coaches felt their ultimate level of success would have been possible without that relationship and help. The question is hypothetical and Steve Davis gave the honest reply, 'Who knows?' A few athletes (11 per cent) were not sure and usually said that it would have been a lot more difficult. For example, Al Oerter replied: 'It would have been very difficult. I probably would have wound up in sport in some way because of my size and strength, but I don't know if I would have been able to enjoy a sport as long as I have done. I would probably have been in baseball or football and have been long retired by now.'

Jayne Torvill and Christopher Dean also said that it was a difficult question to answer. Christopher is the creative one who puts the programme ideas forward and then they work on it together. Betty Callaway and Courtney Jones are advisors and friends and their opinion is valued on the choice of music and ultimate performance.

Eighteen per cent felt that it might have made some difference but that they probably could have reached the top in their sport without significant coaching assistance, Lester Piggott saying that he thought it just would have taken longer. Several of the team sport players, such as Bob Cousy, Bryan Robson and Gareth Edwards, said that they were able to develop their individual skills but needed the coach to develop the team situation. The remaining two-thirds (68 per cent) believed that they would not have reached the level they did without the assistance of their coach and they usually cited at least one good reason. Of course, many reasons have already been covered concerning the coach–athlete relationship. Nevertheless, further insights were given into why their relationships were valued.

Ken Read said that there was no way he would have reached the top without his coach Scott Henderson. 'He'd work and work at something until he thought we had it and then he'd shift to the next thing.' This step-by-step approach requires a great deal of patience on the part of the coach but is invaluable for the athlete because under pressure, the athlete reverts to what is second nature. If the fundamentals are sound and have been repeated correctly enough times to have become second nature, then the form will not give way in the most important tests.

Bobby Charlton was another who said that he did not think he could have reached his ultimate level without his coaches Jimmy Murphy, Bert Wooley and Sir Matt Busby. Of Jimmy Murphy, Bobby said, 'I never went on the field without thinking of him. I supposed he brainwashed me but, just as you learn to ride a bike, it becomes second nature. Anything from a professional point of view that I did as second nature was something that Jimmy Murphy taught me, whether it was marking, doing a one–two with someone and getting a return pass, or whether it was a shot on goal, there was always something there that Jimmy Murphy had worked on with me.'

The fact that a coach can become a part of an athlete's thinking was mentioned by Steve Ovett several years ago. In recent years, Steve has had a close friendship with Matt Paterson who has also given him advice, but in the early days Steve was introduced to the sport by Harry Wilson. When Steve was only eighteen, he said that he could hear Harry yelling at him, even though Harry was not physically present. It was an experience which I had personally encountered in my time with Billy Smith. While training alone, there would come a point of tiredness where the need and temptation was to slow down, but the acquired conscience from my coach was strong enough for me to feel his eyes on me and hear his voice encouraging me not to ease up until the end of the session. The expectations and will of my coach somehow had become ingrained and merged with my own will and self-expectations.

O.J. Simpson valued the coaches who expressed their caring in various ways. 'In high school I was kind of a tough energetic kid, and Jack McBride helped with a little direction, for example he said, "To get respect you have to accept responsibility". First you have to accept responsibility for yourself. You can't say, "I'm man enough to live up to the punishment because I knew I was doing wrong". You've got to make the decision, if I knew it was wrong I shouldn't be doing it.' O.J. went on to relate that while at the University of Southern California, he had received instruction from the head coach John McKay, and from one of the assistant coaches, Marv Goux. They both expressed care and support while opening up opportunities for O.J. to develop his talent. And finally, while with the Buffalo Bills, coach Lou Saban based the team's game around what O.J. could do offensively.

Being in the right place at the right time was considered to be important in the fortunes of these athletes. Lynn Davies said, 'I'm pretty convinced that if Ron [Pickering] had not come to Wales as national athletics coach, I would not have continued in the sport.'

Another important aspect taught by the coach was making the athlete think like a winner. Those achievers who win do not waste their time thinking of the reasons why it might not be possible to achieve a goal; they do not give such negative thoughts the time of day. The focus is on the ways of achieving the next step. Billie Jean King said that she was given practical suggestions as well as a role model by a Wimbledon winner. 'Over a period of three months, Alice Marble taught me how to think like a winner, yet she was nice. I knew what it was to be around a champion and how a champion thinks. The first thing she said was, "You get too close". She talked about the face of the racket in relation to the ball. I devoured her scrap books.'

One of the greatest gifts a coach can give is a sense of belief in the athlete. Frank Brennan worked with Billie Jean on strategy and focussing. 'At fifteen, he told me, "You're going to win Wimbledon one day".' Finally for Billie Jean, Lew Hoad helped to put everything together. 'I gave up my job at twenty-one and made the commitment to be number one. He changed my serve, forehand and strategy. It consolidated my game. It was a tough period, ranked number four in the world, and during one game I served thirty-five double faults. People questioned why I was changing and I said, "Because I want to be the best".'

Knowledge both of the physical and psychological may be gained in conjunction with academic and scientific research or it may be simply the application of common sense. When Valeriy Borzov was asked if he could have reached his potential without his coaches, he gave a firm answer of no. Valeriy had been taught the basics by his school coach and then he had learned about the workings of the body and mind from a professor at his sport institute who worked with him for twelve years, from 1966 to 1978.

Less sophisticated but equally helpful was the role of Pat Burgess as described by Lucinda Green. 'There have been masses of people who I've put my trust in and have been the cornerstone on which to build, but the person who has seen me through the longest and has been the most helpful of all is Pat Burgess. She is no world trainer of any sort, she just trains in a back field over tin cans and poles but has this wonderful quality of common sense which so many people lose when they start learning techniques, and an ability to know what a horse is thinking and feeling, and to see why a rider isn't getting on and why that horse isn't going. She's a really gifted person.'

Coaching rewards

Before closing this chapter on the coach–athlete relationship, it is worth asking the question: What does the coach get out of all this? In many cases they will get as much, if not more, from the experience as the athlete. It is a very true saying that in giving, one receives. In fact both parties do give and when each knows that the other is devoting their best effort, mutual respect and allegiance is gained, and a closeness is established. Trust is also established when the athlete knows that the coach is not trying to exploit him or her by 'living off' their sucess, either financially or through self-glorification.

All of the coaches referred to the value they held in their personal relationships with their athletes. This is quite possibly the most important element in the long term. The mutual effort towards a common goal brings a closeness and sharing and thus enhances communication. This makes the process valuable in itself, regardless of the outcome. All the better if it results in a winning performance, but if there is an intrinsic worth in the endeavour, then both parties gain and grow by the experience. There are several factors which contribute to making the relationship valuable. The situation evolves over a considerable length of time during which there is a sharing of the spectrum of emotions: joys and sorrows, frustration, despair, humour, hope and elation. The goal is shared and the endeavour is mutual. In the close coach–athlete relationship, the coach can become totally consumed with the athlete, and their projected aspirations become one and the same.

In many cases, the gifted athlete will inspire a coach to learn more about the sport or event, bringing about a mutual learning experience; indeed the coach will often learn more through working with a gifted athlete than working with one of lesser ability. A young athlete who has the necessary ingredients to go to the top kindles an enthusiasm in the coach and an eagerness to work with a would-be achiever. The coach's role then is to work the athlete but also to preserve the athlete's enthusiasm. My coach Billy Smith said, 'If the athlete is force-fed then the enthusiasm can be chipped away. You can parallel enthusiasm with motivation. When the enthusiasm is at its highest, the performance will be the best. It almost overrules physical logic, too. Enthusiasm is the key.'

It is worth noting that Fred Housden, coach of many British Olympic athletes, and my hurdles coach, intentionally took on athletes of all abilities because of his own added learning experience in how to teach at all levels.

Pat Clohessy coaches Rob de Castella and he views his role as a pleasurable teaching experience – 'To educate the athletes to beome more self-reliant and to understand their sport better, rather than to make them dependent on me, particularly a long-distance runner. On the creative side, the coach should back his judgement. He has more experience and has got to lead, but you need to explore different initiatives.'

Tom Tellez has coached Carl Lewis since 1980. He saw the necessary ingredients as going beyond pure physical talent. 'There are other kids who have just as much ability. He's got a lot of ability but I think there are other athletes who have had or do have right now as much ability, but I attribute his success to his parents, his home life and his stability. I think they created a sense that there are no limitations to what you can do if you want to. The Lewis children were brought up with that idea. Anything is yours if you want it and are prepared to work for it.' Later he added, 'I think our personalities kind of hit. I'm not a dogmatic kind of coach, I tend to work with the athletes. I don't like to overwork kids. They have to be self-motivated. I work on mechanics. You prepare the athlete mentally by preparing him physically.' He then spoke of what he gets from it all. 'You plan something . . . you conceive of a model . . . we've built this model and he is the model and he's doing everything well . . . that's the thrill I get out of it.'

I asked Billy Smith when he started goal-setting the Olympic 400m hurdles for me. He replied, 'Oh, first or second day.' His wife added, 'I was in hospital having given birth to our first daughter, Susan, and he came in and said, "There's a kid named David Hemery who showed up at camp today. He needs work. He really needs work, but he's got great technique, he's going to be good, I'm telling you, really good." I said, "How good?" It was almost like he was afraid, he kept saying, "I don't know, I just know he's going to be really good" and he sat there rubbing his forehead, he was just so excited.' One reason for a coach being nervous before the relationship starts is that 'with opportunity comes responsibility' and Billy said that he did not want to mess it up.

John le Masurier was big enough to be self-critical of his lack of experience in 1960. He said, 'I think I nursed Mary [Twomey] too much in competitions in this country. It's a great temptation to go out and see where the foot comes on the board in the run-ups prior to competition. It was a lesson we learned from. It was better after Rome to say, "Right, you're on your own. Go out and do it and I'll watch you from afar. I'll talk to you beforehand and I'll talk to you afterwards." She had to learn to do it herself and be self-supporting.' For John, one aspect which meant a lot to him was the friendships which he had with his athletes. 'Mary and my wife would have long chats on the phone. I think it's very helpful if the people you're coaching are individuals you want in your home. Mary, Vic Matthews, Sue Platt, we were one big happy family really, and I think that was an advantage.'

For Ron Pickering, 'The great joy days were the training days. The competition days were always the stress days.' Ron worked out in the weightroom with Lynn where there was an element of mutual challenge. Ron said, 'It took three years before he could out-lift me – and it took another year before he could beat me at everything.' Ron used his verbal dexterity and wit to goad Lynn to the next level of effort. For example, Lynn would be asked to demonstrate for some assembled coaches and Ron would climb all over him verbally. 'He and I knew it was humour but the crowd didn't and he would get such sympathy from them. I can remember the phrases, "Yes, 25 ft 4 in – that's grade three for clerical workers in Outer Mongolia! Do you think these people have travelled 150 miles to see a grade three performance of that sort? Don't you think they deserve to see you at your very best? I mean I've seen you on a cold day do things and really, to waste their time . . ." And the banter would go on. Lynn was asked by someone at the front, "How do you feel about that?" To which Lynn replied, "I love it. It brings out the best performance in me and he knows it." I was constantly challenging him, attempting to put him under competitive conditions.'

Unlike John le Masurier, Ron told Lynn that he was on his own prior to the big meeting against the Soviet Union. It was, however, the first time that Ron had had a long-distance perspective of his athlete. From 75m away, he saw errors in movement which he had missed by always being right beside the take-off board. The new visual perspective altered the game plan for the future. It caused a complete rethink of their approach to the event. Ron said that over time, their relationship changed. 'Far less authoritarian, far more man to man, far more intimate, because we were talking about minor adjustments and philosophical discussions, we were not talking about command–response situations. My new role for the developed athlete was to be his eyes when he needed them and to be much more subordinate. My value to him was to use the experience of life rather than my experience as a coach and that is where our friendship developed in that I would expect him to come to me about money problems or marriage, and that was far more important than to create simply a practical and correct environment from which he could develop athletically. The environment became more important than the event and I think that happens in all cases.' Ron also referred to the coach's home as being a place where the athletes came as friends and that they would talk to his wife about things that were troubling them, which they would not have shared with him. He thought that this was because of the coach–athlete rapport, which is based on high expectations of one another.

At times it can be a thankless task and as has been said already, the athletes are at times very egocentric. The strength of the experience is in mutual learning, where both sides recognize and appreciate that the other is giving of their best.

Enthusiasm is generated in the coach because the athlete with all the necessary elements for world achievement does not come along every day. A line from *Chariots of Fire* spoken by coach Massubini says it all: 'You can't put in what God left out.' In many cases, an athlete may have the head but not the body, the heart but not the coach, the body but not the will, so when a good coach meets a willing athlete with sufficient mind, heart, body and will to get to the top, it is understandable why this recognition would lift the spirits, and the experienced coach will see the potential and try to realize it.

CHAPTER 9

ALTERNATIVE SUPPORT

Was there any other person apart from your parents or coach who helped you to achieve your goal? It was at this point that many of the athletes who did not have a coach who had influenced them, named people who were important either as a role model, advisor, teacher, partner, or someone who had given inspiration.

ROLE MODELS Most role models will be unaware of who they are inspiring. They are, nevertheless, an extremely significant source of aims. For children, parents and older siblings are the first and most obvious behavioural role models. However, once the individual is old enough to make a choice of a career or ambition, the impact of another role model may have just as significant an effect.

Jackie Stewart recalled two outstanding drivers. 'Fangio was the great man of racing while Sterling Moss was the epitome of a racing driver.' O.J. Simpson said, 'Arnold Palmer is one of the most well-liked people. He's happy and evidently secure within himself, and once you've reached that state, other people are more comfortable and secure around you, despite your celebrity status or so-called talent. When you meet Arnold Palmer, you say, "I can be like him". Willie Mays did it for me the time I met him when I was a kid. He was my absolute hero and then when I met him, I said, "Man, this guy's just like I am. He's no God, he's just like me, I could be a great ball player". Those are the guys who are secure within themselves and that transmits to the people around them.'

Duncan Goodhew is not at all sure whether Nigel Johnson was aware of being his mentor. A fellow student at Millfield School, Nigel was going to the Olympics, and that became Duncan's goal.

Ian Botham and Viv Richards independently cited Brian Close, during his captaincy of Somerset's cricket team. Viv said, 'I was young and raw and he was the captain. Mentally, he was a hero for me. He would get hit by a bouncer from fast bowler Wesley Hall and he wouldn't rub the spot. He'd just stand there with his chest up.' Ian's comment was, 'I always had the will to win but he certainly helped drag it out of me early on. He taught me one thing above all – that nothing is lost until the last ball is bowled. He only wanted to win and he never asked anyone to do anything he hadn't or couldn't do himself. He lived hard and played hard – a very determined man.'

Barry John also chose to follow an example set by a cricketer. When he was twelve or thirteen years old, he read about one of the most respected West Indies cricketers, Gary Sobers. Gary had decided to prepare himself so that the selectors couldn't drop him no matter what the conditions or what was required. He worked on being capable of bowling fast, slow or spin. He learned to play defensively as well as score dramatically. Barry said that from reading that, he decided to apply the same principle to his own game of rugby union. He worked on being able to kick with either foot and to prepare himself to be invaluable and indispensable no matter what the requirements or conditions.

Jackie Stewart referred to a pre-motor racing teammate who had influenced him strongly. 'The captain of the British shooting team, Glynne Jones, a great character, had a tremendous influence on how I behaved and how I looked at serious competition and how I looked at life. He is a humourist and fun to be with but also a successful businessman.' Jackie spoke of another person who influenced him: 'Bob McIntyre, the first motor cyclist to do 100 m.p.h. around the Isle of Man, attacked his motorcycle racing in such a profound way and it was he who started me on weight training and getting fit.'

ADVISORS Individuals take guidance and receive support from all types of people. Rod Laver recalled that he had had little coaching. 'No one showed me how to hold a racket, but I had advice from Charlie Hollis who said, "If you want to be a champion, you'll have to top spin your backhand". From there, it was done by feel.' The advice gave him confidence to persevere with the top spin regardless of the consequences.

Steve Davis said that his manager, Barry Hearn, was like a brother. 'He helped me mature as a person and grow up a lot quicker. Because of the fact that you only play snooker, there's no childhood, no teens, you're lacking in other ways and you have to grow up quickly and he helped me to do that.' Steve also mentioned that Barry was the one who introduced him to the need for total physical fitness.

Pete Rose echoed this remark: 'When Sparkey Anderson came as manager, I had just won two batting titles in a row and he said, "You can set a lot of records in this game if you start taking care of yourself". That's when I started really taking care of my body in the off season.'

Clive Lloyd was significantly influenced by Fred Mills whom he referred to as his mentor. 'He was a very brilliant man, a barrister, and I always wanted to be a barrister; in fact, he was a QC. He gave me the inner strength and confidence. He looked after me. When I first played first team cricket in Guyana, aged sixteen, I remember the rest of the team going off to the pub at the local hotel. Fred would give me some money and tell me to take my girlfriend out or something, letting me know that he thought I had exceptional ability and not to waste it.'

Gene Upshaw said that Al Davis, the owner of the Los Angeles Raiders, had given him confidence. 'I was elected captain after two or three years and he backed the vote by telling me that it was time to take more of a leadership role and once he'd said that, I started pushing a bit more.'

Some athletes reach a point in their careers where they generally know what is the best for them. However, they value having a knowledgeable sounding-board or someone whose opinions they respect. Joan Benoit Samuelson cited Bob Sevene, the Athletics West coach. Greg Chappell valued Richie Benaud and his brother Ian. 'They are the two blokes I respect most. They're near contemporaries and I know that if I had a problem, apart from going to my father, those are the two who I would have gone to and said, "Listen, I feel as though I'm not doing things quite the same as I was before – have you got any thoughts?"'

Experience counts and Steve Cram is grateful for the reflections of Brendan Foster. 'That extra 10 per cent was very worthwhile. Jimmy Hedley couldn't have told me what it would be like in the Olympic final. Brendan could, so I was lucky.' Clive Lloyd's cousin is the West Indies bowler Lance Gibbs. Clive said that his cousin advised him when he was fourteen not to aspire to play for Guyana, but to set his sights higher, to play for the West Indies.

Another important part that advisors can play is giving advice on personal financial matters, or helping to find financial assistance from another source. Financial backing can be a very valuable asset for the athlete. Harold Guiver was just such an influential person in Billie Jean King's life. 'Harold believed in me from the beginning and said that he would pull together the money to get me to Wimbledon. I said, "No, I haven't earned it yet".' It was not too long before she did. For Rod Laver it was Wally Best at Dunlop in Brisbane who gave financial backing. 'He wanted to know how I'd done and would ask if I needed anything – he was like a second father.'

TEAM-MATES Team-mates and training partners have assisted in a variety of ways. Rod Laver talked about the encouragement from team-mates Roy Emerson and Mel Anderson. 'I worked well to encouragement and I responded well to the positive example.'

Cricketers have no coach at national level, so they rely on advice from fellow team members. Greg Chappell said that both Rodney Marsh and Dennis Lillee had helped him a lot. O.J. Simpson did not make personal reference to anyone in particular, but said that the emotional closeness with team-mates often comes when you have come through hard times together.

Mixed training with both men and women seems to have helped the women significantly. Marjorie Jackson trained with McDonald Bailey; Ann Brightwell with her future husband Robbie and the group of men with whom he trained; Mary Twomey referred to the fun of blatantly taking a flier in starting practice against the boys; Heather McKay, Margaret Court, Billie Jean King and Chris Evert Lloyd all mentioned the significance of playing against males.

PARTNERS Almost everyone in the study referred to the support which they had from their partners. Ian Botham and Viv Richards both cited the understanding and support they receive from their wives. This is very important considering that cricket and rugby tours take the players away from their families for weeks and even months at a time. Without the backing of partners, it would be difficult for the individuals to embark on such trips.

Squash champion Geoff Hunt valued his wife in a role which went beyond normal support. 'My wife helped to keep my performance in perspective and I think that's important. She doesn't tolerate bad behaviour on the court and the odd times where I'd show any form of disagreement, which usually wasn't bad compared with others, she would pick me up on it. She would never come out and abuse me or really praise me. She had confidence in me that no matter what predicament I was in, I was going to get out of it. It was also what she expected me to do . . . because she knew it was what I expected of myself.'

Partner support was as much appreciated by the women. Heather McKay and Margaret Court said that their husbands often travelled with them and not only supported their activities, but were involved with the necessary encouragement in training efforts. Shirley de la Hunty spoke about assistance at home, referring to the work her husband did. 'Without his support, I couldn't have gone on. He was a capable and devoted baby-sitter.'

Chris Evert Lloyd greatly appreciates the support and belief in her as expressed by her husband John. The added bonus in this relationship is that John can also be a valuable training partner.

The most unusual partnership was that mentioned by Lucinda Green: the relationship with her horses. However, on reflection, it is exactly what is required. 'In the case of coaching support, there are so many people who have been vital parts in the jigsaw on the way up, five or six or seven coaches with valuable input, that it's unfair to name one or two in particular. It's the horses that are most important to me.'

TEACHERS Several of the athletes spoke about their school teachers who had played an important role in their initial introduction to the sport. In

Gareth Edwards's case, school teacher Bill Samuel was mentioned as the significant coach, but in most cases the teachers were simply the ones who introduced the sport and kindled an interest in it, either through the way they presented it, or more importantly, through their personality and enthusiasm. There are thousands of such teachers who see young talent and encourage the children in their sporting pursuits. Ann Brightwell named Miss Bromley who taught at her grammar school, as well as Brian Stephens and David Cree, and at the Reading Athletic Club, David Frewin and Keith Horne. Mary Twomey spoke of Miss Saunders at her secondary school, Mr Bromfield at Millfield and club coaches Alf and Mabel Cotton. The chain of people has been there for almost everyone, but their importance often goes unrecognized. It will be noted in a later section that a large proportion of these high achievers saw their progression as a series of steps. The teachers and club coaches have been a vital part in putting youngsters on the first rung of the ladder.

OTHER INFLUENCES Ralph Doubell had the misfortune of losing his father when only fourteen years old. During the interview, he mentioned that his coach, Franz Stampfl, played a significant role, but he also spoke of the support of Howard Toyne, a sports medico, who gave him a job when he needed it. 'Howard referred to me as his son, so there's another person who adopted me and Alan Eustace, a vocational guidance counsellor, less intense but equally a slight father–son routine.'

Daley Thompson has Doreen. 'When I started out, my aunt was really helpful in everything I did; she just supported it whether it was right, wrong, indifferent or anything. She's just been really helpful and supportive – everything you'd expect from your parents and more. So that's been great. If I'd been able to do everything I've done without her, it would have been twice as difficult or perhaps I might not have been able to do it all, because with her, I've always had home stability and all that kind of stuff and I spend so much time away from home. I need someone back there to be solid and dependable. I like being at home, I like my friends and I get homesick.'

Medical backup is another important facet in the sportsperson's life. Ralph Doubell spoke for many athletes when he said just how much he appreciated being held together by the physios. Joan Benoit Samuelson agreed: 'I must thank the doctors who put me back together. People were saying after my knee surgery that I had this miracle cure, electrical therapy, but if Stan James hadn't performed successful surgery, neither therapy nor a strong mind would have helped and the same with Dr Leech who carried out my Achilles tendon surgery.'

Valeriy Borzov believed that the support of the Press, as well as friends, was a positive influential factor. He said that the Press had always been good to him. Significantly, it was not uncommon to hear the Western athletes in this study say that they had stopped reading the papers because too often they were misquoted or run down the the Press. As in other areas, constructive as opposed to negative criticism is far more likely to lead to higher achievement.

Humour

How important to you was a sense of humour and what purpose did it have? The overwhelming response of 89 per cent of all the athletes interviewed was that it was vital and basically relieved tension. Athletes enjoy being around humour even if they are not humorists themselves. David Bryant saw it as providing team unity, especially as a skipper. Lester Piggott said that with all the travel required in his work, a jockey must see the funny side. Carl Lewis sees humour as a form of creativity, while Ken Read felt that it gave perspective.

To Daley Thompson, humour is everything. His humour, however, often gets him into trouble outside the track environment. For example, a sponsor's wife told him, 'Daley, I can't tell you how much pleasure you've given me.' Daley drily replied, 'Thank you, but you'd better not let your old man hear you say that!'

Lucinda Green said, 'I don't see how you can exist without it and still enjoy yourself.' Billie Jean King responded by saying, 'It's essential. You must have resilience, and humour helps that a lot.'

O.J. Simpson mentioned how important it was to keep a team together in difficult times. 'It was everything. The competitive world is intense and humour is a way to defuse that in many cases. It helps you to deal with the ups and downs of sport. Every week someone wins and someone loses. I played with teams that lost most of the time. It was just my lot in life that they gave the best players to the worst teams and though we might have been the most entertaining team, we didn't have enough good players to be big winners. So it was really important in that environment to have a sense of humour and sometimes it kept the team together – you keep the guys light and it keeps the guys working.'

Continuing with American football, Gene Upshaw recalled, 'If you didn't have humour you couldn't compete in sport. You have to be able to laugh when you get knocked on your butt and get up. Everyone gets knocked down but the winners are the ones who get up. That's the key – how fast you get up. You have to be able to laugh, because you have so many chances to cry, you'd better be able to laugh.' Pete Rose said that it was pretty hard not to have a sense of humour when you have played in team sport for so many years.

Mike Wenden thought that it was important to have the ability to step outside of oneself and have a look at the humour of the situation.

Certainly it sounded as if that would be needed in the following illustration which he gave. 'After an epic swim in training, you're lying on the side of the pool, with all the muscles quivering like a jelly and not an ounce of strength left and gasping for breath and the coach walks over with his stop watch and says, "That was pretty good but the next one's going to be better". You've got to have a sense of humour to live with remarks like that.'

Steve Ovett and Steve Cram said that they saw the funny side of things even during training sessions. Ovett said, 'There are occasions when Matt [Paterson] and I have actually had to stop training because we've been laughing so much. I think if you don't have a sense of humour and you can't laugh at yourself, you are not really enjoying it as much as you possibly could. Some of the hardest sessions are when the funny occasions arise. I don't know whether it's because mentally you're alert, you're concentrating and therefore anything seems funny. I think part of you accepts the lunacy of it all, saying, "What the hell are you doing this for?". When training is really hard and people are doubled up on the floor or throwing up, you'll hear, "It's only pain but you'll get used to it". It's not the sort of thing anyone wants to hear, but it's funny at the time . . . Middle-distance runners are very similar and there's an empathy and a closeness that brings understanding of the training or the environment or whatever the circumstances. It only needs something to get you going and it triggers everything off and everybody else can immediately identify with it, it doesn't have to be explained.'

Steve Cram reflected on his need not to make his training too competitive. 'I hate people getting too serious in training. I see lads destroying themselves being too competitive in training and they sometimes get miffed if we're having a few jokes. It helps me enjoy it a lot more.'

In contrast, Herb Elliott took his training time very seriously, saying that he could not remember laughing during the sessions or even finding humour in their intensity.

For all the glamour of national and international sport, it is still a very tense scene. The Olympic Games, for example, come once every four years, and many people aim for them with such passion and intensity for so long, that they become highly charged within their environment. Yet in the midst of the Olympians, one man, Al Oerter, reflected on the scene from a different perspective. Instead of the shared humour with others which he also valued, Al talked from the perspective of one who has been at the top and is then able to relax and enjoy the scene. 'It's always necessary to have a sense of humour. You can't stay in an intense climate, including the Olympic Village, and be unaware of what's going on. There's something about the Games themselves. They're the most intense environment in sport and they're comical at times because these architects build these wonderful venues with award-winning housing and they're wonderful things to behold . . . the first thing the athletes do is hang their underwear outside! In fifteen minutes, it looks like a tenement building. They'll wash out their jocks or their shorts and go out and hang it on a statue to dry!' Al also reflected on what tension does to the athletes. 'It's funny to watch people who were absolutely normal just fifteen minutes before, conversational, talking about their kids back home or about where they're from and minutes later, they're on the floor of the stadium, before the competition – pacing, sweating heavily and looking so concerned. This is to be enjoyed; this is why we're here and why we've worked for four years. If you don't enjoy it, why did you work the four years?' Al was able to reflect on this because he sees the Games as a journey and not as an end in themselves. Each day's training was a step forward, regardless of the final result. Was it possible that he acquired this more relaxed view following his first success? 'Maybe you're right, maybe it was that way my first time in 1956. Certainly, since then, it's something to be enjoyed.'

Oerter is certainly expressing a view which most can see intellectually but few are able to follow mentally. There are few actors or actresses, musicians or dancers, who do not feel nerves at a time when an important performance is about to be judged. Singer Vera Lynn once said that, 'You're only as good as your last performance . . . I didn't really enjoy the feeling beforehand . . . I only felt relaxed after it was over.' It is part of the human response and Al Oerter is certainly a fortunate man to be able to enjoy his competitive times before and during the performance. Few, if any, are forced to compete. They do so because they have to and want to. It is a self-expression, and afterwards the athletes are happy to have fulfilled their task with distinction.

Al is not entirely alone in being able to keep matters in a light-hearted vein, even during competition. Barry John talked about an incident near the end of a rugby union match. He said that his team were ahead by a substantial margin and he knew that making another score was not going to be fully appreciated by the fans. He said that he would rather give them something to talk about and go home with a smile on their faces. So when a high ball was coming his way, he saw that it was going to be very close between him catching it and getting hit head on by a 6 ft 5 in, fast-moving defender. He kept his gaze up toward the ball but drifted to his right. The defender naturally followed him. The ball landed with a thud several feet to one side while he jumped clear of the attacking forward. The crowd loved it.

In their own way, each type of assisting person is significant. It may be through sharing humour at different times, or having a role model to set a standard of temperament or behaviour; it can be a person with insight into talent, taking the trouble to give assistance – or to offer a guiding word or helping with finances; it may be a partner or a friend who understands the struggle or is simply there to go through difficult times with them. The roles are many and varied but the end result is the same – the athlete is supported in mind, body and spirit.

CHAPTER 10

INSTITUTIONAL SUPPORT

Those in the West often think of state support in sport in terms of the Eastern bloc countries where total control is administered by state subsidy of their athletes and facilities. We recoil at the thought of a lack of personal choice, but this is not a completely accurate picture, and it would be wrong to think that we in the West are not providing similar support for our sport, albeit on a much reduced scale. It would be helpful to look at the Soviet system first and to see what expectations their athletes had from sport.

SPORT IN THE USSR Young athletes in the USSR are screened for their physical and psychological aptitude for sport. Those who fit the highly successful sports profile are then given the choice to attend a school. These are normal educational schools which also have a specialist training in specific sports. It is considered an honour to be chosen and offered such an opportunity, similar to being offered a tuition scholarship to university in the United States. Most youngsters willingly accept but it is their choice. Once secondary school is completed, almost all Soviet sportsmen and women will go on to study their sport and related disciplines at university. This has proved to be a very successful system, up to a point. But Jayne Torvill and Christopher Dean pointed out a drawback of such early screening. 'They always get very good performers because they've chosen somebody with the right physique and they always have pretty girls skating, but they almost never get that fantastic, spontaneous performance because maybe it's not coming directly from within them. Some have strong personalities, like Olga Korbut in gymnastics, but we find that they have a lot of very bland people and they work like robots.' They went on to say that some of their top performers have rebelled in some way. 'The Protopopovs defected and Olga herself was very outspoken . . . Rodnina [who was best known in her partnership with Zaitsev] was different in that she's a party member and she chose who would be her partners and she could also decide when to finish skating.'

Due to the large numbers involved, there are bound to be some entering the sport who find that it is *their* form of self-expression, but Jayne and Chris's point was that only if the choice of sport is made by the athletes themselves can one expect to have individuality and personality fully expressed in a performance. Perhaps the choice of sport is being made too early for the generally gifted who could turn their talent to another sport later on. Certainly the screening helps to identify talent and to match them up with well-qualified coaches. But what happens when the sportsperson is no longer in the peak of condition and is unable to continue his or her sporting career?

Valeriy Borzov made a personal comment. He felt that the system in the West was very unfair to their athletes, as they could participate for their country and even win a gold medal but at the end of their sporting career, there was no guarantee from the government, or private sector, of any job. He felt that there must be some amount of insecurity in the minds of Western athletes not knowing if they are perhaps sacrificing their early career days. He posed the question of injustice; while devoting a great deal of time and effort on their own behalf, athletes also devote their energy and talent on behalf of their country, and at the end of the day, can be left with nothing. He reflected specifically on Tommy Smith, the US sprinter, who had won the 200m in world record time at the 1968 Mexico Olympics, and returned home to unemployment. Tommy is now a junior college coach, but Valeriy believes that there should have been no time lag.

It is certainly a point worthy of reflection. One reason that there is not this problem in the Soviet Union is because there is full employment by the State and almost all sports people attend state universities. Many of them will become well-qualified coaches by the time their active career is over. Of course, this may not be wanted by all the Western athletes. However, it would be reasonable to consider that the athletes who are currently receiving a subsidy for training virtually full-time, should have a responsibility to give something back to their sport. It would be a valuable inspiration to future generations if each subsidized athlete took a coaching qualification during some of their free time, so that on retirement, or before, they would be able to visit schools or clubs and teach as well as inspire. It would take financial backing to underwrite their travel and payment, but as trained coaches they would be in an excellent position to engender enthusiasm and to pass on sound basic advice.

SPORT IN THE WEST How do individuals choose the right sport? For most youngsters in the West, choosing the right sport is more by luck than good judgement. If a school teacher happens to recognize talent and has the expertise to assist or direct a youngster towards good coaching, then the young person is fortunate. Usually, the young athletes must rely on the right facilities and decent coaching being close to where they live.

The high schools in the United States are very well set up to afford a variety of competitive opportunities with excellent facilities; however, most of their coaches are teachers who, although they have played in their time, have no coaching accreditation. In most cases, this is not the coaches' fault: few coaching certification programmes exist. The teacher training colleges teach the physical educationalists the rules and general state of play in a wide variety of sports, but even there, no individual sports have instituted a test or specified priorities in coaching and training techniques. Most coaches come up through the ranks of experience: they are usually self-taught and have had no formal instruction. They apply their own thoughts to old methods.

In Great Britain, the situation in schools is not too dissimilar from the US, with the exception of the generally inadequate indoor facilities. However, the emphasis as a nation has always been on clubs. Outside the schools programme, a teacher or club coach does have an option to take coaching courses. Track and field athletics provides an excellent working example with a well-organized programme. A parent or trainee coach may take an introductory, general course which emphasizes basic skills in all events, the avoidance of injury, and above all enjoyment. There are two more advanced levels which amateur coaches may pursue as they become more specialized and experienced.

A disturbing trend in Britain and the United States has been the budget cuts for junior school sport. In several local authorities in the UK, sport in school is played on only one afternoon a week and three different sports are rotated. Ian Botham recounted that his son is very keen on soccer. Thursday is assigned for sport but if it rains, that activity week is cancelled. This happened twice in succession on soccer weeks, which meant that there were nine weeks between the one day for soccer! This is no way to allow young talent to develop.

In Boston, the budget for junior school sport was being cut completely! Sport used to be considered a right within a child's education. The learning of the ideals of sport from Rugby School inspired Baron Pierre de Coubertin to re-initiate the Olympics. Regardless of political point scoring, a youngster can gain so much through sport that a denial of this opportunity is a regrettable and short-sighted strategy. As with any other type of learning, the younger the individual, the easier it is to learn.

SPORTS SCHOLARSHIPS One alternative solution would be private or government sponsorships for school and university coaching grants. There are a few independent schools which offer scholarships. In Great Britain, Millfield School along with other schools in more recent years have given scholarships for the development of excellence in sport as well as for academics, music and art. Many schools offer financial assistance to top academic scholars, a few awards exist for music, and even fewer for art or sport. Lately, one innovation has been the idea of an independent sponsorship. David Lloyd has joined forces with Jim Slater and Reed's School to provide tennis tuition and educational scholarships for a few boys each year. Their aim is to give Britain a chance of having a future Wimbledon champion.

Some independent schools in America give aid to a few talented sportsmen and women, but in whichever Western country one names, the backing usually comes from a keen headmaster rather than from any coherent government policy for the backing and development of sport.

In the United States, there are nearly three thousand colleges and universities, most of which provide a wide variety of sports options. Hundreds of these institutions of higher education partially or wholly subsidize the cost of education for their better sportsmen and women. University teams are provided with first-class facilities, equipment and coaching. Travel is underwritten to participate in local, regional and national competitions. Few talented high school athletes are not offered the chance to study an academic subject of their choice in exchange for representing their university to the best of their sporting ability. It would be difficult to conceive a better opportunity to participate on a regular basis, at all levels of competition, than through the American university system. The problem is, however, that there is practically no club system to progress to once university is complete and only a few, very elite competitors are chosen to play for professional teams. The vast majority finish participating when they are at about twenty-two years old, and if they participate in a sport which has no professional teams or government subsidy, then they are lost to further events. In a sport such as track and field athletics, where the trend is to reach a peak around the mid-twenties to mid-thirties, many of the better athletes have finished competing, years before fulfilling their potential.

The best of both worlds is available to non-American athletes going to the US on a scholarship. In exchange for competing for the university, the sportsman or woman may study the academic area of their choice, assuming that they qualify for that university's entrance standard. Individuals such as David Wilkie and Duncan Goodhew attended universities in America. They were fortunate to find coaches who helped in their development rather than merely exploited their talent on behalf of the team in inter-university competitions. They returned to compete at local, area, national and international levels.

Public sponsorship in the form of donations is another form of subsidy. Indeed, in many Western countries from club to Olympic level, donations from the general public are essential in order to finance the country's athletes and ensure their participation in major events. In the UK, the Sports Aid Foundation was established to assist with personal grants to current and potential Olympians. The founders recognized that an athlete needs assistance in the years running up to the Games as well as during that crucial year. Several Winston Churchill Fellowships have also assisted sports representatives.

Many professional clubs now look after their representatives extremely well. Most professional teams in the West provide substantial backup and support to their team members; top medical and physio attention, insurance schemes and pension funds, and during their limited life at the top, they are comparatively well paid.

In UK soccer, Bobby Charlton pointed out that the better clubs, of which Manchester United is one, require that their young apprentices continue their studies or attend technical or trade school while they are learning their soccer trade. This is a practice with which I strongly agree. Too often the boys who leave school at the earliest possible age of fifteen, sign away their education in the hopes of glory on the field. Unfortunately a large proportion never attain their dreams and have been cast aside with no qualifications. Even a successful professional should have the option of working off the field, once his or her playing days are complete.

COMMERCIAL SPONSORSHIP Commercial sponsorship is another area which can underwrite sporting participation. Many companies are willing to assist athletes, often for the publicity of being known to be associated with them and at times simply for goodwill. Sponsorship in sport has become exceptionally big business for the handful of outstanding athletes at the very top of most sports. Commercial companies have seen the advantage of associating the well-known and admired athletes with their product, for example O.J. Simpson with Hertz 'Rent-a-Car', Steve Cram with Kellogg's 'Start' breakfast cereal, and Jackie Stewart with Goodyear tyres. The products usually bear direct relevance to the sport's personality. Most of the top achievers have their own agents who link them with the commercial opportunity, usually for a commission in the region of 20 per cent. The biggest and best known of these is the International Management Group run by Mark McCormack. Sponsorship is now a key ingredient in the presentation of sporting events. Several events now bear the name of the company or product in their titles. This is particularly true in Britain when the event is to be televised.

The danger which has become apparent in negotiations for the televising of the 1988 Olympics, is that the tail can begin to wag the dog. The request was that the finals of the track and field athletics events at the Seoul Olympics, be run during US television's prime-time. That would mean athletes contesting finals in the early hours of the morning which in most cases is not going to produce optimum performances. There is also the problem that as agents force the appearance fees up, the distribution of available money to the athletes who are nearly elite as well as the up and coming athletes becomes less. Without good competition, there is no great contest, so it cannot be in the long-term interest of sport to extort unreasonable fees for the very best. However, without the money that sponsorship brings, many sports would have their programmes drastically reduced.

CHAPTER 11

SOCIAL LIFE

The athletes in the survey were asked whether they thought that they had sacrificed anything in order to pursue their sport. Nearly two-thirds (64 per cent) thought that they had not. Most of these responses were similar to the one by John Havlicek who said, 'None I regret'. Pat O'Callaghan put the same answer the other way round: 'I would regret it if I hadn't done it. I would always have wondered what I might have done.' Rob de Castella said that he had foregone things, but did not consider them sacrifices as it was what he wanted to do; that may be a subtle distinction, but it probably helps put the question into perspective. Individuals who did not want to devote themselves to becoming the best could often be seen accepting an extra pint at the pub; to refuse would have been a sacrifice to them. To the athlete aspiring for the top, saying 'no' was not always considered a sacrifice, because it was what he or she felt was right and would help the quest towards the goal they had set. Everyone has to make choices as to what they will do with their time. These achievers made their sporting goal a top priority and other things, in varying proportions, were fitted around that aim.

Rod Laver said, 'I wouldn't call it sacrifice. I could have got a better formal education or spent more time with my family, but my friends are spread around the world.' Billy Beaumont spoke for most sportsmen and women when he said that the rewards outweighed the sacrifices. But he said in his case, both business and social life suffered.

The social sacrifice in many cases included the family, and several athletes said that their families sacrificed as much as they did. As was mentioned previously when referring to partner support, several sports involve individuals or teams travelling for extended periods. Rugby and cricket tours were mentioned as lasting weeks and even months, but the tennis circuit is now virtually a twelve month proposition. The US professional sports have extensive 'road trips' scattered throughout their seasons. Today, sport at the top is not too considerate of home time. For Ken Read, pursuing the best meant travelling from Canada to Europe and when the Europeans went home for two to three weeks between races, he could not. Obviously, family life went by the board. On the subject of skiing, Carl Lewis's coach pointed out that Carl had sacrificed his winter hobby in order to avoid being reckless. Speaking during the winter before the 1984 Olympics, Carl said, 'There's no way in the world you'll catch me on skis because if you've got a goal you don't want to have anything divert it.'

Both Chris Evert Lloyd and Marjorie Nelson referred to the loss of their teen years, but each also said that they felt amply rewarded. It was their choice and they could have stopped if they had chosen to. Marjorie mentioned the same aspect as discussed by Pete Rose, that there were not the same distractions as one has today. She said, 'There was no TV and we didn't have motor cars. It was nothing to do a hundred miles from Sydney – bus to school, walk to training and walk home from training. But doing without helped build character. The discipline made me a better person. I think we all need discipline and I think that helped to form my character for later years.'

Mike Wenden was amusing when asked if he sacrificed anything. 'No. Yes – a stretch at the boys' home!' He also referred to a few percentage points in exams. This is a point worth noting. To be a competent athlete while at the same time study for a degree and have any social life, places a heavy demand on the student–athlete. The same applies when trying to combine progression in a work career with elite training. If the athlete is going to try for the top, the physical preparation has to be the number one priority. It requires considerable additional effort to pursue absolute achievement goals and retain a balanced life. Is it an impossible target?

One prime question to be answered is whether it is necessary to have an imbalanced life in order to achieve any significant level in sport. These sportsmen and women were asked whether they considered that their sport caused their lives to be imbalanced in any way. 80 per cent of the athletes said that they had managed to retain a balance, while most expressed their belief that their sport had added to their lives rather than the reverse. The 20 per cent who felt that their life had been imbalanced, pointed out that it was chosen rather than forced on them.

However, it is concerning to read about ex-world boxing champions becoming alcoholics and penniless down and outs; and individual waste is in no way confined to that sport. One must question whether sport does provide the essential elements for learning about life. The answer is that the lessons are there for the taking, but the key as with many aspects depends upon those who are guiding them: family, coach, manager or friend, and whether they themselves have the perspective that sport is there as a learning experience. This group of achievers was fortunate to have had a good degree of support and constructive advice on retaining a balanced view of themselves and their sport.

Ideally one would like to think that the top athletes are able to set an example similar to Renaissance Man, integrating mind, body and spirit. Seb Coe, the only man to have retained the Olympic 1500m title, expressed the view that it is not only possible but essential that the athlete is encouraged to be as mentally and physically balanced as possible. Indeed, Seb is one who has demonstrated that it can be done. He has his degree, works for the Sports Council, is interested in music, art and other sports, and does several promotional activities. About his sport participation, he said, 'I'm inclined to feel that far from taking me into imbalance, sport adds a sort of balance to the equation.'

Ron Pickering expressed his opinion that it was important to let the young athlete know that it is possible to reach the top and qualify to do other things. 'There is no track and field athlete who cannot get to the top with a balanced programme of work of two hours of intensive effort a day. Now I don't mind them taking four hours to do two hours of intensive work. I don't mind them telling me they spend all day training – I have yet to see it! But I still want the aspiring athlete to know that it is possible to be a first rate carpenter or a damn good brain surgeon and be a damn good athlete at the same time.'

Mike Wenden was another athlete who managed to do it all. Mike swam competitively until he was twenty-four years old, and by then he had represented Australia in two Olympics, winning two golds and a bronze in Mexico; he had a degree in commerce, was married with two children and was working. 'In terms of a normal person, I was quite different, but then you have to ask yourself if you want to be a normal person.'

Shirley de la Hunty was in the same category as Mike and arguably went one step further. Competing until she was thirty-four years old, the arrival of her third child halted Shirley's trip to her fourth Olympics. In the meantime, she had obtained a doctorate and was working. She won medals in all three Games, and three of her seven track medals were gold.

When this balanced view of achievement was lost, Barry John decided to hang up his rugby boots. He said that it got to the point where he did not know what people wanted of him. He was expected to be an after dinner comic; he wanted still to be one of the boys but he was expected to stay physically fit and as it is an amateur sport, he had to work as well. Barry said that there are four parts to life; family and social time, work time, personal time and sport time. When sport became too large, he dropped it. He was being called King Barry and while at one public appearance, feeling tired and haggard, a little girl curtseyed to him. For him, that was it: he knew it had gone far enough.

The vast majority viewed their life as enhanced by their sport. When O.J. Simpson was asked about imbalance, he replied, 'The opposite, sport led me to lead a more spiritual life. I'm not overly religious so I say that in the sense of taking care of and paying homage to one's body and for me everyone's temple is their body and because of the nature of sport, it has forced me to lead a cleaner and more spiritual existence.'

Gene Upshaw pointed out the opportunities which are made possible by success in sport. 'Doors are opened. It gives you an entrée to congressmen, the country club group, or your local bar and the guys you grew up with. You get a good cross section and it's up to you to take advantage of it.'

Whatever imbalances there may have been, the response came back that at least for this group, the experiences of sport were worthwhile. In Daley Thompson's word, 'priceless', and Chris Evert Lloyd said that she would never trade it. Bryan Robson said that rather than cause an imbalance it had given him sides to his life that he probably would not have had without soccer. 'It's a fantastic job to be paid for what you enjoy doing.' Bobby Charlton would not wholly agree with Bryan that one does not have imbalance. His view was that the professional players have so much done for them that they are sheltered and cosseted. 'Everything was done for you. When you've finished and you have to start doing it all yourself, I think some of the lads have found it very difficult to adapt.' He realized that organization was necessary for the team, but he thought it would have helped many players if they had been given more personal responsibility.

Rod Laver put forward the view that most people would stamp his life as imbalanced. He readily agreed with the term saying, 'It was tennis morning, noon and night. You slept it, you ate it but that was never forced on me. I would get up at 6 o'clock in the morning to ride my bike, eight or nine miles sometimes to get to the club matches. We'd play all day and people would say, "Weren't you tired after cycling all that way?" Well, that wasn't even thought of. It was just the opportunity to play.'

Travel, and having to live out of a suitcase, was viewed by Lester Piggott as producing an imbalanced life. Another drawback is the delay in developing any other career. Peter Snell was one of several athletes who felt that their career progression was slowed by participating in their sport, but it was the chosen course and it was not regretted. He showed how times have changed in terms of pre-sponsored amateur athletes. He said that during his competitive days, he did not leave work until 6 o'clock in the evening. Had he been given time off before the Rome Olympics? 'Yes, I was given an extra half-hour at lunchtime. An hour and a half was enough to get in a speed workout.' Since his three Olympic track golds from Rome and Tokyo, Peter has gone on to receive his doctorate, and has been doing research and teaching at Texas University.

Although questions in this survey investigated athletic rather than academic intelligence, over 40 per cent of these sportsmen and women obtained undergraduate degrees and some have further degrees. For example, Ralph Doubell received his MBA from Harvard, J.P.R. Williams is a medical doctor, Pat O'Callaghan is a veterinary surgeon, and Shirley de la Hunty has her doctorate in statistics.

Lucinda Green made the following observation which is very true. 'Sport is a university of life really. You may go to university and learn an awful lot about the Greeks or the Romans, but this following of sport can teach you so much about life because it's never going to go as you expect it to. Among other things you are going to have to learn to take very many disappointments and learn to take success, which is just as difficult sometimes.'

Selfishness

There is widespread belief that athletes are often selfish individuals. In many ways, that implies that they are not very nice to know. The definition of selfish is being deficient in one's consideration of others, thinking chiefly of one's own personal profit or pleasure. Yachtsman David Forbes openly described himself in that way, leaving his wife to bring up their children without his help. Placing sport above personal relationships seems excessive behaviour but it prevented Rodney Pattisson from marrying. He stated simply that he chose sailing over marriage.

Bob Cousy, in his book *The Killer Instinct*,[12] said the following: 'Perhaps I put too much store by competition. If I had to do it over again, I told myself, I would look for a better balance between the competitive and non-competitive sides of life, giving more time and attention to my family, and the non-competitive pursuits – reading, reflecting and helping others . . . but doing something about them is another matter.'

There are many athletes, and several were cited in the last section, who would not see themselves as selfish and they would say that it is certainly not necessary to be inconsiderate towards others. The term which is perhaps more appropriate in describing many athletes is egocentric. The very nature of their endeavour and the ends to which they have to go almost forces that state upon them. Intentionally, they place themselves in the centre of a pursuit and much of their mental and physical effort goes into self-improvement. Not only are their thoughts often on themselves, but so is the attention of their coach and supportive cast. In such a situation, it takes a very balanced person to keep themselves and their needs in perspective. No doubt that is why Barry John related the value about going to the hospital and seeing children whose bones were crumbling and looking so ill. This insight allowed him to see his own difficulties in their true light. Yes, the quest is important. It is one of the few remaining frontiers open to everyone. We cannot all explore space or the structure of sub-atomic particles, but we can see how much our personal frontier can be moved, and for a few, that means being at the frontier of human endeavour. When the individual is an athlete and is at the forefront, striving, public attention is massively focussed. Whether it is the world land-speed record attempt by Richard Noble or Steve Cram on the track, humans focus their attention on what can be achieved. As fellow humans, there is an identification with achievement. These individuals represent all of our needs for self-mastery and mastery of our environment. In so many ways, people are confined and restricted by choice and otherwise, so when achievers break new ground, they lift the horizons for all of us.

As a result of this interest and public attention, the individual is under added pressure to produce. The focus of the athlete is in many ways forced to be egocentric. The sportsman or woman is often in the position of being the 'body' under discussion, whether that discussion is about their effort or execution. They are being channeled and manipulated or indeed they are doing it to themselves, all in an attempt to better their performance.

In fine-tuning the body, the slightest twinge means that the 'machine' may not be ready for absolute service. When this sense or concern is put into words, the athlete is seen as a hypochondriac. However, to the athlete, anxiety about health is easily justified. The athlete's life, emotionally, physically, psychologically, and even financially, is largely bound up with trying to improve. If anything or anyone comes in between the athlete and his or her goal, then it has to be avoided or removed. The whole self-image of the athlete is tied up with being in top condition. Is it any wonder then, that with this thought uppermost in the athlete's mind, he or she will often appear imbalanced? For Ron Clarke, the Australian distance runner, it took a shock situation to give him a balanced perspective. He had been attempting to break the world 10,000m record and had come very close, but failed on successive occasions. He was on a training run on the beach and in frustration at his inability to achieve his target, he came to a standstill at the top of a sand-dune. As he looked out over the sea he noticed some creatures flopping and squealing at the edge of the water; then he saw a ball and so he went closer to investigate. He saw that they were not animals at all, but a group of paraplegic children, laughing and squealing with delight as they attempted to play volleyball, with the water supporting their paralyzed lower limbs. Ron said that he looked again at himself; here he was in the best condition of any runner on earth, yet carrying a burden of frustration. This simple experience changed his whole perspective. He came away determined to enjoy his health and strength and be thankful for it. Ron recalled this story at the end of his most successful season, having broken not only the world 10,000m record, but also half a dozen other records besides.

Sociability

The athletes were asked how they got on with others generally; and with teachers, opponents and peers specifically. 78 per cent said that they had no problems getting on with anyone. The words used to describe how they got on generally varied, but the intent came across as being the same. It was apparent that, in most cases, these athletes got on well socially. They were relaxed within themselves. Steve Cram is a typical illustration. His response to the question was, 'Very well, I'm a social animal'. With one or two exceptions, those interviewed were not pushy people. Their communication was straightforward, honest and often tinged with humour. They were enjoyable people to sit down with and reflect with, on general issues as well as those which involved their quest for achievement. It should be noted that no one said that they did not get on at all well with other people. Within the 22 per cent who did not simply say 'very well' or 'fine', some explained their communication problem areas. Daley Thompson referred to not getting on well with authority. 'I hate being told what to do. I don't mind being asked but some people are a little more pushy than others.' Duncan Goodhew said that in his younger days, he had conflict with life in general.

Some of the responses were mixed. Shirley de la Hunty said 'relatively well'; Seb Coe said 'reasonably well'; Relph Doubell replied 'fairly well'; and Ed Moses and Pete Rose said 'pretty well'. Pete went on to say that he thought people did not like him because he is aggressive and makes a lot of money. 'People are very jealous or envious of those who make money. They don't like McEnroe, they don't like Connors and they don't like me because we're confident, cocky and good. There was a time in my life when I worried about how every fan felt about me. When I held out each year for more money, there were negative comments in letters and on talk shows, but those people aren't going to care about me when I'm through playing. They're not going to worry about paying my bills. Now I just go about my business. It's amazing how many people don't like me because I'm aggressive and I make a lot of money.'

Gene Upshaw is the executive director of the National Football League Players Association. He said that he respects authority and that the only thing he asks of anyone is that they respect him. 'When you play against an opponent, you play hard, you play tough but you don't play dirty; when you walk away, you want him to respect you and that's the only reason I'm in this job. Number one, they respect me and number two, they trust me.'

Marjorie Nelson said that she felt humbled by the respect and consideration shown to her by her competitors. In the track and field athletics finals in the New South Wales championships in Australia, it was announced that she had been in an automobile accident. Her competitors got together and decided to wait until she had recovered before contesting the sprints (which turned out to be three weeks later). Marjorie said, 'One of those girls would have been the new champion. That humbled me, to see what they thought of me as a person.'

Several athletes made the point that they still had many of the same friends with whom they had grown up. This was true even for a jet-setter like Jackie Stewart who has moved countries.

Ann Brightwell reflected on the competitive side, saying that there was mutual friendship and respect but that she would not have liked to share a room with the person she was going to compete against. Both Billie Jean King and Chris Evert Lloyd said how difficult it was playing against friends. Billie Jean rationalized the situation by pointing out that it would not be a battle with a friend but a focus on and battle with the ball.

Some sportsmen have had quite open confrontations with their administrators: Ian Botham is just such an example. He is aware of taking some raps for others and that in turn, some peers have taken raps for him. His view is that the reason for the conflict is that too often the administrators of British sport have lost touch with the realities of today. In cricket, the view is still held that you do not complain about an umpire's verdict. Ian complained that the administrators do not stand up for the cricketers. To them, it is more important being a good loser.

It seems to me that he has a point, as there is a generation in Britain who have grown up believing their own words – that they *are* good losers! At the turn of this century, Britain introduced a number of new sports to the world. As the British were winning consistently, they preached the importance of being a good loser and proudly became humble winners. And when they did lose, it was not hard to act as a good loser because they knew that they were in fact winners. Time has changed the luxury of this position. Over the last fifty years, relative affluence has opened up opportunities in sport for many individuals throughout the world. State and private money has increased sporting facilities and coaching available often to a greater extent in other countries than it has in Britain. If Britain or any other country is wanting to compete at the sharp end of international sport, then they are forced to travel the same road. There is a requirement for provision of quality indoor and outdoor facilities, highly competent, qualified coaches and professional sports administrators, who know and understand the requirements of support and backup for every level from introductory fun to striving for excellence.

Was it important what others thought of you, and did that change? One of the issues which females have often had to face has been the stereotyping of physical success with masculinity. Some sports have been inherently more acceptable than others: for example, gymnastics, diving, and dance and figure skating all allow the female to project her body gracefully. At the other end of the sporting spectrum is ice hockey and rugby in which female participation has been suspect. Attitudes are changing but in the recent past, if men and women have competed against each other in sport, the unwritten rule for the female was, 'never beat a man'. The female was expected to be passive and gentle and was allowed to cry. If she was relatively strong, assertive, confident, tough and did not cry, there must be something wrong with her! It takes many years to alter social bias, but the successful female athletes of the last thirty years have forced some enlightened change. Physiological research has also helped. For example, it is now known that the greater quantity of active burning of fat in the female body makes them more suitable than men for ultra endurance performances. For centuries, men assumed that weakness was a female characteristic. Until 1964, the longest Olympic track event was 400m and it was not until the 1984 Games that a women's marathon was finally included.

The responses from interviewing the female athletes show their awareness that they represent the image of their sport as well as themselves. Heather McKay said, 'The image of sport is important. I always tried to look as good as I possibly could and as feminine as I could. I'd play the game fairly, and with good sportsmanship. I would put myself out if I was asked to do something for the sport because I felt that a lot of people had put themselves out for me.' Shirley de la Hunty commented, 'Two things I felt I had to prove as a young woman in the post-war period. One was that I was feminine and an athlete, and the other was that I was intelligent and an athlete.'

Margaret Court said that because of her shyness and sensitivity, she stopped reading the Press. 'In those early days, I'd open the papers and they would say, "Big Maggie, the Amazon from Australia" because I was the tallest girl playing tennis and I lifted weights, and the Press could never understand that. But where you're twisting and turning, the strength from the weight training prevented a lot of injuries . . . As I matured and got older, the press comments didn't mean so much to me.'

The vast majority of the athletes, 88 per cent, did think it was important what others thought of them. Both Clive Lloyd and John Gilmour referred to the responsibility they felt for their image in sport. Clive said, 'As an example for youngsters, you've got to conduct yourself in a good manner because you never know who the people are who idolize you. People look up to sportsmen whether you like it or not . . . I'm not really different, but some of the younger sportsmen don't want the responsibility of acting correctly. Kids need to have heroes, someone to look up to, admire . . . more so now. You can help people! As a person, well liked because of what you're doing, you sign autographs, open things or whatever. They expect that their heroes should maintain certain standards. 90 per cent of those idolizing expect you to live to high standards . . . and if you have to be smoking, drinking or whatever, do it in private.'

John Gilmour said that years ago, it was not important what others thought, but it is now because he knows that he is a living example for others. He is demonstrating that most people can remain physically fit and competitive whatever their age. It is important to him what others think as he is crusading for the upper end of the age spectrum. 15 per cent of the group who said that it was important what others thought of them, commented that they enjoyed being liked. Peter Snell thought that he probably placed too much emphasis on what others thought of him. Both Wayne Gretzky and Bryan Robson were bothered by unjustified criticism. Wayne said, 'I take offence over some things written. My parents say don't worry over what other people are saying. I'm saying, "How can they say that? They don't even know me!"'

Another 13 per cent said that it was more important being liked earlier on in their careers. Jackie Stewart said, 'It gradually became less important.' Rob de Castella personalized the view. 'Yes, it was important what others thought of me, but it was more important what I thought of myself. I kept it in perspective. You could get caught up with a lot of public pressure. The attitudes and expectations of my coach, my wife and family, and my training partners meant more.' Des Drummond also felt that a person must face themelves – 'but it was more important what I thought of myself'.

Three of the athletes qualified whose opinion it was that they cared about. Both Daley Thompson and Ian Botham said: 'Only family and friends.' Herb Elliott said, 'The ones who I did care about, did matter – the rest of them, I didn't give a damn.'

Five of the achievers, Duncan Goodhew, Viv Richards, Lester Piggott, Steve Ovett and Al Oerter, said that it was not important to them what others thought of them. Duncan explained his perspective. 'It was as a kid I learnt, because of having no hair, that if people were so narrow-minded to think a certain way and not give you a chance, then there was no point in worrying about it, but I suppose I've always wanted to be a nice guy basically.' Al Oerter said that he found secondary school years and going through puberty very difficult, but that from the mid-teens on, 'I just have not given a damn what others thought; if I did I'd have been a football player, driven a large car, this kind of nonsense . . .'

Two other athletes gave qualified answers. Ed Moses said, 'Not so much, I'm a loner.' Shane Innes said, 'It was not that important, but I did try to be good.'

Whether or not the top athletes like it, they are going to be role models for others. A few seem unaware of their influence, although several see the implications of their success making them heroes. The fact that sports heroes cut across sex, race, religion, politics and class means that they could have a significant role to play in social integration.

Wanting to please others is probably a relatively common human trait; however, in the light of the finding that athletes are often selfish or egocentric, it seemed a worthwhile question to ask. If their response was positive, they were asked who it was that they were trying to please. One of the aspects which came out in discussion was that inevitably the prime motivation to do anything is for oneself. It can be reasonably argued from a religious–philosophical stance, that one is acting for the glory of a creator, God. It can equally well be extended to say that if God is in all things and man is made in his image, then man's quest for the positive development of his talent is both for the glory of the Almighty and for self-expression. A view from Eric Liddell in the film, *Chariots of Fire*, was that he could feel God's power running through him. In personal, egocentric terms, there is a school of thought which says, 'If it feels good, do it'. Either way, it comes down to wanting to satisfy one's own desires and needs.

In the religious form, the quest is elevated to a spiritual plane and this will be discussed later on in the book. If a person is from the Soviet Union, it is done for the benefit of the State, the party and for the good of the whole nation. In Hitler's call to the Germans, it was all for the Fatherland, and in the West, the spirit of freedom enables the personal choice to be one for personal satisfaction.

Maslow made the point that in terms of human striving and need-fulfilment, unless the individual is travelling on a self-fulfilling path, he or she will be frustrated and discontented. In religious terms, that fulfilment would include the application of the parable of the talents.

Of course, pleasing oneself does not preclude pleasing others, and 92 per cent of these achievers said that they wanted to please others through their sport participation. There was a very strong bias towards pleasing parents. They were specifically mentioned by 63 per cent of the athletes. In some cases, the response sounded like a revelation – 'Deep down, I really always wanted to please my Dad, or my mother'. Usually it was simply 'my parents'. This underlines the closeness of the family ties for most of these athletes and also shows that they appreciated the support shown them by their parents.

The next most frequently mentioned person, 21 per cent, was the coach. This is also not too surprising as in the close coach–athlete relationships, it became a joint venture. There was a partnership where the intent and aim of both individuals was fused into a goal to break new ground together.

There were several who mentioned more than one person, or a group of people. Apart from parents and coaches, there was mention of spouse, team-mates, training partners, friends, managers, sponsors, owners, fans, everyone and anyone! Shane Innes was the one who used the term 'everyone', but in the context that if she did her best, she would be making everyone happy. Peter Snell and Rodney Pattisson used the same expression, wanting to please 'anyone'. Snell also said that he had great difficulty saying no to any requests. Duncan Goodhew also said that he never wanted to let anyone down, and Steve Cram thought that he may have gone a little overboard in trying to please 'everyone'. He had allowed himself to be exploited, slightly; an easy thing for any new arrival in the limelight. Rarely are sports people prepared for the blitz of media attention which follows any exceptional performance. If the image is suitable, then the athlete can be hounded by requests to do everything from more competitions to speech-making; from opening supermarkets to judging beauty contests; and from advertising dog food to endorsing religion. The image of a winner may be short-lived but it is very powerful. It elevates the spirit of man, opening up human horizons. No doubt that is why advertisers in the West use the known achievers and also why the Eastern countries spend so much to improve their image through the success of their sports people. Valeriy Borzov was one of those who also said that he wanted to please 'everyone'.

Apart from family, Bryan Robson specifically mentioned the fans. 'Not just my own club but all soccer fans.' Pete Rose only mentioned the fans, in spite of what he had said earlier. 'I like to please the fans, because really all I am is an entertainer. I have fun. We're nothing but grown ups playing a kid's game, and as long as you can maintain the kid attitude and your kid enthusiasm, there's no problem about getting old.'

Jayne Torvill and Christopher Dean are the only ones in this group who are marked by others in order to determine their measure of success. Not surprisingly, their focus for pleasing was on the judges.

Finally, on the positive answer side, John Gilmour wanted to please others by continuing to get the results expected of him. 'I hate to let others down. I have high expectations of myself. Why should I give it away because of age? I feel no different after a race than I felt ten to twelve years ago. [John was born in 1919.] I know that some people are racing today because of my attitude. I hear the comments, "If he can do it then I'm sure I can". Even from some of the younger blokes. People talk about hurting themselves by exercising, but you work a muscle and it gets stronger – and the heart is a muscle.'

Quite a few of these responses show the extent of responsibility felt by the athletes: not only for themselves but for a wider circle or cause.

Just five athletes commented that they were not aiming to please anyone but themselves. Coe: 'I wanted to please myself.' Ovett: 'No, not even family. I just did it because I wanted to . . . getting the best out of myself for all the effort I'd put in.' Bob Cousy: 'I just did it for myself.' Daley Thompson: 'It's just too much hard work to be doing it for someone else. You can only want to do things so much and you know how badly you're going sometimes. You wouldn't do that for anyone, other than yourself.' David Forbes, however, was the most extreme in his statement of self-orientedness. 'Totally selfish. I think you're doing it for your own egocentric feelings. I'm quite open. I'm quite selfish about the bloody thing and I'm quite sure my wife would say the same thing.'

There is little doubt of the work effort which success entails, which in turn requires motivation to come from within the athlete. It also follows that unless they enjoyed what they were doing, they would not make such extreme commitments. David Forbes reflects the end of the spectrum which sees his efforts purely in terms of self-gratification. No one claims selflessness, but the majority seem to approach the effort in a social context. They are not pursuing their ends in a totally isolated mental framework, but it is done for more than just personal satisfaction. It is also apparent that most feel personal enhancement from the fact that they are sharing the intensity and motivation with others.

PART 3

PSYCHOLOGICAL FACTORS

CHAPTER 12

Athletic Intelligence

'Athletic intelligence' is a term I have used to summarize some attributes necessary to perform sport well. There are several types of intelligence. In the West, the IQ test has become almost synonymous with the level of academic intelligence of a youngster, but according to educationalists today, these tests measure how well a person does on IQ tests! There has also been confusion as to the intent of such tests. In general, they were supposed to give an indication of general aptitude in a relatively narrow range of formal educational skills. However, it is necessary to look at the term intelligence in a wider context. Certainly if youngsters living in a highly industrialized urban country were thrown into the outback or a jungle as a test of their intelligence in survival, very few would pass. Intelligence is not limited to qualifications in the academic sense alone. There is recognized genius in music, art and drama and no less than in the more physical performing arts of dance and sport. Creative genius is apparent to all who have watched Larry Bird play basketball; Lester Piggott ride a horse; Jackie Stewart drive a car; or Torvill and Dean perform on ice. Some ball players 'read the game' so well that they always seem to have more time than others or they have the repeated ability to find a space in order to receive a clear pass.

John Havlicek made a comparison between Larry Bird and Albert Einstein. 'Larry has been called the "hic from French Lick" [which is his home town in Indiana] because he doesn't use the right words in speech from time to time. Put a basketball in Einstein's hands and he wouldn't know what to do with it, but if you put a mathematical equation in front of him, he'd devour it. Put a maths equation in front of Larry and he'd say, "What's this?" but give him a basketball and he's an Einstein. Lots of people judge athletes unfairly because of their actions off the field of play.' Larry's exceptional skill is apparent in every game but a particular illustration of the genius to which John refers was witnessed by millions who were watching one of the Celtics' games on television. Larry put the ball into play under his own basket and took off at full speed towards the other end of the court. A full court return pass was overthrown and was going out of bounds under the opponents' basket. Larry, still running, left the floor heading out of bounds. In mid-air and in one quick motion, he caught the ball with his right hand, passed it to his left hand which had not yet passed under the back board, and successfully shot the ball off the backboard with sufficient spin to score. Bob Cousy's commentary at the time was, 'You can't teach that! It was impossible! Absolutely fantastic!'

Gene Upshaw stated that an unintelligent guy could not understand an American football playbook. 'For one thing it's 415 in thick and there are calls, changes and audibles. You have to store a tremendous amount of information on play options and if it's changed at the line of scrimmage, you have to pass it on – everyone's talking and you have to know what the blocking assignment is on that particular play and make sure that everyone else is blocking the same way. There are no dumb athletes any more. That's gone.'

Having made some initially humorous remarks, Billy Beaumont appeared to disagree with Gene but he subsequently redressed the balance. The rugby scrum is not an easy place to be in. Billy said, 'Playing in the second row doesn't require a lot of intelligence really. You've got to be bloody crazy to play there, haven't you, for a start. There's no point in giving it a lot of deep thought! The intelligence that's needed is to know how to train well; to react within the team; to read situations; you've got to be quite sharp . . . the ball is constantly moving and you have to switch and change all the time.'

The sections which follow attempt to identify some of the mental aspects which have made a difference to the athletes' performance levels.

Mental involvement

To what extent was the mind involved in playing your sport? The unanimous verdict was couched in words like 'immensely', 'totally', 'that's the whole game', 'you play with your mind', 'that's where the body movement comes from'. There was an added element for Lucinda Green as she has to not only be in tune with herself but also with her horse. In the same way that a coach must be sensitive to the mood of the athlete, Lucinda spoke of the awareness needed for success in the equestrian world. 'You've got to read your horse like a book. You've got to know exactly what he's thinking and exactly how he's feeling and not think, "Oh, today we're going to do such and such because that's what my rough programme says, so we'll do it". He might not feel like doing it. I think you've got to be totally in tune to be successful with a horse. To me the root of success is how in tune you can be and how you interpret being in tune. You are always looking at the horse as you walk to the yard and asking yourself, "Does he look happy, is his coat right?" And when you're riding, you're thinking, "Is he feeling right, is he happy?" You're always asking yourself questions, you never just sit there. I suppose it's through experience that you know when it's not quite right and little danger signals warn, so you change the food or do something different with the exercise or give him a week off.'

Shane Innes referred to the need for body awareness, being in tune with her muscles and the need for concentration on what she was doing on each stroke and recovery, in every inch of the pool. Arnold Palmer gave a response which was alluded to by many of these athletes. Given the physique to play, he said, 'You play from the shoulders up – it isn't all important, just 90 per cent . . . and it may be over 90 per cent.'

Athletes used other sports to describe similarities. Jackie Stewart said, 'I saw the sport like a giant snooker match where I always put the other drivers in a position where they could not retaliate, I would always have them behind the ball. If they did retaliate and therefore involve me, they would be the ones who would be the most embarrassed. They would be the one going off the track or hitting the barrier.' Steve Davis and John Newcombe compared their sports, snooker and tennis, to a game of chess. John described it as follows: 'For two, three or four hours there is a great battle of minds going on, which is like a chess game and also an enormous physical contact of minds. It's gladiatorial really – one on one, thousands watching in the arena and millions more on television, and here's two people standing on Centre Court, firing tennis balls at one another but it's really firing rockets from the mind and using your ability to hit the ball to take that message from your mind. So there's a huge clash of mental prowess out there on the sportsfield. Your game is the weaponry you have to play with.' Steve Ovett likened the contest to an animal stalking its prey. He used the term 'cunning' and 'having the understanding of other animals'.

The mind was applied in both a theoretical and practical way by Shirley de la Hunty. She said that she enjoyed learning to do things. 'I enjoyed thinking out the bio-mechanics of how to run faster, clear the hurdles better and to work the scientific side of it. I learned how to generate intense concentration and intense adrenalin and was also able to adjust my body balance so as to get the maximum out of my run. I balanced my strength against the ground so that I lost no impetus at all. The first thirty metres were critical. For hours in my room I'd mentally rehearse this. There's not much room for error. I ran 11.3 sec for 100m and I was just delighted with that. It stood as a world record for nine years.'

What can be learned from the experience of those who demonstrate athletic genius? The answer is much. The average performer may have been born with slightly less natural ability, but several of the items which follow can be used to develop the thinking and talent of all levels of performer.

From a general initial question of what they saw as necessary to have athletic intelligence, many of the athletes responded that they had tried to find out all they could about their sport or their event. They tried to learn from their coaches and had read all they could from books – history books and biographies as well as instructional books and they also spent time talking to those who had experience.

It is perhaps most surprising that coaches with eager young athletes do not direct themselves or their fledglings to the people who have most recently been at the top. I was quite surprised that almost no local coaches had asked Billy Smith what sort of programme he had evolved en route to producing an Olympic champion. Steve Cram expressed the same surprise saying that he was hungry for information. Steve said that he talked a lot to experienced athletes and coaches. Most of the information divulged could be left, but the odd helpful thing picked up made the search worthwhile. 'Everyone needs to learn and yet no one is asking, "What do you think about this?". They don't take the opportunity to learn.' Certainly it is not possible to have one programme exactly suit another individual – the physique, physiology and temperament of each individual is different, and the aptitude at birth may not have been as great, but there is a wealth of experience from which to learn. Young athletes should not be shy to ask for advice while it is available to them. Gene Upshaw said that he believed the ability to be coached was the key to athletic intelligence. 'When a player's become uncoachable, they don't stay around too long.'

O.J. Simpson said, 'To be great at any sport you have to be a student of your craft and you have to love your craft.' The athletes who have made it to the top were all eager to learn. John Newcombe said, 'I talk to some of the top juniors and you can tell if the kid's got the potential to be a champion because when you're talking, you can almost feel them absorbing everything you say.'

Seeking knowledge extends beyond how to perform. Many American teams spend hours reviewing films of their coming opponents, looking for weaknesses or clues to give any advance notice of what the opposition are about to do before they do it.

Jonah Barrington's method was to make extensive notes on his squash opponents, even the ones he was not playing, and keep them on file. 'I could refer back, say five years, and would always find there were common denominators with a player throughout their whole career. So I could make myself aware of them and prepare before a game; I'd never leave it to the last moment.'

Only three achievers said that they were slow in adapting to new skills.

Mike Wenden and Duncan Goodhew said that they found it difficult to change swimming techniques, while Lucinda Green said that she felt unable to change her plans quickly during a cross-country event. She added, 'And as far as teaching me goes, anyone who has tried will tell you, it's a nightmare, because I find it very difficult to re-adapt.' Ed Moses said that he would work at it and Des Drummond said that only tackling came easily.

Apart from those few, all the rest, well over 90 per cent, were what is often referred to as 'naturals', i.e. they learned the required movements fast and naturally. Bob Tisdall actually used that term to describe his athleticism.

From my own experience as a coach, I know that academic intelligence does not correlate with athletic intelligence. One study said that in general, top athletes have a little above average academic intelligence but the spectrum is varied and therefore analogy pointless. During my seven years of coaching hundreds of students at Boston University, I discovered that it made no difference whether or not the athletes were good at their studies: some who were receiving top honour grades had great difficulty translating verbal descriptions or physical demonstrations into personal changed actions. Others may or may not have been average in their academic performance, but they picked things up as if they had a mental picture even before the instruction was complete. These were generally the better athletes.

Tom Tellez said that he thought Carl Lewis was an athletic genius. He only had to see another athlete attempt something or hear a few words from Tom, and he was able to execute the new action. This does not mean that it instantly becomes second nature, but the action was almost a perfect imitation. Herb Elliott had such a clear communication with his coach that he picked things up before Cerutty finished what he was saying. Shirley de la Hunty pointed out that since she has been coaching, she has found that the athletes who can pick things up faster than others have a greater chance of reaching their potential, particularly in technical events, because they can move on so much faster and more can be covered in every session.

Christopher Dean said that there was such clear communication between himself and Jayne Torvill that it would only need a word from him. 'Some people say something to us that I see straight away. If Jayne doesn't quite understand, I can just say one word and Jayne will understand straight away, because we think along the same lines.'

Arnold Palmer referred to being able to copy easily. 'I could watch a good player like Sam Snead, who had a great golf swing, and could go and concentrate on what he was doing, and then in my own mind, maybe not in yours, but in my mind I could go and swing the club just like that.

And that was all I needed. It didn't matter whether I was doing it but I could imagine that I was doing it and I'd get the results I wanted.'

Gareth Edwards referred to watching the third-year students doing hand-to-feet somersaults across the gym. He was simply able to go and do it after watching them. Gareth was so aware of his body, that as long as he had an idea of what to do he could execute the action. Bobby Charlton used the same expression in describing his soccer skills: 'I just did it'. Greg Chappell described athletic intelligence in the following way: 'What the mind generates, the body fulfils. It's probably 90 per cent of the game at top level. All those that get there physically can play the game, the ones that are able to stay there and perform at a high level for a long period of time are the ones who can do it mentally.'

There had to be a slightly different element to learning for Jackie Stewart. He pointed out that motor racing requires perfect coordination between hands, feet and eyes, but unlike other sports where you can observe how it is done, the cockpit of a racing car is such a confined space that you cannot even see how the others do it. 'I liked the way Jim Clark performed. I thought he was smooth rather than busy. He never seemed to be in a hurry to do anything. It was always a nice, smooth, gliding motion and he never seemed to be going quickly, whereas the others looked spectacular but never seemed to be going anywhere. If there was nobody else on the track they looked wonderful, but I realized that controlled motion and the elimination of heroics was a very important ingredient. Therefore, I applied myself to becoming smoother and smoother and as a result, the physical movement was cut down. But it took a lot out of me to make that happen, so I was draining one side to play up the other.' In order for Jackie to learn his skill, he had to observe from afar and sense what was needed to execute his image of a 'Jimmy Clark' performance.

What are the attributes necessary to have things come naturally? Inevitably there are physical factors such as physical coordination and the right bodily structure for their sport. There are emotional factors too, the nerve to try, as well as emotional stability, but perhaps the greatest key to success at the top is having the mind for it. These athletes had mental control and could use their imagination to see and feel themselves performing an action before they did it. This ability will be discussed more fully in the following chapter on 'creativity, visualization and imagery'.

CHAPTER 13

CREATIVITY, VISUALIZATION AND IMAGERY

Did you always think that you were going to achieve at a high level? This question was asked to see if the dreams of youth were present in all those who reached for the top. More than half, 57 per cent, answered positively saying they had always thought that they would reach a high level. A few said it as if they saw it as their destiny. Herb Elliott, Wayne Gretzky, and O.J. Simpson said that there was 'no doubt', 'no question' and 'I never had any doubt'. John Newcombe said, 'I knew it was my destiny'. Sebastian Coe responded, 'No age, five or six, I knew', while Daley Thompson said, 'Yes, at something'. Several others sensed that a high level of achievement was for them, but only when they were a little older. Peter Sterling said that he wanted to do well by the age of seven, but he had no doubt at all by the time he was thirteen. For Duncan Goodhew, the realization came when he was fourteen years old. He stepped out of the pool one day and told his school mates that he was going to the Olympics. Billie Jean King was eleven when she first held a racket. She said that she knew from the first day that this was it, she was going to win Wimbledon! John Konrads felt the same way. 'I was probably afraid of the feeling but nevertheless had it. From eleven or twelve I was saying to myself, "One day I'm going to be world record holder or world champion".'

Gene Upshaw referred to dreams but unlike the others he did not really believe that it would happen for him. 'I wanted it to happen. I dreamed about it but I never thought it would happen to me. When I was drafted in the first round I couldn't believe it was happening to me.'

Just under half the group gradually realized their capabilities to achieve. They described their experience in terms such as 'it evolved' and 'it was like steps', or 'there was just a gradual progression'.

Steve Cram confided that he had only set short-term goals, but he also mentioned an important turning point in 1981 when he was racing Steve Ovett at the Talbot Games in London. 'I didn't want to go past him in the home straight. I felt I shouldn't try to go past him. After the race, I made the conscious decision saying to myself, "You're now good enough to beat them if you really want to".' It was a changed attitude about his own capability. A very similar deferment had taken place in the mind of Ben Jipcho the 1972 Olympic steeplechase champion who had not felt that it was right to try to pass the great African runner Kip Keino in a 1500m race. Both Steve Cram and Ben Jipcho had not yet taken the final step. At the times they were referring to, they were still thinking of *them* rather than *us*. As Steve Cram pointed out, it takes a conscious recognition that one is just as capable of competing with the people on the next level up. The way in which people perceive themselves affects their whole approach to doing anything. Margaret Court referred to her experience as a series of pleasant surprises. Jean Benoit Samuelson is another who never thought that she would achieve the heights she has in spite of the hard work she was prepared to put in, but she did not see herself as different. 'I really enjoyed long distance running and was willing to work hard at it. I don't think it was innate talent by any means . . . I still consider myself an ordinary everyday person.'

Lynn Davies drew attention to the fact that motivation can determine success and that if your aim is enjoyable for you to pursue, then you will be more motivated. 'I was tremendously motivated towards sport – I wasn't motivated academically. I believe if you spend two or three hours a day over a long period of time at something which you enjoy doing, you become very good at it regardless of what it is, but you have to tap what it is that motivates you, that you enjoy doing.'

It is apparent that either from when they were young or by way of a gradual progression, these athletes have accepted a very positive view of their capabilities. In most cases, they see the top as just another plateau which they have found attainable. Sometimes, it was a frightening thought of taking those first steps but in each case they were willing to make the effort and had the confidence to face the next challenge. Whether a person is in sport, business, or any other challenge, gaining the confidence to achieve anything is critical to success. Confidence is often only gradually acquired.

What these athletes did consciously or subconsciously was set themselves a goal or target, and it would probably be helpful here to say something about this. It has already been stated how important it is that the coach and athlete have similar levels of aspiration. It is also invaluable that the goal is set individually or in concert with a coach or team, but it must be pitched at the right level. Set too low and the motivational value is lost. There is no challenge if something is too easy to attain. Equally unproductive is the goal which is set too high. The individual or team can be tempted to give up because the target is unattainable. At best a good effort is made but the result inevitably is failure. A realistic yet challenging target is therefore the aim.

It is usual that very high achievers have a dream, a hope, even an aim to get to the top, but it is not enough to have only a long-term target. The attraction of next week's or next month's challenge, even next year's goal, can be a significant motivating factor in the difficult times ahead, training and preparing. Greg Chappell progressed this thought even further. 'Wanting to have a successful cricket tour of England, I thought I'd just take it game by game and then break it down to innings by innings and then break each innings down into components of ten runs. The measure of success for a batsman is to make a hundred runs, but rather than thinking about getting a hundred, I would think about getting ten. When I'd got ten, then I'd be able to give myself a mental pat on the back, "Well done, you've achieved your first step, now the next step is to get to twenty", and so on to achieving the overall target.'

Sixty per cent of the athletes were able to give specific dates or ages when they truly felt that they had the capability of setting a goal to make the top. Most of them were two or three years away from their greatest achievement but the time varied up to twelve years in advance of realizing their goal. The remaining 40 per cent stated that their progress was step by step or that their success just evolved. The aim for the top had not been a long-term aim, it just became a natural progression.

Lynn Davies certainly had the latest revelation of a goal to win. He was more than half-way through his Olympic long jump final! The realization added more than six inches to his jumping and he won by less than two inches. The build-up to that was as follows. 'I had worked very hard in the winter before the Tokyo Games, and in May I won the Inter-Counties for the first time with over 26 ft 4 in and the 100 yds in 9.5 sec and I achieved a new level of self-esteem as an athlete. I walked into the Tokyo stadium feeling I had a right to be there, whereas at the European Championships two years before, I was letting things happen, I wasn't controlling the situation at all. In the Olympics I was aiming to make the final and possibly the bronze. I went in thinking there was no beating the American, Ralph Boston or the Soviet, Igor Ter-Ovanesyan. The weather conditions were really bad and the performances were all down. I thought I could jump further than was being jumped in those conditions, and suddenly I had a perception of their vulnerability. I was sitting there watching them, perceiving that it was possible to beat them. It was then my fifth out of six jumps and I jumped into a six inch lead. It showed that the bad conditions had been having more of a psychological than physical effect, and the others came back to within two or four inches, but it was too late, I'd seen the opportunity and snatched it.'

Rob de Castella said that he set the goal of winning the World Marathon Championships when it became feasible, but he added that he didn't like to set goals. 'Irrespective of what you achieve, you should be able to feel totally happy and satisfied with it provided you've channelled all of your energies and effort into it, irrespective of winning. Of course, everybody would like to win, everybody would like to set a record but that's a bonus.'

The athletes were asked whether they saw their sport as a form of self-expression. In most cases, athletes are expressing their thoughts in a physical form, but the question was asked to see whether the athletes thought of it in that way. Shirley de la Hunty was very clear in her positive views. 'Yes, very much, it's a big reason for having sport in society. Just as much as dance and ballet, singing and art, it's an art form, it's creative. Perhaps we should be finding different ways to make it more creative, but it's a self-expression, an art form and must be seen as that.'

Bob Cousy spoke for many athletes when he said that sport had helped bring him out of his shell. It has been stated that the vast majority of these athletes classed themselves as introverts, but many of them referred to the effect which sport had had on them. Bob said, 'I think it had great impact as a growth tool. I think you do absorb a lot of every day beneficial lessons that can be applied to the rest of your life. All the things we're aware of, the dedication, sacrifice, working with other people, taking instructions, how to be a good loser and a humble winner, the whole lot. I think you absorb this almost in any form.'

Des Drummond pointed out the benefit of having a socially acceptable outlet for aggression. 'It allowed me to express myself physically where I couldn't verbally and to let my aggression out on the field. It's been good like that.'

Creativity

The athletes were asked also whether they felt that they were creative in experimenting with their training or technique. It has been said that the need for creativity is one of man's basic needs. Listening to a radio interview, I heard a professor criticizing the pursuit of sporting excellence on the grounds that it often involves little creativity and is repetitious. If this is so then both the coach and athlete are to blame. Certainly there are constraints within an event or sport, and practice must involve a certain amount of repetition, but in fact the opposite is the case, as with control comes freedom. Once the fundamentals are sound, then they can be used as building blocks to allow for individual creative expression.

Barry John said that he was constantly attempting to be creative and experimenting with his play, kicking drop goals with either foot, and catching the ball backwards if they had a substantial lead in the game. He said he tried to make the game fun. His rugby union team-mate Gareth Edwards, having a soccer background, could kick the ball into touch wherever he liked with either foot. 'I didn't think anything was impossible. I worked on the reverse pass, going one way and the ball going back the other, and a few different things like bringing the ball around behind my back.' Gareth referred to this last move as schoolboy stuff, but it was enough to confuse the opposition at international level!

Wayne Gretzky credits his father with part of his creativity. He said that his father had been clever in giving him a lot of different things to work on in both training and technique.

Perhaps the most obvious exhibition of creative art in sport is ice skating and the performances by Torvill and Dean. Jayne said, 'Christopher is very creative. He's the one who comes up with all these weird and wonderful ideas which I have to learn how to do. We both think along the same lines, that we want to do something new every time.' Chris said, 'At the end of the day it comes down to the discipline of training technique. However, I think of our bodies not just from a physical point of view but also in terms of shapes and designs, the lines our bodies are creating. I see pictures in my head.' Chris added that he can be watching a film and suddenly he would see something which could be integrated into their programme. He would mentally note it, then go back into the film. Torvill and Dean have recently included ballet as part of their creative learning work. They are not alone. Other athletes are turning to this discipline for added strength, balance and flexibility. Steele Bishop includes ballet as part of his multi-disciplined training, which also includes cycling, swimming, exercises for balance and coordination, stretching and orthotron work. He said that people laughed at the extent to which he went in his quest for improvement, but now he has a clinic where his chiropractor and occupational therapist are working on the full fitness of mind and body for a variety of athletes. These include cricketers, cyclists, ballet dancers, golfers, tennis players, marathon runners, track and field athletes and footballers.

Visualization

Creativity comes from the mind and visualization has a great deal to do with creative thought. A Californian-based company called Syber Vision recently published a series of tapes based on interviews with achievers from all walks of life.[15] Visualization was considered to be the most important aspect these achievers had in common. They sensed with the greatest possible clarity the successful performance of their ambition. At times this involved using all their senses, they would imagine the sound, sight, touch, taste and smell of the coming challenge and its successful outcome. This group of sport's achievers was therefore asked if they had ever used visualization or mental imagery. 80 per cent said that they used this mental exercise. In several cases they had never talked about it, but for most it had just come as second nature; others had learned the skill but for a few they still had to execute the task physically. Jayne Torvill said, 'Chris can picture moves of where we are and where the legs will be, whereas I can't picture them without actually doing them.' The mind becomes accustomed to an action by physical practice. The concept of visualization is that in addition to an athlete's physical practice, he or she can perform valuable practice by rehearsing an action in the mind. It is important that the action is as close to perfection as one's mind can conceive the body's performance. This action has three advantages. Firstly, the process allows the athlete to have 'been there' before the event and therefore some of the fear of the unknown can be resolved. The athlete will be more familiar and at ease. Secondly, the required competitive action has additional practice time in perfect execution, i.e. a successful personal outcome. Thirdly and perhaps the most important, the individual is convincing himself or herself that an improved and successful action is possible. This means that one is working not only on improved physical action but also on an improved self-image and that can increase one's self-confidence, and confidence is all important in performing well under stressful conditions. The mind is rehearsing personal control of successful actions. Of course, this process can be applied to all areas of life, personal or professional. The imagery part of this exercise in sporting terms allows the mind to take the body into differing competitive conditions. For example, varying weather (if the competition is held outdoors), different opponents, differing surroundings, varying ground conditions, and so on.

It could also be possible that there is a need to take the pressure off by mentally being somewhere else or simply by mentally moving inside one's physical system and slowing things down. Many people are still unaware that they can substantially control their heart rate and other automatic systems through a variety of relaxation techniques such as deep breathing and also by visualization. The point of this is that individuals take control of themselves and have a better chance of determining their future. The athletes who have no mental picture of what they would like to do in varying conditions are more likely to have the pattern and outcome of the contest dictated to them.

Mental rehearsal

There is not a sport or an activity to which mental rehearsal cannot be applied. Dr Christiaan Barnard, the world's first heart transplant surgeon, said that he believed man could achieve anything within the scope of his imagination. I heard him say this in a speech during a dinner in 1966. It struck me that the first four-minute mile by Sir Roger Bannister had first to be mentally conceived as possible, similarly for man to walk on the moon, it had to be thought of as a serious possibility. All that then remained was the hours of dedication and intelligent application of time, effort and resources to achieve the goal! The thought helped me in my own quest of bettering what had been done before in my event of 400m hurdles. In the months prior to the Olympic Games, apart from the hours of physical practice, many more hours were spent mentally rehearsing the effort distribution, pace judgement, stride pattern and hurdling technique for a successful attempt to break the existing world record, which I hoped would be good enough to win the Olympics. Even while lying down, the visualization was so clear that my pulse rate and breathing would come close to what I would actually experience in a race.

Des Drummond related how he visualized successful moves the day before the game. 'The night before, I see and feel myself scoring and making tackles: you hit a good player coming onto you full on, and you stop him in his tracks – it's a good feeling, physical contact.' Peter Sterling gave almost exactly the same account: 'Lying in bed at night, for a while I'll be looking at myself doing something at full speed, doing it correctly and simulating the situation in my mind as close to a game as possible. I'm sure it's helped my game, but if I only think that it's helped it's worth it. The only time I see myself defensively is if a man gets loose and I come up with a good tackle but it's mainly when I've got the ball in my hands, I think of doing something that's directly involved in what I'm going to do . . . sometimes your sub-conscious comes in and you do something bad, so you repeat it without the error.'

In motor racing the driver has the problem of controlling a potentially lethal situation. Jackie Stewart said that the greatest requirement was to eliminate the sensation of speed. 'What I did was to de-synchronize to the element of speed, where it was all slow motion.' In an interview for *Playboy* in 1972,[16] Jackie had said that he was always impressed when he saw Rod Laver return a serve. Even when returning a 'cannon ball', there appeared to be no rush. He returned it almost as if it was an insult that one should send such a 'dribbler' into his court. 'That's what I mean by synchronization, and that's more than just fast reactions. I can't see one of those serves. In my case the synchronization is to a race track.' Most people have travelled in a car for extended periods at some speed and find that the sensation of any great speed is lost. The cues seem to be coming in slow motion so that when one leaves a motorway exit and slows down to 25 m.p.h., it feels as though one could open the door and get out. In cold anticipation, Jackie Stewart eliminated the sensation of speeds approaching 180 m.p.h. before the start, and thereby dominated the early laps and took control of the race.

Billie Jean King said that her own rehearsal was of what she would do once the ball came onto her side of the net. Her focus did not include the opponent, just how she needed to react and what she would have to do.

Steve Cram, on the other hand, liked to put himself in the shoes of the other top competitors, such as Seb Coe, Steve Ovett and Said Aouita. He liked to have game plan options. He would imagine how he thought they might like to run the race, and how he would like to run it. By the time he had run through the possibilities he had a few options. 'I think that's good because then when I get out on the track, I've been through it and I don't suddenly have to think, "What am I going to do now?" If you react too slowly your chance has gone. Things happen very quickly in the 1500m and these days you can't give anybody two to three yards.' It is perhaps unfair to make comparisons at this elite level, but it may be significant how often the vastly talented pair of Coe and Ovett have run themselves into tactical trouble. They are two of the 20 per cent who did not use mental rehearsal or imagery. They both expressed, and exhibit, a heightened awareness while running but react to their surroundings rather than having rehearsed options.

At every major sporting event, there is the tension relating to the occasion. Prior to coming on to court at Wimbledon, John Newcombe would mentally rehearse the first five to ten minutes so that it was familiar. 'I'd imagine walking onto the court, tossing for serve, photographers are out there, go down, I'm going to serve, he's going to return like this. He's going to serve, I'm going to return like that. The night before I'd just run through in my mind and make a check-list on everything I knew about the guy, any titbit of information and then I'd go to sleep.'

Advance planning is a common thread. Arnold Palmer said, 'My most successful events were those that I had carefully planned and imagined throughout the entire day – imagining what you're going to do, how you're going to do it, what the course is like, which is similar to saying what's the opponent like and how you would attack him or the golf course.'

In the same way, Lucinda Green said that she walks the cross-country course before an event. 'You start getting the science right behind you when you walk it and soon before I start to ride, I will find a completely quiet place, shut my eyes and think. Starting from the beginning, I'll go right through and see every single bit of land I'm going to cover and every single approach at each fence, like a film.' Ann Brightwell used the same analogy of film, but in her case it was watching herself when she was high jumping. 'Like a little film section, I could picture every part of what I did and break it down.' Ann had started as a high jumper, had her first international in the long jump and became Olympic champion over 800m. Ann referred to the simulation of races during training. She said,

'Every training session bore some kind of resemblance to how I was going to feel at various stages of the race.'

Steele Bishop introduced an additional element which he used in conjunction with his mental rehearsal of the coming race. He said, 'There are pressure points just above the bumps above your eyebrows. I'd shut my eyes, lie back and go through the race, exactly how I'm going to ride it, and win it. The pressure points were usually weak at first and uneven. The more I went through the race, winning it and how you're going to do it, the stronger and more balanced they and even the pulse, became. Once they were strong I was in a very positive frame of mind, alert and ready to go. And it made a big difference to how well I rode.'

Al Oerter used to visualize the Olympic competition during his training sessions in the weeks leading up to the Games. 'I've always been able to simulate competition. I may be by myself out in the field but very easily I drift into a simulation of an Olympic discus event, I can mentally picture myself competing with the other people in a training session.' He added a positive philosophical note. 'Some people compete because they have a compulsive need to beat someone and like getting someone else down – that's negative and will ultimately force someone out of sport. But those people who use competition as a natural extension of the training environment, just to test their capabilities, they become positive and and bring you back into the sport. If you don't think you've done as well as you possibly could, all you do is go back and change the training programme and if you improve, the programme is working and you push it into a higher gear.'

Even from these few descriptions, it can be seen that there was variety in method and intensity. Some athletes watch themselves as if they were watching a film, others are able to take it much further and live the event in great detail. The more senses used the greater the impact on the system. Sensory experience can be a powerful tool for anyone wanting to fulfil their potential.

Imagery

How can imagery help one to control nerves before a big event? How can it assist an athlete's preparation? One aspect of imagery is to help the athlete come through difficult training sessions. Herb Elliott said that on training runs where he wanted to slow down, he would call up a mental picture of Merv Lincoln, another fine Australian runner, who would be on his shoulder. Herb would not allow himself to slow down or to be passed in this imaginary race.

The emotional stress before competition can be extreme. Jackie Stewart described how he felt and how imagery was used to defuse the tension. He said that prior to a Grand Prix race, the image he had of his emotional state was that of an over-inflated beach ball, he felt as though it could bounce out of control. During his emotional countdown towards the race time, he would gradually deflate the ball. If bounced, it would come back to his hand. This process continued until the ball was completely deflated and Jackie was virtually emotionless. 'By the time the race came, my rubber ball had deflated; I wasn't going to get jokes and I wasn't going to get angry either.' Jackie had eliminated all emotions and was clean and cold on the starting line. He had become almost numb, a protection of his nerves against the atmosphere of tension and anticipation before the race.

Duncan Goodhew used imagery to centre on his target and to keep himself focussed. 'I broke my race into quarters. I visualized my target times on a big wall of paper and I'd smash through it into the next one.'

Soviet athletes are prepared psychologically before competing. Valeriy Borzov spoke of his autogenic training. To control his nerves before his Olympic 100m semi-final, he used the rehearsed image of a forest and a river, relaxation being the key point. The different moods required for each occasion were linked to his own experiences in life. High points with great emotion and successful outcomes, and very quietening times of complete emotional relaxation. Before the final, his thoughts were uplifting ones. Visualization was of success, winning in perfect form of course! Valeriy said, 'For success, first athletes must have talent, second they must work and third they must have control of the mind.'

One requirement for all sports is that one feels comfortable with the surroundings during the competition. John Newcombe related how he had been introduced to a few things that helped. 'Let's say I had to play on the Centre Court: before I left Wimbledon the night before, I would walk up to the back of the stands and look down on the court and I'd imagine my arms enveloping the net posts and the court, and I'd close my eyes and have a mental picture of the court and myself being one – familiarity, so that when I came out to play there I felt right at home.'

In many sports such as golf, basketball and baseball, as well as several others, there are chances for success or failure in every attempt. Any run of negatives can create psychological pressure which in turn can tighten the athlete physically and adversely affect his or her performance. Daley Thompson said that he spent most of the last two or three days before competition lying down. 'I spend an hour or two going through every decathlon event and in each event putting myself in a pressure situation. For example, I imagine myself standing on the high jump area having had two failures and the bar is at 2m 10cm, so I've been there before.' He said he knows how he is going to approach it and will not be afraid of it because he has actually been there. This practice may well have saved him in Los Angeles. He had two failures at his opening height in the pole vault, then successfully cleared the bar on his third and final attempt. He expressed his relief to the world with a back flip on the landing area.

Pat O'Callaghan used imagery during his Olympic hammer competition. In training he had used physical targets. He would walk out and place flags at the distances he knew his competitors had thrown in the summer prior to the Games. 'I'd walk about saying to myself: "Three throws to qualify for the final". I never left the field without beating those fellows flags . . . You can reverse that, when they're shouting at you at the Games, you can stop and think, remember the flags outside.' The image of the contestants' flags was used to get him 'psyched up' in training, and the same image was used to calm him down in the pressure of competition. He knew he could surpass the flags – he had been there before.

Prior to major competition, nerves can cause athletes to go 'over the top' and lose their self-control. On the warm-up track in Mexico prior to my Olympic final, I was sitting down to change from my jogging shoes into spikes. As I looked up I saw the pre-race favourite, Geoff Vanderstock of the United States take a practice start around the first bend. He flew! I felt my throat tighten and recognized the first stage of inner panic. I knew that it was vital to maintain my sense of personal control. The grass on the infield was damp so I left my shoes off and while taking an easy stride, took myself back to where I was running in a few inches of water, on the firm sands of Powder Point Beach in Massachusetts. The sun was on my back and I felt the sensation of my body flowing with health and strength. The image was so strong that my mind was totally blank as to what I had just seen and I was back on to personal performance. Imagery can be used to heighten or lower emotion. It can be applied to real or imaginary situations. As long as the individual is in control of the imagery, it can be a valuable and powerful tool. It should be noted, however, that it can be equally powerful in a negative frame of mind. Certainly in everyday life the imagination can be used just as effectively to think of reasons and create images as to why something cannot be accomplished. I had a personal experience of creating a negative reaction without intending to do so. Prior to the Munich Olympics in 1972, I thought that it was important to face the possibility of losing. It was a thought that I had never before entertained but as I was older and possibly past my prime or so I thought, I considered that it would be a prudent and a mature thing to do . . . so I ran race after race mentally imagining that I was beaten and although I anguished for a couple of months over being a loser, I came to terms with it by saying I was just going to try my hardest and do my best. The result was that when it came to the time of the Games, my self-talk had taken away all the adrenalin needed for fight or flight. I made the final, but came to the start line completely flat. I tried pressing my nails into my hands saying, 'Wake up, this is the Olympic final', and the conditioned response came calmly back, 'Yes, and you're just going to try your hardest to do your best'. It caused an uncontrolled response from me during the race. I put in a sustained all-out effort early on, where normally I would try to conserve my energy while still running high on adrenalin. I realized my error too late and found myself treading water in the home straight. I hung on for a medal but the gold was gone. I have no idea whether I could have won that race. Injury had also been a factor shortly before that Games, but I am very well aware that the negative mental rehearsal had an overwhelming bearing on my subconscious on the crucial day – so much so that I could not consciously alter my emotional level. It is often said, 'As you train, so will you race'. I believe one must add to that, 'As you pre-think, so will you react'! If one wants to gain positive results, positive thinking is one key element.

CHAPTER 14

CONCENTRATION AND CONTROL

In competition, how would you rate your ability to concentrate on a scale of 1–10? Never one lacking in self-confidence, the response from Daley Thompson was predictable: 'Twelve!' Daley was certainly not the only one to exhibit confidence in this area of concentration, Lester Piggott, David Forbes and Ed Moses used the word 'total'; Gene Upshaw and Ken Read said 'absolute'; and Herb Elliott referred to it as 'dramatic'. Twenty-one others said things such as 'very high', 'in the eight or nine range'. Joan Benoit Samuelson rated herself nine and added that it was her strongest asset.

For most people there is a limited period of time in which concentration can be razor sharp. Des Drummond passed on his experience related to tiredness in the game when he said, 'I used to get tired in a game when I wasn't mentally prepared. My concentration used to last for forty minutes and the game's eighty minutes. If you have a positive view of the game before you go into it, you can last longer.'

Bryan Robson tackled the same problem of total concentration from another stand point. He said that the more tired you become the harder it is to concentrate, underlining the need for a high degree of physical fitness.

Greg Chappell learned to concentrate for the minimum amount of time necessary. 'When batting it was when the bowler turned at the top of his run, I would concentrate until nothing further could happen, until we'd taken our runs or we'd established that there would be no runs from that ball. Then I'd switch off until the bowler got back to his line. If you concentrate the whole time you'd be mentally exhausted.'

The conscious breaking of concentration was clearly seen in the play of Arnold Palmer and Lee Trevino. Both men are able to laugh and speak with the crowd between shots and then go back and completely lock in to the task of the next shot. Ian Botham attributed the longevity of Lee Trevino's career to that ability to relax in between shots. Ian likened it to his ability to turn on and off on the cricket field. He also showed how his ability to concentrate but carry on a conversation won him a battle. 'In one game against Northamptonshire, a good mate of mine Geoff Cook was trying to intimidate me by fielding really close. So I thought, right I'll play him at his own game. I'd just come in to bat and they had a spinner on and just as he came in to bowl, I started talking, "Have a good night last night, Tosh? It's nice down here, isn't it?" I wasn't looking at him, so I wasn't going to get out. He went! He was wasting his time! I had won!'

Rob de Castella pointed out, 'It's easy to concentrate on something you enjoy.' Of his competitive concentration, he said that it was at about a six when it didn't count and a ten when it did. Billie Jean King was another for whom the concentration varied but it was the pattern in which she played. If she was going to be beaten, it was in the early rounds. The further on the tournament progressed, and the further into each game she went, her concentration moved towards ten.

Billy Beaumont said that he concentrated well because as a forward, he was always in the thick of things. He added with a bit of humorous needle, 'Whereas if I was a winger, I might have been day dreaming and thinking about how I could keep my kit clean for next week!'

Only two athletes were harsh on themselves. In both cases it was because of a break in concentration while competing. Bob Tisdall said that during the Olympic 400m hurdles final, commentary over a loud speaker above where he was running said, 'And it's Bob Tisdall in the lead'. Bob said, 'I never should have heard that!' Duncan Goodhew had a greater reason for concern. He said that as he turned, half-way through his swim at the World Championships, he said to himself, 'Come on Duncan, you've got to do well, your mother and step-father are here all the way from Britain, you've got to do well. I wonder what we're having for dinner tonight?' At which point he realized that he wasn't quite concentrating fully on what he was doing. In his Olympic win he said that only in the last 25m was his concentration absolute and everything was right.

Gene Upshaw related how the intensity of concentration on the game stayed with him. 'Once the coin was tossed I was in it, absolutely, and I didn't come out until the next day. I just got so involved that after the game I'd just keep replaying it, thinking if I had done this . . . What usually happened was a few guys would get together and have a beer and talk about it and you didn't come down. It was midnight before you came down.' This intensity level is quite common among the highest achievers and will be discussed later in this chapter.

Focus of attention

What was your focus of attention while you were competing? Inevitably the range of answers was diverse because the sports varied so greatly; however, there are many similarities within groups of sports. A useful perspective comes from sports psychologist Robert Nideffer.[45] Using four quadrants he illustrates what is required of each sport (see *Figure 1*). The parameters on one axis represent a spectrum from broad to narrow focus and on the other, internal or external focus. A broad focus would be required of any athlete who takes in a reasonably wide field of vision, for example a basketball player who must see where all the other players are moving so that the pass is directed to the man or woman who is in the most likely position to lead to a score. A narrow field of vision is required by a darts player who is aiming for one particular point on the board. An internal focus is often held by the distance runner who is monitoring his or her energy output and effort distribution. An external focus would be held by the yachtsman who must constantly be conscious of outside elements.

Although this illustration is a helpful representation of the focus of attention, it must be remembered that this is only the primary focus. Taking the 400m hurdler as an illustration, the hurdler's primary focus of attention is in Quadrant III, narrow–external, because the focus and primary concentration is on the coming hurdle. However, at different instants focus is in each of the other quadrants. For example in Quadrant I, the broad–internal focus is constantly reviewing the stride lengths required to reach the next hurdle in the proper position for a rapid, balanced clearance. There is also assessment of the effect the wind, track conditions and pace is having on the stride pattern for clearing the next

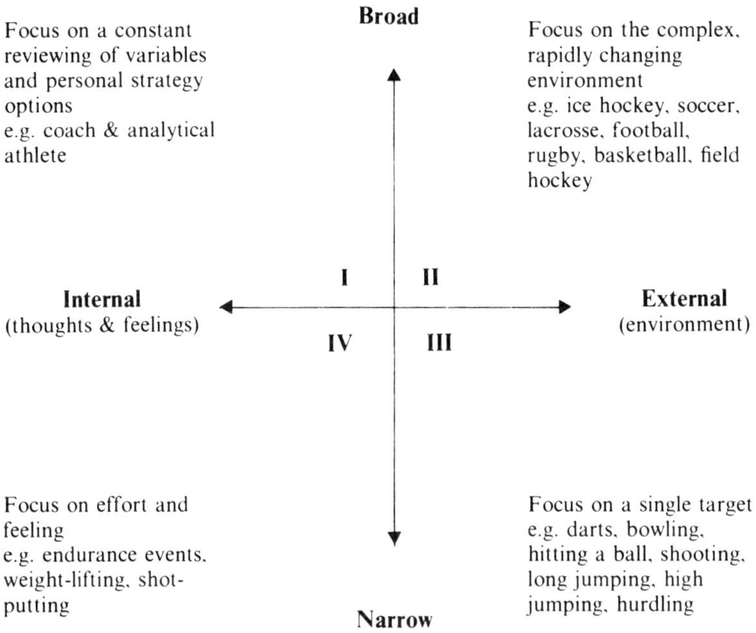

Figure 1 Parameters of focus of attention.

hurdle. Also one has to see whether the pace chosen is sufficient to maintain good position against the other competitors. In Quadrant II, the broad–external focus is assessing where one is in relation to all the other competitors in the race. In Quadrant IV, the narrow–internal focus is on personal pace judgement and effort distribution. At any one moment in time, any of these factors could be critical. The point being made is that the athlete is not only executing one function or concentrating on one focus when competing. It is important to prepare for as many eventualities as possible, so that in the main, it becomes automatic, and he or she competes in calm but alert awareness.

As mentioned in an earlier chapter, the Salford University researchers maintained that selective attention accounted for the predictive mental state of competitive cyclists. In this study the cyclists were being taken into stressful fatigue. There are different ways of dealing with feelings of discomfort. Some may choose to distract themselves by thinking about other things. Most top competitors have learned to accept the feelings and allow the mind to focus on where the discomfort is located and assess it accordingly, perhaps on a scale of 1–10. Identifying the place and the degree of discomfort is very helpful in dealing with the associated feelings. Frequently it allows the athletes to realize that they are really not in as bad a state as they originally thought. The whole point of allowing oneself to move into this 'discomfort zone' in training is that at times it is necessary if one intends to modify the body and to make muscles stronger as well as more efficient. If one is in a sport where this is part of the necessary training, then the body and mind gradually learn to build up a tolerance. Herb Elliott believed that his training was, for the most part, producing an adaptation to pain tolerance. I recall a female university student taking up the public call for fitness. She had never before done any stressful physical activity. By the time she had jogged half-way round the 400m track, she panicked because she felt a strange sensation of rapid, gasping breathing. Through inexperience, her neurophysiological pain threshold was unusually low: in contrast, Herb Elliott's had become exceptionally high.

Returning to Nideffer's 'focus of attention' theory, what must be recognized is that requirements change and the athlete must consciously control the change in focus. Billie Jean King said that her focus would constantly switch from a broad perspective, assessing where the opponent was on court in relation to the ball, then rapidly narrowing her perspective to focus on the ball. The same is true of most other ball sports; the parameters must be broad until the requirement changes as the player receives the ball, at which time the attention is focused on the object.

An added problem for individuals such as the American football quarterback players, is that generally their focus narrows when pressure of tension increases.[17] Those who follow American football will often see the quarterback trying to force a pass between two defenders, when there is another man waving his arms about in a completely wide open spot. That quarterback, under pressure, has narrowed his focus and is unable to maintain the necessary wider vision.

Billy Beaumont said that his focus was primarily on the ball and the opponent . . . and sometimes on the referee!

Gene Upshaw said that he had an internal and an external focus. 'Internally, I was doing my job to the best of my ability. Externally I was dictating to my opponent that I was the best at what I did and whatever he did, it was going to be wrong.'

The middle-distance runners have to maintain a minor focus or monitor on their internal response throughout the race, but in general it must be a broad external focus. In the light of the fact that neither Coe nor Ovett uses mental rehearsal, it is not surprising to see the exceptional degree of awareness with which they run their races. Coe said, 'You're concentrating on what you're doing and have an awareness of whatever else is happening around you, sensing how other people are breathing, whether they're breathing hard and whether their feet are coming down heavily – that way you respond to a break. The one thing about 1500m and upwards is continually being aware of how somebody is responding to what you are doing. If I look back to the 1500m in Los Angeles, there was an occasion when 250m from the tape, I felt Steve Cram wasn't responding as well as he should have done and that made me realize that if I could perhaps hit him with two or three more surges before we got round to the bottom bend, each time the response would be slightly less. I throw those surges into races just to see how people respond. It's that and also it's just concentrating on not allowing other things to start clouding what you're trying to do.'

Any contest where the competitors are moving towards the same finish line with no lane restrictions, whether it is a foot race or with bikes, automobiles, yachts or horses, there is a need for a broad focus of attention. Lester Piggott left school at fourteen, with sporadic attendance for another year. He said that he and academics never really got along, but in terms of his trade his intelligence is unquestionable. Illustration of this was given when he answered this question on focus of attention. Lester said that he sees things that are going to happen before they happen. His focus is on the other horses and jockeys around him. He said that he would be taking in how much space there was between the inside horses and the rail and between the other horses; he would be focused on what the other horses and jockeys were going to do before they did it. He would be assessing how much each horse had left, and aware of a jockey getting ready to make a move, and he would attempt to cover the action before it happened. He would know the form of each horse from reading the form book before going to the start and he knew from past experience how the other jockeys raced. He said that he had a minor focus on his riding position and how much energy his own horse had left, but the main focus was anticipation and knowing his options. His racing record sets him apart. Where most would be holding on and trying to steer at 40m.p.h., Lester gives us a focus on racing genius.

Ken Read said that he identified strongly with Lester. He said, 'Your focus of attention is on yourself, your space and your positioning, how you're riding the ski itself, how it's reacting, but you're planning ahead, five or six seconds, which at 80m.p.h. is quite a distance. You're planning your trajectory, how you plan to come into a gate, coping with the terrain, working with the centrifugal force, trying to get a good curve and gliding the skis as well. So your focus of attention is ahead of you as well as around you and within.'

Awareness is another important factor in where to place one's focus. Seb Coe's awareness often had to be on those behind him, and while leading down the home straight in the 1500m final at the Moscow Olympics, he kept control of his position by watching the shadows of his competitors on the track!

One of the most famous commentary lines in basketball was from Johnny Most, where in the seventh game of the 1976 NBA playoffs, with five seconds remaining, he screamed, 'And Havlicek stole the ball!' John Havlicek told me what he did. The opposing team had the ball out of bounds. (In basketball the players must put the ball back into play within five seconds.) John's particular genius was defence. He saw the ball being given by the referee and John was watching and covering his man, with his back to the passer but at the same time he was counting 1001, 1002, and by 1003 when nothing had happened, he knew that the passer was in trouble. He turned half-way so that he could see the passer out of the corner of his eye while still focusing on his own man. A second later he saw a poor pass being made and reacted quickly enough to deflect the ball to one of his own players, who ran out the clock. Boston won the game and the championship. If John had not counted, he would not have had a clear sense of the most important focus at that instant.

In games like squash and tennis, the way in which an opponent approaches the ball can tell much about the coming shot. This means reading the game before it happens. Jonah Barrington said, 'If you are taking in what an opponent's doing with his racket swing and with his body, it's much easier to assess what stroke he's going to play. When the ball is on the other side of the player, so it's not visible, you have to anticipate what's about to happen through what's taking place with the body and those who read that better and earlier than others will immediately be far better players.'

During the first British Superstars, former England soccer captain Bobby Moore showed how slow he was over 100m, and by exposing that, he told us that his athletic intelligence was extremely high. During his career, he read the game so well that he was always in the right position when the ball came into his field of play. Reading the game on a soccer field requires a broad focus of attention, combined with a cool head. One technique which works is to 'imagine you had more time'. Bobby Moore always looked as though he had that extra time.

David Forbes said that he made sure that he set pin-point priorities before a sailing race but as there were an infinite number of variables, his technique was to relax and not to focus. He could then automatically respond with an open mind. In contrast, Rodney Pattisson said that he was thinking all the time, reading the wind, studying the tide, watching other boats, keeping on a permanent look out and constantly changing the feel of the boat with the strength of the wind.

Cricketers often have to face balls delivered at close to 90m.p.h. Greg Chappell said that he focused on the face of the bowler until the bowler reached his delivery stride. 'Then I'd look for the ball and then the hand and try to watch it come round, particularly focusing on where the bowler was going to let the ball go. You're picking up the angle the ball leaves the hand, your brain reacts to the length and line from the down and sideways angles, giving you a fraction of a second to react. Eye-sight's not important, it's reaction.'

Athletes who are in their own lanes such as sprinters and swimmers have to create a focus which will draw them out. They may be able to react to the challenge from others but it is also necessary to have a personal target or focus. For Ed Moses it is the hurdles in his lane and how he feels, but he added that in competition everything was automatic. Duncan Goodhew said that when he was at the start he would focus on a point. 'There is a cross at the end of the pool and I used to stare at it and physically try to draw it towards me. I was concentrating absolutely so when I actually entered the water, I got a real feeling of speed with this cross coming towards me and I focused to nothing.' Duncan explained that because of this, elements of the race were practised in training and they became 'one'. Then he practised clearing any extraneous thoughts from his mind while competing, which combined to produce a 'focus to nothing'.

Duncan Goodhew's description of 'focusing to nothing' and allowing his inner-being to simply execute the known action is very similar to the actions taught in the 'inner game'.[21] Timothy Gallwey has attempted to bring some of the thinking of Eastern religion, namely Zen, into Western sport. There are two basic principles, 'trusting the body' and 'quietening the mind'. Too often the Western coaches tend to over-instruct, even telling the athletes what they should be thinking and doing, rather than asking them what they are experiencing and feeling. Tim Gallwey has pointed out that we often try to correct ourselves or our pupils by forcing changes which create muscular tension and thus interferes with the natural flow of action. Instructed correction is often not the fastest or most permanent method of learning. His method is to increase awareness. For example in tennis, the server may be aiming for a certain spot. The method of correction comes not from trying to force a change in the service action but simply and carefully to observe where the ball is landing in relation to that spot. The player is asked to trust that the body will make the necessary inner corrections as long as the player carefully observes the balls' landing positions. Tim points out that the body taught itself to walk and talk and yet our egos want to take over, when in fact we do not know what alterations are necessary to achieve our target. The role of the coach in the inner game method is very Socratic. Learning takes place through questioning. The coach asks the player to focus his or her attention in such a way that learning can take place. The player replies by telling the coach, 'I was too tense'. This is non-specific. The coach should reply, 'Where do you feel tense? How would you rate it on a 1–10 scale?' By putting your focus on the area of tension when you next feel it, invariably the tension melts away. The player is asked to keep his or her competitive mind in the present and not to dwell on self-critical aspects or past mistakes. Tim's teaching parallels the thought that inside every acorn is an oak tree. Once someone has a vision of how to perform an action, assuming that they are physically capable of performing that action, there is no reason why they cannot learn how to perform that way.

Intensity with control

If an occasion is very meaningful, whether it is a social encounter, a business deal or a sports contest, there is almost always some apprehension. In the case of the high achieving athletes, for a period of time their top priority has been focussed and centred on achieving a goal. There is a heightened sense of anticipation, responsibility, and in many cases, anxiety. The ones who walk tall in these situations are those who have managed to withstand the pressure and maintained emotional and mental control.

From discussions with this sample of top athletes, they believed that it helped immensely to be capable of high emotion. A competitor without emotional intensity is not going to live long in any competitive arena. It may sound like a dichotomy but the intense emotions must be more than matched by the ability for self-control. If there is intensity without self-control, either players erupt and are doomed to disqualifications, bookings, penalties or fines or they 'choke', cracking up under the pressure of the occasion.

During the World Snooker Championships in 1984, Steve Davis appeared on television as cool as ice, but when I interviewed him, Steve said that he was a very emotional person, and that he might be shaking like a leaf inside as he walks to the table but he would never show it. He said that he thought there was a need for that emotional intensity within every great athlete but that true greatness came from their ability to control that emotion. This summary was repeated to all subsequent interviewees and was unanimously supported.

David Bryant's sport of bowls would be seen by many as a quiet and relaxing game; however, David said that his sport was all about pressure: who can take the most pressure, being able to apply pressure, and choosing the right time to apply it. 'One good shot or one lucky one can completely wipe out five minutes of good careful build-up by you, and there's no outlet. You can't get stuck in as you could on a soccer field. The pressure is all in the mind. You have to have great self-discipline and take it squarely on your shoulders and rise above it.' David referred to the qualities of Bjorn Borg and Chris Evert Lloyd, citing them as ideal professionals. They never let their opponent see when they were getting to them. David said that he will always appear confident although he accepted that one can lose. He quoted Borg as saying, 'If you're afraid of losing then you daren't win', but David and almost all the other top athletes are at their best when the pressure is greatest. Frequently they produce an unbelievable comeback when they are in trouble.

The pressure referred to is a strange phenomenon because it mostly exists in the mind of the athlete. Nevertheless, the athlete is only too aware that the outcome could determine his or her future. Since the days of the ancient Olympics in 776 BC, sport has carried a high degree of prestige. Today, many lucrative financial contracts can depend on the outcome of events, as well as any appearance fees or prize money that might accrue. However, money is not in the mind of the competitors when they are about to do battle. The emotional pressure is caused because the athletes have invested themselves entirely in the outcome; their self-image, self-esteem and credibility are laid on the line. Those who intend! to win usually do. Many would like to but the intent is missing. The mental or emotional pressure comes from the uncertainty of the outcome and the fact that the outcome has such personal importance. There is a strong desire not to let themselves or anyone else down. The emotional pressure is so great that it is rather like having a baby; they want the end result but they would often rather not embark on delivery!

When discussing intensity, O.J. Simpson referred to anger as being a powerful force. 'I'm a firm believer that anger makes you strong, so you've got to build up a certain amount of anger. It's just a matter of where you direct it. I used to direct it inwards. I ran a play and was tackled by one or two guys. In the stand they might say great run but to me, I didn't make it all the way for a touch down. I shouldn't have let that last guy or two guys get me. I used to channel that anger in. My team-mates would say, "Leave O.J. alone on the bench!" By myself I'd be concentrating. I was trying to reach a state of clear vision, where I could see it all . . . my biggest yardage was usually gained in the fourth quarter.'

The need or desire to prove oneself is a strong motivating force. The response may be fear or anger or enjoyment of the challenge, whether self-imposed or from another person. Whatever the root cause of the heightened emotion, the key to success is learning to maintain mental and physical control.

Personal behaviour control is also important and is reflected not only in performance but also in behaviour around the competition. Rod Laver reflected on the lack of control of some of the leading tennis professionals. To rectify this he thought that penalties should be increased. Like a great number of the viewing public, he said he would like to see tennis introduce a similar code of behaviour to that required of the professional golfers and that the penalties should be strict enough to be effective. He pointed out that in many cases, a monetary fine is of little or no consequence to a player who earns a great deal, whereas a substantial time ban from tournament play, including one of the Grand Slam tournaments, could have more impact.

Almost inevitably the name of John McEnroe came up in conversations on personal control. Everyone had their own views as to whether his outbursts were gamemanship or involuntary. Billie Jean King said that she identified with John as a perfectionist because she had suffered from similar outbursts. 'One side of me was telling me to shut up for making such an ass of myself and the other half was still going, telling the guy where to get off. Afterwards I'm totally upset with myself for being such a jerk. I can feel part of me trying to bring myself back but it's like a volcano going through an explosion. Afterwards, I get over it quickly and I'm sorry I did it. I think John's that way. I saw him yelling at Cliff Drysdale for putting Fred Stolle on a rival television network at the same time as the Davis Cup. He was going crazy. One minute later he was back, apologising and saying he shouldn't have said those things.'

John Newcombe saw it differently and said that McEnroe never behaved like that against Borg. 'I think it's his way of creating a presence on court . . . [to] dominate the occasion. My way of doing that was in the way you played the game. If someone hits a winner against me, I'd say, "great shot" and smile and then come back and play the next point like it was match point. It was just a subtle way of letting the opponent know this guy's not afraid of me. I was leading the applause and then attacking.' John said he wished he was still at the level to play McEnroe. He said, 'The first thing I'd do when he starts bitching about calls, is wait until he'd finished, then I'd walk up to the umpire and ask for the referee and I'd say, "My opponent's trying to intimidate the linesman and trying to put me off by stalling and I ask you to stop him straight away." I'd say it loud enough so it went into the microphone for the people to hear. I wouldn't talk directly to him until I'd finished, then I'd say to him, "Look, John, every time you do something, I'm going to do something. You want to see who's the best tennis player, get on with the game or do you want to carry on with this . . .?" I don't know whether he understands this himself but what happens out there is that when he blows up, the whole centre of attention is on him and the umpire and referee. His opponent's down there unimportant. Everything is centred on John and it's a tremendous psychological presence. Almost every time he does it he breaks serve straight away. That's why I'd wait until he'd finished his show, then I would become the presence so when we resumed play, we'd be even, but I'd finish up with the presence being on me.'

Time has been devoted to McEnroe as his name was brought up by a number of athletes as an example of how not to behave because he lacks personal control. Each sport has its problem athletes, but the percentage of these achievers who did not care about self-discipline and behaviour was negligible. Quite the opposite, Heather McKay reflected on the worlds of squash and racketball. She was concerned about the deterioration of court manners in a few of the younger players. There was a definite bias towards old-fashioned standards. In the final chapters, there will be further reflections on standards related to cheating, gamesmanship, drug-taking and other disturbing issues which face the players of tomorrow.

It has been outlined previously how relaxation, concentration, focus of attention, mental rehearsal and imagery can all help the athletes to maintain control of themselves. Without that control there is a possibility that they will go over the top. It can be graphically demonstrated, as seen in *Figure 2*.

Arousal is a term which today has strong sexual connotations. Here, however, the term refers to the automatic response of the nervous system to the athlete's mental state. The anticipation of competition can produce a great deal of stress and anxiety as well as pleasure. Some of the physical responses to stress are increases in muscle tension, breathing rate, pulse rate, urination, sweating as well as feelings of nausea and so on. Prolonged concentration becomes more difficult with increased stress.

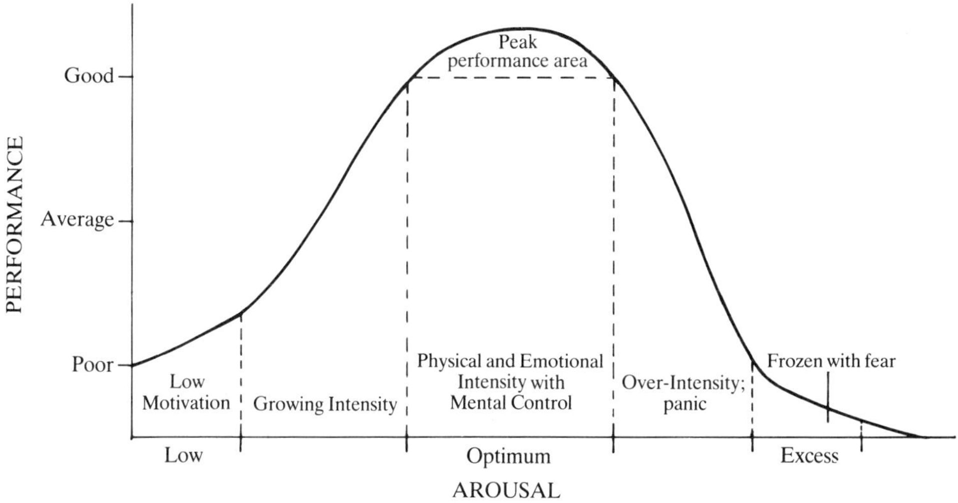

Figure 2 Performance curve.

The mind tends to jump from one thing to the next. If the tension and anxiety go unchecked, performance can be negatively influenced. An extreme example of the result of fear was given by Bob Tisdall, who told a story about a fellow student at Cambridge. 'The mind controls the fear which is very important. Too much and you're scared stiff. This fellow had failed to get a blue [varsity colours] during his three years at Cambridge, so he stayed for a fourth year, especially to get it, and he froze in the starting blocks in the finals. We had to pick him up and he was stiff, like a corpse.'

The purpose of discussing the topic of performance under stress is to draw attention to the fact that there are techniques used by top athletes and others, which allow them to control their arousal levels. Illustration of the use of imagery was given by Jackie Stewart, deflating his imaginary beachball. He took away his heightened emotions. Borzov used images of being in a relaxed environment and also used the repeated self-suggestion of a winning self-image. Progressive relaxation uses the technique of tensing muscles to bring awareness to them, and then consciously relaxing them. Mental rehearsal was used to give the athletes a sense of personal control and mentally letting them experience the idea of a successful performance beforehand. The focus of attention was on personal control and not on what others were doing. Concentration was helped by good physical conditioning and having a clear view of the intended goal. The goal is set at a realistic but challenging level. Self-confidence certainly helps to control stress levels, and it is no secret that confidence comes from having done the preparation work. All of these factors can assist the athlete to remain at the top of the performance curve.

Perhaps not in their sport but certainly in other areas of life, these athletes will have experienced 'going over the top'. An illustration in the academic world might be going into an exam having only read half of the assigned books, reading the questions and panicking, thinking, 'My God, I know nothing!' Of course, a host of other factors may have been responsible for an individual not to be ready for his or her test. In the case of the athlete, apart from laziness, other reasons can include injury, bad coaching advice, or unrealistic goal-setting.

It should be noted that there are two separate conditions of anxiety.[59] Trait–anxiety refers to the perceived level of danger or fear which we all carry around with us on a daily basis. Some people are more highly strung and will jump if a door slams unexpectedly. Others are quite laid back and take life very much as it comes. The other anxiety level is referred to as state–anxiety, which is the response or reaction to a particular occasion or state in which one is centred. Obviously a World Series, a Cup final, a Super Bowl or an Olympic final will produce a heightened state–anxiety level. If individuals have high trait–anxiety levels, it will not take much state–anxiety to nudge them over the top of the performance curve with the resulting decline in performance. For the highly strung individual there is even greater need for control techniques, but in all cases there is a need for control of anxiety levels. Before a big event, the athletes need to understand what they must do to maintain control. In many cases the coach can help by being calm, and reinforcing a positive view of the athlete's capabilities. In most sports there is time available to communicate with a coach. If there has been a situation in which the player made a costly mistake, his stress level will have been increased. The role of the coach is to control his athlete's personal upset and to help put him or her back into a personal state of control.

For individuals like David Bryant and Billie Jean King, who said that they were more likely to lose in non-pressure situations, the chances are great that in areas where they see little challenge they are relatively low on the arousal performance curve; when the pressure rises, their concentration is intensified, their focus of attention is narrowed to the importance of the task at hand, their control is maintained and the performance is dramatically improved. Although this was not put to the test, it would be quite a safe bet that the pattern just described would fit most of these high achievers in sport.

Pressure often starts to build up some time before an important event and consequently, many people have difficulty in getting to sleep because their minds are racing. Shirley de la Hunty spoke of a technique which she developed for getting to sleep. She mentally watched her brain, encircling it and every time a thought escaped she pulled it back. In no time at all the brain gave up and she would be asleep! Shirley also related what every athlete knew: how hard it is waiting for the start of their event. 'But I learned to quieten my mind and instead of being frightened by that awful waiting feeling, I learned that it was my friend really. It was my build up. I'd been foolish not to recognize it as such. World records were created in that sort of scene, instead of the avoidance pattern I'd followed.'

The field of biofeedback gives an individual equipment which enables them to measure a physical response to the symptoms of stress. There are tapes on relaxation and mental rehearsal techniques, various pieces of apparatus which either visually or audibly give a read-out of items such as pulse rates or finger tip sweat response. The individual has sight or sound contact with the equipment and can learn how to reduce his or her own stress levels. Valeriy Borzov referred to this as autogenic training. It has a growing following among those who are concerned with stress management.[66] The mind is considered to have the greatest part to play in improving performances in the future. The value of biofeedback is that it provides a measureable method of analysing personal control. It may not be wanted by all athletes, but certainly there is no harm in ensuring that one has internal control. It is particularly helpful for the athletes who are having trouble maintaining personal control of their nerves. The feedback from the machines will be able to assist in determining whether better control is being established and which form of visualization or imagery is the most helpful. The equipment simply gives indications of the degree of control which one is achieving. In the past, no such information has been available to the coach or the athlete.

CHAPTER 15

PRE-COMPETITION

Did physical or emotional relationships affect your performance? For many years, the world's Press have congregated at sporting events where some of the world's youth are on display in excellent physical health and attractive condition. Most people find a well-toned body appealing. It does not take long before one or two openly friendly women cause rumours to fly around the world, about sex at the Olympics or whatever the particular gathering may be. These tales were certainly enhanced in the sixties when a certain US diver and an even more successful Australian swimmer found that pre-competition sex relaxed them and they performed better in the pool.

Steve Davis said that he felt a mild ongoing relationship actually helped him at the time of competition. Ann Brightwell said the same, citing the fact that Robbie and she shared the same athletic interests and so their personal relationship was an asset. However, as the day of Olympic competition neared, there was a difference – Robbie preferred to be aloof and Ann would have liked more support by being with him. Peter Snell related that such activities never seemed to affect him. Some of his best races were run when he was on his honeymoon!

However, it would be accurate to relate that there is less sexual activity at an Olympic Games than there is on any university campus. It is also fair to say that in every large group, athletes and non-athletes, there will be a cross-section of personal habits. The responses of the athletes who had to peak for one special occasion, such as a world championships or an Olympic Games, differed from those who compete in frequent league or other competitions. The responses of those whose sport is a regular fixture was that life proceeded as usual. The coming competitions made little difference to how they normally led their lives. Most of the individuals who were peaking for a long-term event said that they usually abstained from intimate relationships prior to those events; this ranged from a day or two up to several weeks. The reason behind this abstention was that their emotional focus was needed to produce a peak performance on the day.

It is understood that with any meaningful human bonding, emotions are tied in with the physical aspects of the relationship. The question of emotional upheaval was asked as a separate question in order to get the athletes' reactions to a situation of emotional distress such as a quarrel or news of misfortune. The question was asked to find out whether their subsequent performance was adversely affected. More than three-quarters (77 per cent) of the achievers were able to shut themselves off from their problems or concerns once they entered their sports arena.

Wayne Gretzky and John Havlicek both used the expression that they were able to 'block out' everything else. Seb Coe said that he had the ability to just switch off. Ralph Doubell said that he shut himself off from everything else. Greg Chappell said that he was not greatly affected, but for the couple of years when he had his worst performances, he felt that emotional problems did disturb his concentration.

As one who was affected, Joan Benoit Samuelson said that although she felt that she was an emotionally stable person, upsets certainly did alter her performance so she attempted to avoid situations which might hamper her emotional or physical state before a major race.

Clive Lloyd mentioned an aspect which was relevant to several sporting individuals who came from small villages or small countries – that they felt somewhat overawed by a move into the big time. He mentioned that he felt that the West Indians in general did not see themselves as good enough. That inferiority complex has been something which Clive has attempted to turn around. He started with himself, working on attaining a professional attitude which was needed when he lost his place on a team. Having conquered his complex, Clive dedicated himself to helping other players gain belief in themselves and their capabilities.

Being mentally prepared for an important event is essential. The athletes interviewed were asked whether or not they were able to distance themselves before a competition. As an important event nears, was there a need to put a cocoon around themselves in order to focus and concentrate on their performance? It is the most difficult time for the performer: similar to entering an exam, with the results being publicly put on display. Inevitably there is apprehension as to whether the preparation has been sufficient. Fears are magnified at such a time. Questions circulate in the head: is the body in a good enough condition? Will any recent injuries inhibit performance? Will the body perform as one wants it to? Will the performance live up to one's personal expectations? What about the fans, the judges or the clock?

One way in which many individuals behave before major tests is to avoid involvement with other people. Of this group almost three-quarters (73 per cent) said that they took themselves away from distractions either mentally, physically or both. Often the reactions are involuntary as Lucinda Green pointed out. 'I don't mean to distance myself but I think I do. It's not done purposely but I notice people saying, "Mind what you say because it's only a week to Badminton". So I then realize that I must have been difficult.' For John Gilmour the involuntary avoidance mechanism manifested itself in the need to sleep. This is actually quite a normal physical reaction to avoid trauma. The desire for additional sleep was mentioned by several athletes and sometimes came after a vivid mental rehearsal of the coming event.

Gareth Edwards was one of those for whom it was business as usual, but he explained that he was almost in a dream world, detached from the current situation. He would be greeting friends in the hotel lobby before going across the street to Cardiff Arms Park to play; 'I'd talk to them and see them but I didn't see them.'

Some individuals needed to be quiet and by themselves for only the last half an hour or so before their match. John Newcombe said that at Wimbledon, he would retreat into the toilet because it was the only quiet place. There was too much noise in the dressing room. J.P.R. Williams said that the team would change about thirty minutes before the game. By then he liked to have all the preparation done. He said, 'I liked to have half an hour or an hour before I went to change, just concentrating on the game.'

For Wayne Gretzky, the lead-in time started the previous evening. He said that the night before a game he would have some food at about 7 p.m. and by 8.30 p.m., he would shut his door and unplug his phone. 'I can't carry on a conversation on the afternoon of a game. I'm awful.' Late in his career, Bob Cousy also used a cloister routine, locking himself away in a hotel room for some time alone to create artificially tension within himself. He found that worked, especially as he was getting older and the competitive fire was dimming.

Individuals' comments varied as to the amount of time that they needed prior to competition. It was often more prolonged for those who were tackling a long-term occasion such as the Olympic Games. Lynn Davies said, 'I used to cut myself off. For a week or so I was anti-social. I just wanted to be by myself leading up to an event. I think it's part of the process. You train very hard and you withdraw into yourself. I think you seek inner strength and you can't share yourself with people. If you want to be the best in what you are doing, then it's probably got to be the most important thing in your life at the time. If you're going to be number one – you can do other things but the focus of your attention has to be on competing.

Jayne Torvill and Christopher Dean both avoided socializing the week before competition. Jayne said that Chris would only say 'hello' or 'good morning'. Chris replied that he avoided long conversations. They both declined invitations to join a group for lunch preferring to eat alone together or with their coach Betty Callaway. If they were caught at a table, Chris's desire to escape was high. Jayne said, 'In a way I don't show it. It's obvious that he doesn't want to talk to someone and he leaves, but I'll stay and be a little more polite and say, "How are you and how's it going?" and all that and I'll make a bit more of an excuse why I'm not going to join in. As long as we're in competition we like to be quiet.'

At the other end of the spectrum are those who need to socialize and want to talk in order to relieve tension. As can be imagined, this can cause problems on a team when other members need solitude. Three of those interviewed, Billie Jean King, Marjorie Nelson and Viv Richards, all liked to mix and needed to talk. In the middle are those who simply lived life as usual. This group, just over 25 per cent of those interviewed, did not separate themselves from encounters with others although in some cases they were aware of becoming a bit edgy. Steve Ovett mentioned this last point, but in general he felt that his balanced and more relaxed approach to his competitive encounters had helped him to perform consistently over a ten-year period.

How did you spend the day of competition? In a sport such as cricket, competition progresses throughout the day, but with most sports, there are hours of waiting and apprehension. The question was asked to see what the athletes did to occupy this time.

David Bryant spoke for many saying nothing was overdone; it was a time to settle oneself. Gene Upshaw said that he took it easy. 'I didn't have to beat the locker to get psyched up. I started psyching myself up during the week. Pre-game I was loose and calm, playing cards . . . I was ready.' Gretzky, Gilmour, Snell, Moses and Coe all talked about taking a doze during the day. Gareth Edwards said there would be a team talk at 11 a.m. Following that he would talk with his parents whom he met in the hotel lobby. There would be tickets to distribute and autographs to sign while all the time he would be preparing himself mentally, not wanting to fail. On the way to the field he would move down the corridor alone thinking how he would feel on the way back. He said it was a case of wanting success.

Bobby Charlton referred to his routine as business as usual, and J.P.R. Williams said that he would try not to do anything different from the previous week. Both he and Bobby mentioned getting enough sleep. For a weekend match, Bobby never went out for a drink after Wednesday of that week, and J.P.R. said, 'No alcohol for the week before competition. I don't say it made any difference but mentally it was important to me, it got me in the right frame of mind.'

Many of the athletes referred to their day being made up of small segments of activity. Billy Beaumont indicated a number of activities such as watching television, having a short walk, talking and checking the kit for the match. John Konrads mentioned that music was his main pastime. Rob de Castella and Jackie Stewart liked to read, while Rodney Pattisson said that he would go for a run in the morning to clear his system from the night before; then there was a great deal of equipment checking to be done. Billie Jean King said that she was very conscious of enjoying the process of getting ready for the day's play.

Each in their own way occupied their minds and bodies in what might be termed planned trivia, being active with time-consuming activities until it was time to move into the serious business of competition.

In physical terms, there is a general belief in reducing the volume and intensity of training in the lead-up to competition. Most athletes work towards a peak in preparation for any major event. Athletes who drive themselves right up to the day of competition are only draining the emotional resources available to them. Soviet research has shown that following a long period of training, a week to ten days of light sessions will allow the athletes to produce their best performance in explosive events.

Do you see yourself being able to adapt to sudden change during or just prior to competition? For example, what would the outcome be of a changed start time, a delay because of the weather, altered conditions, equipment failure or other similar interruptions?

Ken Read said that he was bothered to a limited degree and saw that as one of his faults. Both Wayne Gretzky and Steele Bishop said that they were upset by changes because they both liked routine. Lynn Davies said that it was never comfortable to have things changed on you.

Bobby Charlton made the distinction between playing conditions and other aspects. He said that he was never thrown by frost or other pitch conditions, but that because he had been in a very stable club where changes were not expected, it threw him if the managers changed or coaching techniques changed. He would adapt to it but not overnight. The other 92 per cent all agreed that they felt they were very adaptable to change. Gene Upshaw said, 'You have to be.' Geoff Hunt reflected that he was adaptable because he changed his style for different players. Steve Davis also said he was adaptable to sudden change but he did not like it.

Throughout history, man has always had to adapt in order to survive. It is not unreasonable therefore to assume that sports people would be adaptable and be able to cope with pre-competition changes. However, it is quite common to see the physical manifestation of an athlete's panicked thoughts: the actions become hurried and jerky, and the deliberate calm and control have been lost. It is a matter of mental control under stress. In general the high achieving athletes have been adaptable and have coped well under stress. What actions they took to achieve that state of control will be discussed later in Chapter 17 under 'getting an edge'.

Coping with pre-competition stress

A few of the athletes said that they did not feel under any stress. Pete Rose said, 'I never worry, it's fun.' Daley Thompson was the same, saying, 'I love it. I just look forward to it,' while Al Oerter said, 'That's what all the training's about.' All of the athletes interviewed were the ones who dealt very well with stress, either they did not feel it or they coped well. They held together and performed best in the highest pressure situations.

The techniques of controlling stress have already been discussed in previous chapters dealing with mental rehearsal and imagery. It was also mentioned that these athletes felt that their exceptional physical preparation gave them a great deal of self-confidence. Prior to competition many of the athletes liked to be on their own, collecting themselves and their thoughts, whereas a few liked to talk a lot to calm themselves down. Reference has been made to the benefit of self-control gained through relaxation and autogenic training. A few athletes have resorted to prayer for help. Many of the athletes referred to maintaining a routine on the day of competition. In a lot of cases, athletes referred to the excitement of 'being there' and the performance curve illustrates how important it is to have some arousal to improve levels of performance. Billie Jean King said, 'I like the pressure, the challenge – it's exciting; I chose to be here!' Al Oerter's comments were similar, loving to be on the hot spot in the Olympic discus circle. Jonah Barrington declared, 'I love the competing. I get fired up, no panic.'

Lucinda Green spoke for many who have questioned why they compete as the feeling of nerves is so uncomfortable. 'It's just a question of keeping control of yourself; you come into the start box and you still say to yourself, "Why do I do this?" It's stupid in many ways and you wonder why you're doing it . . . but the nerves are important. Some genuinely don't have them but I don't know how they get anything out of themselves.'

Herb Elliott said that stress was one of the unpleasant pressures of competition and training. 'Nevertheless, I was aware of the strength that you develop out of nervous tension. I used to try to get away into a forest to feel the serenity and the greatness and the distraction, if you like, of things that have been there for hundreds of years, to take my mind off tiny little insignificant events like winning a running race. There was quite a lot of careful handling of yourself mentally, to be able not to ignore the importance of the event but at the same time not to get it out of perspective.' Others spoke of their ways of coping with stress and what they had found worked for them in bringing out their best performances.

Bob Tisdall's evening before an event was pretty laid back. 'I went to bed and read Edgar Wallace and smoked my pipe!' Ian Botham referred to music taking him over before he goes in to bat. 'My metabolism is slowed completely – a pre-death state. I can be totally unaware of my surroundings, someone could drop a cup and I wouldn't know. Someone has to kick me to let me know a wicket's gone and it's time to go. The music matches the mood of the day.' Jackie Stewart mentioned that he would avoid eating heavily. Certainly the anticipation before a major test will often inhibit the desire for food. 'I just have a very light breakfast. I never eat before a race. As soon as I had food in my stomach, I'd feel satisfied and the edge would come off me, I'd get lazy . . . less aggressive and less desirous, less hungry, . . . I wanted to hold that strength. Some skiers told me that they didn't want to shave or shower because they felt that the hot water seeped away some of their vitality. If they did shave and shower it was with cold water; the hot water takes away the edge. Although I might not have a cold shower, I certainly wouldn't lie in a hot bath.'

David Bryant expressed his thoughts on holding together under pressure. 'It's a discipline of doing things right and the way you do that is firstly to have confidence in the mechanics. To that you apply your concentration. You must be able to read the conditions in which you're playing and you must be able to pick things up quickly, which comes through concentration.' For Pete Sterling the requirement for holding together under stress was as follows: 'Confidence in your ability, confidence that you've done the preparation, confidence that you're better than the other side, confidence that if you do the simple things right then you'll win the game, and not panic . . . We just thought if there was time on the clock we could still win the game.'

Lynn Davies said that in his experience, many athletes try to do too much training prior to a major championships. Lynn has acted as team manager for the British Olympic team. 'It was an effort to restrain some of them in the last week before the Olympic competition. I now realize that if one took a week off and did nothing, it would probably be better but it's hard to recognize that at the time.' The point made by Lynn is that many athletes who have been training intensely throughout the year do not have the confidence to do very little, but if they did, they could produce a higher level of performance.

Gene Upshaw made the observation that pressure was self-inflicted. He placed pressure on himself. He said that the easy part was getting to be named to the 'All-Pro Team' and being the best; the hard part was staying there. 'Each year I tried to be better than the last time and by the way I played, I wanted to let my opponents know that they were playing against the best.'

J.P.R. Williams had a similar philosophy to Gene. 'I think you've got to be self-critical, especially when you've stayed at the top for a long time. You have to work on little things. It's easy just to go through the motions and people probably wouldn't notice that you're not trying the odd thing and it's very easy to be lulled into being very safe and not doing anything spectacular. On the other hand, you can get criticized unfairly, you're trying everything and you have extra people marking you and the critics say you're not doing anything. I think once you stop learning something, then you should start worrying!'

Ken Read spoke of the time directly before competition. He would read a good book and follow a routine for the day but when he arrived at the course, there was a pre-race routine. There would be a warm-up and relaxation time with a bit of horse-play to avoid thinking about the race, but at some point he would go into his cocoon, thinking intensely about what was to come. 'During the last few minutes before the race, I concentrated on rehearsing the run – two minutes at race speed – then I relaxed and tried to drain my mind so that it became blank and ready to race.'

Lester Piggott pointed out that the frequency of racing precluded him from getting too nervous. 'When you're doing it every day I don't think it comes into it – if you start worrying too much you can't get the best out.'

Most of these sports achievers had interesting illustrations of their best example of coping with stress and these can be found in the athletes' biographies at the end of the text.

CHAPTER 16

COMPETITIVENESS

Were you competitive on your own as a child? The answers to this question may show us the key to the greatest difference between those who play for fun and those who *must* achieve. 92 per cent of the achievers challenged themselves. It was not a one-against-one race to the nearest tree, although that undoubtedly was also a part of their experiences, but it was an inner-drive, a quest for self-improvement and self-challenge.

I reflected on this topic with my brother John, who eloquently pointed out that he saw one basic and significant difference between us: from the age of six or seven, I had set myself abstract goals which had no finite limit. For example, I would beat the number of consecutive jumps on a pogo stick and be pleased each time I broke my own record. My brother on the other hand wanted to complete a task and move on. He was happy with the bike race around the garden with a clearly defined finishing point. He was never interested in any similar open-ended obsession with beating the previous target, regardless of the time and effort involved. From my point of view, the enjoyment was in managing to achieve the new record breaking performance, the number was almost irrelevant, but the process of struggling to extend the limits was infinitely appealing. In one sense this is the essence of the intrigue and challenge of pursuing any world record. There is always a new frontier as proven by explorers who have driven themselves to unforeseen levels through the ages. Sport has a similar appeal of new discovery, both in personal terms and for the human race. The striving touches many areas such as endurance, speed, strength, balance, coordination, control, creativeness and skill. To some degree there must be a parallel in the make-up of the explorers and those who enjoy reaching for the outer limits of human capabilities. It would appear that this inner competitiveness is innate. It was with these individuals as early as they and their parents could remember.

Illustrations to prove this point were plentiful. Herb Elliott said, 'If I got a three-wheeler bike I'd try to see if I could ride it on two wheels and then when I had a two-wheeler I'd try to ride on one wheel and then there were course records . . . yes, I was fiercely competitive, with myself as well as with others.' Steve Cram's response was, 'I'm awful, I time myself driving to training every day.' Ken Read said, 'Ski jumping helped. One would gain confidence to push out a little further each time, pushing your limit out. That helped so much in downhill – you ski within your limits but you're always trying to stretch them.' Arnold Palmer said that he was out playing with a club from the age of three. 'I recall the days when I started out shooting in the sixties for nine holes when par was thirty-five or thirty-six, and I can recall breaking fifty for the first time and forty for the first time. I was doing that by myself, constantly.' John Havlicek said, 'As early as seven or eight I'd roll up a sock and lie on my back on the ground, throw it and catch fifty times with no movement. If I had to move to catch it, I had to start over again, just to gain control.' Rod Laver described how he built a backboard in his yard and put the boards in vertically. 'They warped over the winter, so I had to hit the right ones to get the ball back. I accepted the challenge, I wouldn't tear it down.' Heather McKay remembered volleying the tennis ball against the wall and beating the number she had done before. She would also mark the garage wall at squash court tin height and do a figure of eight routine, where one strikes the ball to hit off the front wall onto the side wall, back to her and then onto the front and side wall on the other side and back to her again to complete a figure of eight. Her record is ninety-nine consecutive hits and she added, 'I still count!'

Geoff Hunt was challenging himself as a child by seeing whether he could walk around the outside of his house on his hands. Greg Chappell referred to some creative game playing. 'When I was about eight or nine, I listened to the Davis Cup on the radio. Rosewall and Laver were playing for Australia against the Americans. Australia won the rubber on this particular afternoon and I went and grabbed Mum's tennis racket and ball and went and hit against the back wall for hours.' As most kids do, he imagined himself to be one of the winning players and he set up a challenge. 'I picked out a few bricks and set myself the target of five in a row otherwise I lost the point. I'd set myself the target and then try to beat it. I've done the same thing practising with a golf ball for cricket. I was having a game with myself but in essence it was catching practice. At the foundation level of the house there were bricks and a ledge. If I hit the foundations just right it would come back alive at waist to chest height. I'd try to get five in a row without it flying off at different angles; it was great reflex and catching practice.'

Ed Moses and Steve Davis took it out of the physical realm. Ed would challenge himself to see how many books he could read over the summer holidays. Steve challenged himself playing patience or space invaders. Barry John challenged the use of the word 'competitive'. He said that he did those self-testing and challenging things for inner-satisfaction.

If there is some innate quality of competitiveness in these individuals, what is it that makes one spirit different from another? From the same parents, in the same location, with similar treatment and similar genes, children in the same family are very different. They may hold the same values but the personality traits and the spirit of each is unique. Have the spirits of these individuals had past life experience in which they have learned competitiveness or is it due to a chemical difference in the brain? Whatever the answer, there is little doubt that those who are involved in competitive sport accept the implicit challenge within their activity which brought out the competitive side of their nature.

Did you have trouble passing up a challenge? The question was asked to see whether or not the athletes were motivated by challenges from others. The vast majority, 83 per cent, said that they did have trouble passing up a challenge. Mary Twomey recalled how she was always in trouble, not just joining in when the boys said, 'Let's see if we can walk on this branch without holding on', she would say automatically, 'I can', but often she was the initiator. 'Let's see if we can knock on this door and get away before they get us.'

Most of the answers were positive. Steve Cram said that even when challenged to arm wrestling by much bigger and stronger fellows, he would still accept the challenge. 'There's no way I'm going to beat them but I'll always give it a try.' Steve Davis referred to playing things which had some element of skill such as darts. 'Not for money but for the thought of doing it. I dived off the top of a boat in Hong Kong for the sake of a dare. I'd never dived in my life but it was great fun and it wasn't that dangerous.'

Several individuals gave a qualified yes for an answer. Peter Sterling, John Havlicek and Ed Moses said that they would not have trouble passing up a challenge if it was dangerous. John added that he accepted challenges to gain the respect of his peers. 'I remember playing "tackle" football at eight playing against fourteen year olds and I'd get "my clock cleaned" [annihilated]. I didn't want to do it but I did it to gain respect.' O.J. said that he would accept a challenge if he considered it worthwhile but that he would not be drawn into fights.

A few athletes gave the qualification that they'd accept the challenge if they felt that they were in with a chance. Unlike Steve Cram, they did not see much point in accepting a challenge in which odds were less than 50–50 at the start.

Bryan Robson applied a challenge to recover from injury. Following a shoulder separation, he was unable to lift even a few pounds held at arm's length. His team-mates and physio were ribbing him about his weakness. He took this as a challenge and secretly took home the weight so that he could work at the exercise over the weekend. He returned on Monday successful.

Many referred to the fun of challenges and their unwillingness to give up. Seb Coe referred to a session with his club Haringey. 'I was in no shape to run fast, I was strong and fit but it's club policy to break the middle-distance group into teams for a mixed relay. There were about six or seven groups of four and I ran with a fourteen-year-old girl, a twenty-four-year-old girl and an eighteen-year-old guy. The better runners have to go twice and the course is about 400m on a hilly course around a rugby pitch – just a stupid thing, my team was about 200m behind and I just went out and literally had to launch myself to get over the line to win the bloody thing, and I felt absolutely like death warmed up. I was spreadeagled in the mud and the kids were standing around while I was quietly passing away.'

Seb's story made me recall a sand-dune relay with a similar outcome, involving my coach and four athletes, two per side. There was nothing in the race at stake but the fact that a challenge had been set and accepted. It was the 800m men against the 400m hurdlers. The race ended at full speed down a sand hill, legs like rubber from the previous loops. The result was a dive for the line to ensure a win, a bloodied knee and absolute exhaustion. The level of our competitiveness bore no relationship to the lack of importance of the occasion. As Seb said, 'You just have to do it.' It is strange but the enjoyment of the occasion, the effort and the win were as important an achievement, in terms of personal fulfilment, as many top track results. It has a lot to do with giving everything to the effort.

Lucinda Green applied the question of a challenge to her work with horses. 'I find it difficult to admit defeat with a horse. It's only just beginning to sink in that not every horse has star quality, as not every person does. I've been lucky because I've got through doors with some horses and nobody else has and I've found that they have got it, which made me feel that I could get through with every horse. I've wasted a great deal of time with some very mediocre horses. In my particular game I find it extremely difficult to give up with a horse because you are always wondering if you're not giving up with a star.' In a way Lucinda has illustrated an important point. If enough time and effort are concentrated then there is a chance to go through doors which were never thought possible. It was once said to me that each person has their own gold medal level. It is a statement worth remembering. The end results may not produce a world record or an Olympic gold, but if life's challenges are accepted and a commitment is made to try, then a gold medal can be gained in personal terms.

Within the 17 per cent who said that they had no trouble passing up a challenge, Gene Upshaw said, 'I decide when to accept a challenge', whereas several of the others said that the challenge was only with themselves.

To win or not to lose

Was a desire not to lose the positive stimulant or was the aim to win stronger? It is after all, the opposite sides of the same coin. It is not asking if the athlete was afraid to lose or that they even thought about it. The question assumed that they won reasonably consistently and asked whether they avoided the thought of losing by making sure they did not lose. In a sense this competitiveness was based on fear; it was an unacceptable thought to lose, so it had to be avoided. Fear can be just as great a stimulant to performance as anger or ambition. 37 per cent admitted that part of their success was due to the motivation not to lose. More than half, 53 per cent, said that they simply aimed to win and the other 10 per cent were just out to do their best.

Barry John mentioned that a desire not to lose could produce a defensive attitude in some team sports and thereby take away from the game. For example, packing the defence in soccer may produce a draw but it does not make for a very interesting or entertaining game.

Perhaps the best way of describing the avoidance of loss as it is intended here, is that the athletes see that they have their backs to the wall and will fight very hard and long to avoid losing. It is still the will to win but it is taken from the perspective that they are never willing to accept defeat. Gene Upshaw said, 'We seemed to always be behind in the last minute or so and we always won. We felt that as long as there's time on the clock we could win. You have to think you can never lose. All you need is the will to win.'

All the tennis players interviewed said that they hated to lose. Both Rod Laver and Billie Jean King spoke of the initial intent which was to win but that they both played better when they got behind. Rod said, 'Even if it was 5–1 to my opponent, there's still a chance. If you believe that, sometimes the other player tightens up a bit and that saved me a few times, not giving up. Also when I got behind I'd give them a rough ride. I wouldn't pull up and play safe if I was losing. I'd make the loser or the winner. I'd put it on my racket. I'd also concentrate better and things look a bit easier from behind . . . not that it was intentional!'

Billy Beaumont pointed out another avoidance issue when he said that he wanted to avoid any team loss being attributable to a mistake by him.

Gareth Edwards said, 'In the end the more success I had the harder I'd work at it not to fail, and that was a motivation. I enjoyed success . . . not to pick up the headlines, but just knowing that you've done it and no one can take that away from you.' Steele Bishop was another who tried to avoid losing. He said that if he did lose he would be very angry with himself, but that no one would have known it. He also made sure that he would never make the same mistake twice. Herb Elliott's practices taught him to win at all costs and to die rather than lose. He said, 'In training I had a sense of accomplishment afterwards that I had managed to beat my own weaknesses and my own desire to slow down.' Rob de Castella was sorry that the feeling of fear had become associated with avoiding losing. The negative aspect was that this pressure was not coming from inside him but from the Press and the public. 'It was fun in the old days, being unknown and an underdog, because if you won then there was an extra thrill. Going in as favourite and always being expected to win can produce a fear of being beaten which initiates some sort of primeval motivating force. I don't think that that's good, succumbing to pressure. Competing should be for ones own satisfaction and enjoyment, regardless of the public pressure, but that's easier said than done.'

Lynn Davies saw it in a different light. He referred to the fact that sport at the top level is a self-imposed stress which is alien to people's natural inclination. A lot depends on the perspective of each individual. 'One person may perceive the Olympic final as being a life or death situation for them, whilst another person might simply be happy to be there. Certainly at that level of equal physical talent, the one who wants to win most will win. It's the ability to place enormous stress on oneself to do it. I think the great athletes take losing much more to heart than most people. Losing is worse than dying because you have to wake up the next day! Yet the other side of me is the physical education lecturer, believing in the value of sport for bringing out the best in people, character development, personality growth and everything else but that was not the part of me that enabled me to win athletic competitions. I don't condone teaching the philosophy of winning being all-important, but you must recognize that unless an individual possesses that hate of losing and that feeling of discomfort with oneself, then one loses.' Lynn's statement refers to the athletes having their self-image so much tied to their athletic performance that they need to win in order for that self-image to survive. The fact that the Press and public are so quick to put in the boot makes the athlete quite vulnerable.

For more than half the athletes interviewed, the desire was to win rather than avoid losing. Ed Moses, who has the longest winning streak in sporting history, said that he was doing just what was needed to win and doing that kept it simple for him. Arnold Palmer saw the challenge in personal terms – to prove that he could win. Clive Lloyd pointed out that in cricket, there are no trophies for second place!

John Newcombe was aware of criticism of those who failed to win and pointed out that the person to satisfy is oneself. 'The belief in myself instilled in me a pride that carried across to the tennis court, that every time I played I was going to give 100 per cent and because of that I had no fear of losing. If doubt or fear that they might lose enters someone's mind, if the other person does not have any fear of losing, they are not afraid to lose, then that person will win . . . I'd give at least 100 per cent so there was no fear of losing because if I lost, that meant the other guy was just better than me on the day. The most important thing was when I sat in the locker room after the match. I was happy in my own mind that I'd given it my best shot.'

At times sport has been strongly equated to battle. It certainly has been represented in that light on many occasions. It is hardly surprising, therefore, that the term 'the killer instinct' has been applied to finishing off an opponent. Both David Bryant and Bob Cousy used the phrase, Bob even using it as the title for his autobiography. This could be looked at as killing in self-defence. In terms of personal development through sport, trying to kill or crush the opponent is a negative intention but this is how it was seen. David was milder than Bob, referring to the stage in a bowls match where he senses that the other team are starting to crack under the pressure. He feels a bit of the killer instinct when he sees a chink in the opponents' armour: 'I'll say, "Listen boys they're keyed up, I think they're cracking; if we can lift our game now, I think we've got them."'

Bob Cousy recognized the instinct within himself but also saw the problems of carrying it too far. Referring to his book, he quoted the following passage: 'The killer instinct has brought me success as a player and as a coach, but it also tempted me to run over people, to break the rules, to neglect my family, to neglect myself to the point where I was on the edge of physical and emotional breakdown . . . I'm no longer so proud of the killer instinct. It can do more than blow away an opponent. It can kill the moral sense, the happiness of a family, even the man himself. It is not an instinct I can get rid of. It is something I must live with as best I can.'

Mike Wenden saw that there was a need to change the social viewpoint on sport. He felt that in Australia (and it is certainly not limited to that country) the view is, 'You either win or we don't want to know you.' He recalled the hammering Steve Holland was given by the Australian Press, having gone to the 1976 Olympics as the 1500m freestyle world record holder. 'He bettered his own world record time by a couple of seconds but a couple of other characters swam even faster than him and he wound up with a bronze medal. How can it be said that he let everyone down?'

No one should ask more of an individual than to give 100 per cent effort to the attempt. If that results in a personal best under the most intense competition, then the performer has achieved their personal gold medal level, even if that does not result in a win or a medal. This book is about those who were fortunate enough to win consistently. In one respect they are fortunate because they have not had to face too many insults from the Press and public as they were winning. The written word has immense impact and an individual's confidence can be rocked by a few ill-chosen phrases. All those who pass judgement – or even offer 'constructive' criticism – should bear in mind that to reach the top, an athlete must put in years of dedicated work and effort, often without reward.

All athletes interviewed can be classed as winners by any standard; they won consistently and well under the most serious competitive conditions. However, how should a winner be defined?

Tom McNab, ex-National British track and field athletics coach and author of *Flanagan's Run*,[32] said, 'If we define a winner as someone who tries their hardest to do their best, then we can have a lot more winners.' If one only sees winners as those who finish first and everyone else as a loser, then one is labelling 97 per cent of those who make it to an Olympic Games as losers. They are already the few out of hundreds of thousands who have aspired to achieve that level.

An analogy with music may help us to see the absurdity of calling someone who achieves second place a loser. If one had to make a decision as to whether Isaac Stern or Yehudi Menuhin was the world's best violinist, how could you classify the one placed second as a loser?

No plaudits need be omitted for the actual winners. They deserve their full recognition. However, there is no moral justification in denegrating or dismissing all the supporting cast. All! the finishers in the New York and London marathons receive medals. Recognition of accomplishment is what is needed. If one is capable of finishing first, then go for it, but athletes and coaches should appreciate personal improvement and ultimate effort. Kip Keino, Kenya's great middle-distance runner and winner of the 1968 Olympic 1500m and the 1972 Olympic steeplechase titles, said that he never felt bad about not winning nor would he ever look down on someone who finished fourth or fifth. He knew how hard each person in the competition had worked to reach the level of being in the race.

It has been mentioned earlier, but it is worth repeating. There are two ways of looking at competition. One way is to see competition as a kill or be killed situation. You tread on your opponent to reach the next rung on the ladder of success. This is a hostile and cut-throat version of sport. At times it is the way things are but it is not a perspective which should be fostered. Someone once wisely cautioned that you had better be nice to your rivals on the way up because you will be seeing them again on your way back down!

The other way is to view competition as a challenge which brings the best out of each competitor and as a result enhances the overall performance level to a degree which could not have been reached without competition. Individuals or teams are competing for the same prize, with the recognition that only one can finish on top but that there would be no event without other contestants and the better the challenge, the more enjoyable for contestants and fans alike.

On a few very special occasions, Press, public and contestants alike have recognized a contest where there was no loser. The competition itself was more important than the outcome. It happened in a baseball World Series (1975) in which Pete Rose was playing for the Cincinnati Reds against the Boston Red Sox. The seesaw battle gave an emotional lift and earned praise for spectacular plays by both teams. The same was true for a brilliant game in 1971 between the New Zealand All Blacks and the Barbarians. It happened again in a mile race in 1981 in which Steve Cram and Steve Ovett were locked in a sprint finish battle for the final 300m. Our perspective on winning has been severely clouded by the over-abundance of attention, praise and rewards usually showered only on the winners.

There is nothing wrong with the desire to win. Neither is there harm in acknowledging the achievements of those who show the way and are taking the fresh steps at the frontier of sport. It is the 'all or nothing', 'winner takes all' approach which is so unhealthy. This does not mean that one should settle for second best. Striving for excellence is the ideal. If one has the talent to try for the top, then that should be the aim. The request is for a more balanced perspective in recognizing the efforts of all involved; the gesture which symbolized this happened at the 1982 Commonwealth Games. Following two days of competition, Daley Thompson persuaded all the protagonists to attend the victory ceremony. The first three place winners received their awards, but all the contestants shared in the applause and recognition of the moment.

All the achievers interviewed recognized that they were very competitive when it came to sport. There was also a part of themselves tied to the outcome of the contest. Finland's Lasse Viren, 5000m and 10,000m winner in the 1972 Munich Olympics and the 1976 Montreal Olympics, told Ian Stewart, Britain's 5000m Commonwealth and European champion, that at Olympic level he believed it was the person who could least face losing who would win. The competitive situation sets off the alarm system and adrenalin flows. The two natural responses are fight and flight. Perhaps the individuals who see themselves as aiming to win really are seeing themselves as fighting, and those who are 'running scared' are literally taking flight, avoiding the 'chasing bunch' catching them. In both cases the competitors are harnessing the additional power and controlling their efforts successfully.

Reaction to mistakes or losses

How did you respond to mistakes, losses or other setbacks? There are generally three steps involved in a physical mistake. The first point is that the individual must not dwell on it during the game. J.P.R. Williams explained, 'You have to put it behind you as quickly as possible.' The second point is that it must be a learning experience. Wayne Gretzky said, 'If you learn from mistakes, you become a better person. If you don't learn from what you've done wrong, then you're defeating the purpose.' Olympic long jumper Mary Twomey highlighted another facet. 'You have to have the losses to appreciate the wins. The important thing is to be able to handle them, deal with them and carry on, and not give up.' The third point is coming to terms with the fact that the losses are disappointing. Tennis star Chris Evert Lloyd: 'You have to care about losing. It has to mean something to you. It used to take me three days to get over it, now it's only a day.' Bob Cousy referred to it as feeling as though there had been a death in the family – winning was so important. Some found it easier than others to bounce back. Barry John said, 'I had one golden rule from a young age; if we lost in a big game, I allowed myself one minute to sulk, then that's it. You become a sportsman again and you go and congratulate the opponents and knock it back into perspective. And if you want to examine your performance, you do it later.'

Learning from losses was done by analysing what happened and attempting to see what could be done to improve next time that opponent or team was faced. Sometimes it was simply a case of the opponents playing better on the day, but in most cases the responsibility for not winning was taken by the individual. Gretzky has built-in perspective. 'After losses I always feel disappointed, dejected and feel even worse if I haven't contributed the way I know that I can, but you see we have a mentally retarded youngster who works in the training and locker rooms – he's my girlfriend's brother – and I come into the room and see him and realize how lucky we are. He really perks me up.'

A very different aspect of loss had to be faced by Jackie Stewart. 'Losing a race I was fairly philosophical, there was always another Grand Prix in two weeks and a World Championships every year. I think the most difficult thing to deal with in our business was that of losing friends because most of them went. I lived through a very bad period of motor sport. Most of my best friends were killed – Jim Clark, Jochen Rindt,

François Cevert, Piers Courage, Bruce McLaren. They all died . . . I became shy of creating deep friendships because suddenly they were all taken away.' Against much pressure, Jackie successfully crusaded for better safety measures for all cars, racing and domestic.

Financial incentives

Would you have performed any better if there was increased financial incentive? The background to this question came from two sources. The first was that a great deal of media hype goes into big prize money today and it was wondered if the athletes did in fact try harder if there was more at stake. The second prompt was from watching Jackie Stewart competing head-to-head with heavyweight boxer Joe Bugner during the first British Superstars. The prize money meant nothing to Jackie but the effort being expended could only come down to personal pride and competitiveness. The answers brought out some interesting insights. Only two people gave a straight yes, that increased financial incentive would enhance their performance. Steele Bishop said that he did try harder. 'Definitely, every time I changed sponsors or added a new one, I'd feel I'd got to do something for them. I'm getting the money, so I've got to try harder all round. I'm honest and I'm a professional.'

The other person who thought that it would have made a difference to how hard he trained was Bob Tisdall. However, he did say that he would not have wanted to get involved with money because for him, the amateur way left it as fun rather than as business. 'I would have trained harder but the enjoyment would have become less. As soon as money comes into sport, the fun goes out and the greedier you are, the less you enjoy it. You enjoy getting the cheque but the sport disappears in proportion to the money that's up there.'

Opinion from 88 per cent of the rest of the professionals and amateurs would not support Bob's belief. As professionals they may negotiate for more money but at least for this group, the effort in competition was motivated from within, not by external reward. The view from the amateur ranks was no different. In many cases they would like to see a more open attitude to money being available within their sports but they could not have put in any more effort. Amateur squash champion Geoff Hunt said, 'I couldn't have tried any harder.'

Among the professionals, Chris Evert Lloyd, Billie Jean King and Clive Lloyd all referred to personal pride in their performance being far more important than money. Pete Rose said that he agreed that it was personal pride, but he added that for some individuals, money was an incentive. He said that he did not believe in a four-year contract because those who were not inner-motivated only tried hard in the final year of their contract. Daley Thompson related the same view. 'The reason I'm out there is to do good for myself and to win – that's the most important thing for me, so whether I am getting £100,000 or £1, it would make no difference to me. I have a great deal of pride in my performance . . . I enjoy performing well – that's why I do all the training, so the incentive or motivation of money or people watching makes no difference to me at all.'

Margaret Court said, 'I've heard Chris Evert Lloyd say, and I believe any champion would say, you're not there for the money. I think that if you get your eyes on the money and you haven't got it on goals, you're not going to achieve what you want to achieve. I know that once I'd got the Grand Slam in 1970, I had a baby and then had the goal of getting back to number one in the world. After that I was running out of goals. I could have gone on playing for the money but my heart wasn't there any more so I knew it was time to stop.'

O.J. Simpson pointed out that, in one sense, the size of the purse usually indicates the importance of the match. 'The match is what stimulates the athlete. It's a direct challenge and everyone's watching – public recognition and public attention, not the $100,000, winner-takes-all!' Bob Cousy said that money might make a difference in terms of preparation but he added, 'Viewers attach financial rewards as an incentive but in reality, you never think of it once the whistle blows.'

Des Drummond pointed out that using money as a tool to get more from players can backfire. 'I've seen players trying to perform better because money has been offered as an incentive . . . they end up having a bad game. They should have been prepared to play the game before.'

John Havlicek referred to something which this generation of viewers would have forgotten, if they ever knew it in the first place. He said that when he was playing in the 1950s and 1960s, the Celtics basketball team all had to find off-season jobs. He said that his team manager Red Auerbach used to point out that if they won the Championships, they would get $2500 to $2700 which would subsidize them through the summer! How times and finances change!

Rugby amateur J.P.R. Williams also played professional tennis. He said, 'I couldn't have played any harder. I played tennis for both appearance money and the prize money and it made no difference to me.' Billy Beaumont said that money would not be an incentive to play harder but added an interesting postscript: 'When I put 100 per cent in, I got more enjoyment out . . . but money would probably have made me a dirtier player!'

Money would certainly have made the task of preparation much easier for most amateurs, a view confirmed by Peter Snell. Pat O'Callaghan said that it would have allowed him more time for training. Herb Elliott said that it might have kept him in sport for longer. David Bryant said, 'When you've been doing a job of work all day, often you don't feel like practising, but it wasn't a chore, it was relaxation.' David Forbes made the point that money provides opportunity. 'I've been lucky to have my business and if I wanted to do something I've been able to find the cash to do it. Lots of people have ability but without financial support they wouldn't be able to achieve it.' Mike Wenden mused, 'I liked the feeling of giving at an absolute level. I wouldn't have performed any better with increased financial incentive, but afterwards I'd have felt a lot better!' Marjorie Nelson said that she and her husband started married life with nothing. They had spent all their money going to represent Australia in the Helsinki Olympics!

Marjorie's comment raises the issue of amateurism. Even with increased sponsorship, almost all of today's amateur sportsmen and women are out of pocket attempting to reach a level where they represent their country. The ideal of amateurism is laudable in many ways but the Western sportsperson or their family has the price to pay and that means that some are denied access. Marjorie spoke of the injustice that there are some sports millionaires without a gold medal and of how Jim Thorpe was stripped of his gold medal in the pentathlon !in the 1912 Stockholm Olympics] for once playing a semi-professional game of baseball. Carl Lewis took a similar stand. 'It's unbelievable how amateur athletes are looked down on for accepting money . . . Stevie Wonder signs a $40m recording contract and the world rejoices; I make a token of that and they say, "You dog!"'

There were 8 per cent who were not sure whether prize money would have improved their performance. Rod Laver made the significant observation that if money was riding on every shot in his early days, he might not have allowed himself or been allowed to continue experimenting. 'My game was allowed to grow. I'd be hitting a winner and then the next shot would be into the cheap seats. It finally gelled but maybe I'd never have taken those risks if thousands of dollars were riding on it. Maybe I wouldn't have gone for the shots and played conservatively, but ultimately I would not have developed the shots which were my trademark – hitting top-spin or slice from any angle.' Rod was one of a group of four, who for five years barn-stormed the United States in a mini-van, driving 500 miles, doing pre-promotion, getting the papers to write about it, playing and moving on, and thereby helping to get professional tennis off the ground. Like several others in this group, this story illustrates that if individuals have the courage to take the initiative, they can help to change the course of events.

CHAPTER 17

GETTING AN EDGE

Did you always have the self-confidence that you could produce your best effort when you asked that of yourself? On several occasions the achievers referred to having the 'confidence' in themselves and their abilities to take risks and perform up to expectations. Self-confidence means having a positive view of yourself and what you can do.

Even at this level, there were 13 per cent who lacked confidence in either themselves or their ability. Both Joan Benoit Samuelson and Lynn Davies were testing themselves right up to competition time, just to prove to themselves that they still did have the capability to perform well. Ron Pickering pointed out that Lynn went to do some weight-lifting on the morning of the Olympic long jump final, just to reassure himself that he still had his strength. Lynn said, 'I was never very confident. The whole process was seeking a feeling of mastery and the good sensation that confirmed that the good performance of a month ago was still going to be there in half an hour's time. The constant seeking of reaffirmation of one's abilities.' Joan was also constantly testing, even on the day before competition, taking a hard run just to reassure herself that she was ready and it was still there.

Herb Elliott saw self-doubt as an asset. 'I think one of my strengths has been my doubts of myself: if you're very aware of the weaknesses and are full of your own self-doubts, in a sense, that's quite a motivation.' Steve Ovett said, 'There's always a worry that I'd never live up to the expectations of my friends or whatever. If I had a failing, it's that – that the confidence level in my own ability is very low really.' Seb Coe's opinion was similar. 'I never go into a race believing that I'm invincible.' The exceptions he noted were the 1500m final in the Los Angeles Olympics and his first 800m in Oslo where he said that he felt something special was going to happen. In the latter, he broke the world record running 1 min 42 sec.

Marjorie Nelson said that she was extremely nervous before the big competitive events. Similarly, Shirley de la Hunty said that she never approached a race with confidence; however, like Herb Elliott, she believed that the feelings of apprehension always helped to bring out the better performance. At a different time, Shirley talked about trying to get a mental picture of invincibility which really helped her state of readiness. Lucinda Green said that she still lacked a bit of confidence.

In spite of these confessions, each of these individuals did manage to hold together and repeatedly produce the results under the stress of top competition. In spite of their self-doubts, they maintained the necessary self-control to perform their chosen sport superbly.

Although it could not really be attributed to a lack of confidence, both Bobby Charlton and Bob Cousy said that they could never be sure whether or not their actions were going to be able to flow. They were not worried about their technical skills letting them down, just that there were days when they felt right and everything was fine and other days when it just wouldn't work. This would happen despite being prepared. Research on human bio-rhythms has shown a distinct probability that there are physical, emotional and intellectual cycles in each of us which can account for the up days and down days.[30,60] On the 'critical zero' days, we are three to four times more prone to mistakes or accidents.

Jackie Stewart took his lack of confidence out of the realm of competing and said that he was never going to be secure about having sufficient money. He was interested to hear Paul McCartney say the same thing in a radio interview.

The vast majority of these athletes, 87 per cent, had a very high degree of self-confidence. In many cases this was attributed to their knowing that they were as well-prepared as they could be. With a few, it developed over time. John Gilmour said, 'I'm much more self-confident now. Once you've done the work, you know the body will back you up.' Chris Evert Lloyd said that winning when young brought self-confidence, supporting the view that those who win reasonably consistently from an early age, see themselves as winners, and believe in most cases that they can and will win. It did not make much difference what the early competitive level was as long as they instilled in themselves the vision of being a winner. This behoves both the teachers and parents to attempt to create more situations in which early success can be achieved by more children. Perhaps it is a case of staging handicap races and balancing sides in games so that at different times various youngsters see themselves as capable of winning. Likewise, in training sessions, allowing different individuals the opportunity to lead. Presumably the same theory would work in reverse; if a child never experiences success then he or she will believe that success is beyond their grasp.

Some individuals have always had confidence. Daley Thompson said, 'I've always been confident of doing well. I know whether or not I'm going to win. I have doubts but come a week or ten days before the event, they're all gone. I've never gone into a competition with any doubts. I've always had confidence of putting 100 per cent in and at the end of the day, I think regardless of where you come, you can't do any more than try your best. I believe if it happened to me and I had to lose, provided I performed well, I could take it . . . That's not a proven fact, by the way! I might as well be talking hot air.'

Bob Tisdall's reaction to the question of confidence was instant. 'Oh yes! I loved to go in against blokes who had done better than me and say, "Nothing's impossible, I might beat him". If you go in saying, "He's going to beat me", you're beaten before you start.'

Shane Innes said that she always had self-confidence in her ability and thought it might have come from her father 'brain-washing' her that she was capable of anything. 'He had a confidence in my ability in every aspect,' she said.

Geoff Hunt also said that he always had a confidence in what he could do. 'I went on the court and felt that I could win the matches. Even when younger, I remember playing the top player in the state and I was only about number fifty, but I thought I had a good chance against him and I led him 7–1 in the first set. I'm sure I did that because I played to win. He went on to win it 3–0, but even though I knew winning was unlikely, I still gave myself a chance.'

O.J. Simpson said that he had confidence that he would produce his best effort at the crucial time in the game and against the better opposition. The added pressure brought the best out of him.

Barry John pointed out that it was a willingness to accept responsibility for the outcome of one's actions, which brings up a point that Billy Smith made. 'Most of us in a tight basketball game with one shot left would hope that the ball didn't come our way, so that we would not be the ones to blow it! Yet Larry Bird is begging for the ball; baseball star Ted Williams was dying to be at the plate in the pressure situation.' Two things occurred to me. Firstly, these are the people who perform better under increased responsibility or pressure, and secondly, they want to have control of their own destiny. If they take the ball they are in control. They do not want to leave their destiny in someone else's hands. John Havlicek said that he did not mind taking the final shot, he treated it with the same degree of discipline and dispassion. Every shot was important and therefore all he could do was to try his best on each one. He said, 'I miss the play-offs. I loved the play-offs. I love being under the gun and being in the spotlight where there is a lot on the line.' A very similar description came from Al Oerter; he felt as though the discus circle in the Olympics was the same as being under a magnifying glass with the sun making the spot white hot. 'I love it there.'

Billy Smith pointed out that Larry Bird was the one staying after everyone else had left, taking 100 to 150 foul shots then running laps around the balcony track, all the time . . . even during the play-offs at the end of the season. Bobby Charlton said that he always liked to take extra individual skill practice on his own after the team training sessions. Improved competence increased confidence. Mary Twomey said that there was a mental discussion going on with one side of her saying, 'I could win' and the other side saying, 'Don't get too cocky'. 'The balance reached was thinking I've got a good chance here and I'm going to give it my best.'

Despite the differences in the aspects of confidence which each chose to mention, the belief was always the same. Torvill and Dean said that a personal best was always their aim. Steve Davis had a similar view saying that he always had confidence that he would do his best and not panic under pressure. David Bryant said that he had complete confidence in the mechanics of his game. Steve Cram was confident that he could dig down and find what was needed – 'I can drag it out'. Ian Botham said that there were two things which gave him an edge. 'The belief in myself and the fact that I don't believe any situation is lost until it's actually gone. I believe you've always got a chance.'

Pat O'Callaghan said, 'I felt that whatever the opposition did, I'd do better. It was a state of mind from training.' Like the others, Pat had confidence in his ability and in his body's performance.

Despite Joan Benoit Samuelson testing herself up to the last minute, it is worth recounting a discussion which took place between Joan and one of the Boston University students, Julie White, who had represented Canada at the Olympics, and myself. Joan had a marathon coming up and said that she was worried about having to make a pit stop during the course of the race. She had been having trouble with her stomach on some recent training runs. I reflected on my only concern, as someone who wore contact lenses, that just as the gun sounded for the start of the race a gust of wind would blow some dust into my eyes and the pain would force me out. Julie made an astute observation that we both feared things which were beyond our control. The reverse was true for her as she would often be worried about things over which she did have control. Could the focus of anxiety be one of the factors which makes a difference between the elite and the good athletes? Or is it simply that the highest achievers are more in tune with their bodies and have greater mental control?

Did you do anything special to get an edge on others? Many people wonder whether there is any one thing which made these athletes into winners. Some reporters from a few years ago were so out of touch with what went into any great performance that they would ask questions like, 'What on earth did you have for breakfast on the morning of the competition?' As if there might have been some magic potion which created success. Melbourne Olympics' 800m medalist Derek Johnson became so fed up with such enquiries that he told one reporter that the secret was that he stood on his head in a yoga position and consumed spoonfuls of honey while so positioned. The reporter took careful note and Derek left with the satisfaction that if anyone was foolish enough to believe it, they deserved to have their noses filled with the runny nectar!

As one will have already gathered, there are so many factors which contribute to the overall pursuit of excellence that there is no one miracle element. However, it is my experience to look back and say, for example, that sand-dune running was a significant training edge. It is so difficult to run fast up a long sand hill that it taught my mind as well as my body to hang on despite the discomfort. I also felt that, for me, the hardest way was the best way because I would be mentally uplifted by having gone out and done a session while it was snowing. I would come back in and think to myself, 'I don't think my opponents would have gone out today; that puts me one step ahead or gives me a little bit of an edge.' Most of the athletes believed that their training was doing something special and would make a difference to their performance. Naturally, most related that they placed an emphasis on physical fitness and for some, it was long before it became fashionable in their sport.

Arnold Palmer mentioned that he had learned discipline through having to cut the greens and fairways with his father. He also did physical exercises such as chin-ups with him to build himself up. Lester Piggott ran to gain extra fitness but said that his greatest edge was his good temperament for racing. 'It made a difference on the big occasions because nothing bothered me.' Clive Lloyd stressed fitness for his team but added that the other two things were playing other sports to relax and avoid staleness, and each season he tried to look for something new to do in order to make himself a better player. Pete Rose said that he was one of the first to stay in shape all year round; part of that involved playing a lot of basketball. Chris Evert Lloyd pointed out that she had done weight training before it was common practice, but for her an important edge was that she really enjoyed what she was doing. Heather McKay also said that her fitness level gave her the edge, but added that she thought it helped coming to the British tournament with a tan! Gene Upshaw would begin training the month after the season ended. He went on, 'I'd train on Sundays because I knew the other guys would have a day off. If there was a celebrity golf game to play, I'd train in the morning before the tournament. I'd find out what the other guy was doing and figure out what extra I had to do to get an edge.' The level of dedication is written through every response from Gene and every other athlete.

O.J. Simpson showed an intense application of mental toughness. Of his conditioning he said, 'I ran more in practice and I ran harder than anyone else. Where others would run a practice play five to ten yards, I'd do forty.' An added challenge for O.J. was that he played in Buffalo which averages more snow than Anchorage, Alaska. 'In a game I'd never wear sweatshirts or long-johns, I'd just have my regular T-shirt on because I didn't want to think of it being cold. On the side lines, I'd never go near the heater because I felt once you start going by that heater, when you're away from it back on the field, you'll be thinking about getting back to it. Psychologically you've taken the edge off if you've got a long drive on and you're worried about getting warm and getting back to the heater. When I set the record over 2000 yds in one season, it was 0°F. Two weeks in a row I gained over 200 yds, the first was in a blizzard and the second was so bitterly cold there was ice all over the field.'

Seb Coe referred to his ten years of background work up on the Sheffield moors. 'When it was very, very bleak I would be the only one who would be likely to go out in that weather. Athletes tend to hang on to anything that they feel might give them that little bit of edge and the extra motivation – that feeling of satisfaction that you were out there when it would have been easier not to have been.'

Valeriy Borzov said that he was used to training on holidays and days off and that his training was more intense than the other athletes. He also had special training to stimulate the muscles. This is being introduced more now in the West, but with particular emphasis on rehabilitation from injury. If it is the same piece of equipment, the electrodes are simply placed at either end of the muscle which is to be contracted and the electrical impulse causes the muscle to contract. It can be very beneficial in building muscle condition and size to either wasted or healthy tissue. Both Jonah Barrington and Daley Thompson reiterated Valeriy's point and cited the hours which each of them put in as giving them their edge over others. Jonah referred to his six hours of training each day. Daley would play at sport for part of his day and be intense at other times but training took up all of his day. Billie Jean King referred to the intensity of her two-hours-a-day training involving two-against-one practice. She said that her training was longer, harder and more efficient than the others. 'I didn't think about it so much then, I just knew that if I paid the price, I'd be a better athlete.'

Rod Laver cited an example of how well he pre-planned for tennis, although he confessed that the same did not hold true for the rest of his life. He said that in a tournament at the Spectrum in Philadelphia, matches were beginning at 8.30 a.m. He and Arthur Ashe were challenging for the number one position. Rod had breakfast at 6 a.m. and was on court by 7 a.m., so that he had an hour and a half's practice on the same surface before the tournament. He saw that as gaining a usable edge, especially as he knew Arthur wasn't doing likewise.

Ken Read also had some practical application of preparation which he felt gave him an edge. Apart from his dedication to physical training, he spoke of the times when he was in transit overnight; they might have arrived at noon and while the others shopped, he ran. Also during the Christmas break he would spend some time with his family in Canada doing light training but then would move on to a routine which included readjusting to European time and getting himself ready, knowing that all the others were having a more generous break and would come back a bit off. John Konrads referred to getting a motivational lift through being so fully prepared physically that he gained a psychological high.

The aspect of doing more than the others is a common theme. Steele Bishop would arrange to meet the fellows he was going to ride with down where they were, an hour's bike ride away from his home. He knew and they would know, that he had done two hours more than them by the end of the day. Steele was also confirming an enhanced self-image. He was not the only one to refer to such feelings.

Barry John said that his touch of playful arrogance was based on a strong sense of self-confidence, but he added that you have to be prepared to back it up. 'Although I wasn't the greatest trainer, I still went out on my own when I felt I needed sharpening up, even in the snow and ice on the field by the river. I'd clear a little path through the light snow, of about 100 yards and I'd do twenty to twenty-five minutes to prepare my mind for the weekend game.'

In the cases of Joan Benoit Samuelson and Peter Snell, training was sacrosanct. Peter said, 'It was a sin to miss a day's training. A target would be set, like you've got to try to hit 100 miles a week.' Joan also said, 'I would never sacrifice training.'

J.P.R. Williams, who lived very near to Merthyr Meyer sand dunes, felt that the work there gave him more stamina than most other rugby players. Another edge was that he never missed a high ball and he said, 'I never had to practise catching the high ball because it was ingrained in me by my father. When I was young he used to pump the ball up in the air and I used to catch the ball wherever it went. The tackling was timing and I did practise that. I'd get two people to run at me in the space of ten yards and almost be able to make them pass the ball when I wanted. Normally if you get a two-on-one situation, the two would always get the ball past the one but if you get your angle and approach right, if he doesn't dummy you, you're going to get him and there are occasions when I have quite often taken two men out of the game either by psyching them out and making them pass too early or making them hang onto the ball by approaching as if I'm going for the other person. I think it's something that most people don't practise. I got the other full backs doing it on the Lions tour and they found it a tremendous benefit.'

Viv Richards felt that he got an edge when he played shots which would take the heart out of a bowler, like hitting the ball for six no matter what the delivery. He said that his aim was to keep cool and calm because the longer you stay that way, the more runs you are going to score.

Lucinda Green felt that an edge was gained because she had some land to train on even when it snowed and others were prevented from training. She said that it was a very good morale boost in her favour. Torvill and Dean mentioned that they felt as though they got an edge on their opponents by practising on Christmas Day when they knew that everyone else would have had a day off. Having mentioned this to Daley Thompson, he told me that last Christmas he managed two training sessions, thus gaining a double advantage over his arch rival Jürgen Hingsen!

The special edge for Shane Innes was training with men. She felt as though that gave her a challenge which was not usual for other women at that time. For Wayne Gretzky it was that he was on skates from the age of two! Jackie Stewart said that his special lift came from him gaining the awareness that he was not competing against others but with himself. Ed Moses talked about how he fasted for up to a week and continued to train hard. He felt that his training was more efficient and that this proved one of his theories that people overeat, even when training.

Mike Wenden summarized it on behalf of all the athletes. He said, 'If you can realistically say to yourself that no one else has worked as hard and believe it, then it's bound to create an internal confidence, and that will help in the next trough to get you back in the routine again.'

It must be noted that simply doing more work is certainly not the whole answer. Many athletes have done too much and have injured themselves. Each person must carefully extend their mental and physical capacity.

How did you cope with thoughts of your opponent? Half of them said that they never gave their opponents much thought. Their focus was on themselves and what they were going to be doing. Others wanted to find out all they could about their opponents, so that they would be more fully prepared. This latter group would be using this knowledge both in terms of assessing how they would compete against their opponents as well as in coming to terms with some of the anxieties which might be caused. However, the thoughts given to the opponent would only be used as a tool for better personal preparation. Respect, apprehension, even some anxiety were possible by-products, but their thoughts were not dwelling on any possible negative outcome.

Of those who wanted to deal mentally with their forthcoming opponents, several referred to the situation as one-on-one, even if they had to face several at once. Ed Moses said that sometimes mentally, he would run races one-on-one but that he never worried about anyone but himself. He said, 'Purely for preparation, I might see what would happen if I found myself behind, but when I got on the track, I'd block that out by not allowing myself to be in that position and that's how I'd run. I just energize myself to eliminate that automatically. Whatever it takes to win that's what I do. I get the best out of myself by not expecting an easy race, giving the opponent a lot of respect. Take them seriously but don't dwell on them. It's easier when there's pressure. You don't have time to think, you get emotional and go out and perform.'

Jonah Barrington's coach would talk him through each player, discussing the reasons why Jonah was better than the other player, in all respects of the game. Additionally when it was clear that the opponent was better in certain areas, his coach, during the build-up, would take Jonah into the sort of game that would not play to that opponent's strengths.

Greg Chappell concentrated on the positive aspects of his own performance rather than on worrying about what the opposition might do. Barry John used humour to defuse pressure concerning opponents. He said, 'When the Press said things like, "What about this giant you're playing tomorrow? What about sleeping tonight?" I'd say, "Sleep! Of course I'll sleep. All I know is that he's going to have to mark me and he's got to sleep tonight!" But once you've created that situation, you'd better back it up!'

Shirley de la Hunty said that she was too shy to talk with her opponents. 'They were mythical people in my mind. I didn't want to know them. With Fanny Blankers-Koen, for example, I didn't want to diminish my need to beat her by getting to like her! I didn't dislike her but I didn't particularly want to go and meet her and certainly the opportunity wasn't there.' Bobby Charlton said, 'Opponents never bothered me unless they were particularly close to me. I hated playing against my brother or close personal friends like Jimmy Armfield and George Cohen. Other than that I completely cut myself off. It didn't matter because I knew that they were trying to beat us just the same.'

Bob Tisdall saw competition in a much less cut-throat light. 'Opponents were not regarded as enemies, you regarded them as competitors after the same goal. The object is winning the race, not beating the competitors in it. I was chatting with Lord Burleigh in the tunnel of terror, talking as if we were going out to shoot the same bird. He was defending his Olympic 440 yds hurdle title and I was after it, but that didn't come into the conversation at all. We were just trying to achieve the same thing, side by side.'

Valeriy Borzov was interested in the opponents as people, but said that at the time of the competition, the only thought was on his own performance. This last aspect is true for all the athletes, even those who had studied the opposition in as close detail as possible. Once it was settled in their minds that they could control what they did against their opponents, they were no longer involved in thoughts about them until the contest was over. The only time that would change was where their play demanded a constant reassessment, for example in cricket where a variety of bowling attacks might have to be employed on one good batsman.

David Bryant said something which was alluded to by many but not said in so many words. 'You mustn't be dictated to by your opponents.' While many of the others were coming to terms with how they would control their own efforts and how to focus on their performance, he was stamping his own authority on the game. Not that it always resulted in a win, but at least he was attempting to determine his own fate rather than allowing others to dictate it for him. David said that he was not worried by opponents, his main focus was on how he was playing and if he felt that he was playing at his best, then he was going to win. This statement exudes the sort of self-confidence which made these individuals consistent winners.

My own experience of coping with thoughts of opponents altered according to the level of competition. I liked to see the stadium before running there as it took away some of the unknown. Similarly, I liked to at least know what my competitors looked like and how they ran, so that I had clear images for my mental rehearsal of the coming races. At the time of the Olympics because there were so many top competitors, I decided to race mentally each contender for the gold in a one-on-one situation. If my mind started to run away with the race allowing the other fellow to take control, I would start again until I was sure that, given an equal chance, I could successfully finish ahead of him. Certainly the main focus during competition must be on one's own performance. Coping effectively with thoughts of the opposition is a helpful prior preparation. It can settle the mind, enabling an attitude of confidence and full concentration on what one has to do on the day of the contest.

CHAPTER 18

CONTROLLING YOUR DESTINY

Do you feel that you control your own destiny? The reason for this question was that many individuals simply let things happen. Most of these achievers made things happen. The question was whether they considered that they had control of their lives. Some of them voiced the obvious qualification, they realized there were certain other parameters, but in general they thought that they were in control of their direction. Overall, 89 per cent said that they did feel in control of their own destiny. Half of these simply said, 'Yes'. Some were more forthright, Jackie Stewart and Bob Cousy saying, 'absolutely'; Pete Rose, 'I sure do'; and David Forbes, 'very much so'.

O.J. Simpson said, 'I believe most people can control their own destiny. I believe you get what you deserve in this world.' Wayne Gretzky said that he believed that you make your own fate but also added that luck plays a part as to where you end up. Shirley de la Hunty elaborated on this: 'I think one has a large control over one's own destiny and I guess it can be put in other ways – setting a goal and working towards a goal, not just letting things happen.'

The theme that you can either take control of your destiny or just let things happen was taken up by Peter Snell. He was referring to achievement and said, 'I felt that there were lots of people around that could have done it but they didn't know they could and so I felt I was lucky that I was able to get involved and discover that I could do it. My coach Arthur Lydiard obviously played a part, but there were a lot of other factors as well.'

Valeriy Borzov said that he was in control of his own destiny. Running fulfilled his personal desire and he also saw it as something which helped his country.

Half of those who said yes gave qualifications. Most said things such as 'to an extent', or 'generally' or 'up to a point'. Billy Beaumont and Des Drummond pointed out that their fate lay to an extent in the hands of the selectors, but Des added, 'You control your own destiny to the extent of playing so well you can't be dropped.' Bill also said, 'On the field you control your own destiny.' Mike Wenden said that he could not control a few little things, like the state of the economy, but outside of that he was in control of his own destiny. Lester Piggott made it sound very simple. 'You have to really because it's us doing it.'

On the more cautious side of the fence, Gareth Edwards, Duncan Goodhew, Ralph Doubell and Rodney Pattisson thought that they could not control their fate but that they could influence it. Duncan referred to his belief in deterministic fatalism. He described it as follows. 'It's basically like a tree, you start at the bottom, you climb up and you choose the various options. I also believe that if you have talent, it's sacrilege not to make the most of it.'

The six other athletes who said no to this question answered as follows: John Havlicek believed that he could not control his own destiny to do well. Bryan Robson said, 'No, you could be injured tomorrow.' Both Jayne Torvill and Christopher Dean said that they believed in predetermination. Al Oerter and Bob Tisdall referred to themselves as fatalists. Al said that several people had tried to imply a Messiah-like destiny on his career which he rejected. Bob said that his fatalistic belief was a direct result of having come through warfare.

Ian Botham said that as a player he felt that he controlled his destiny but not the rest of his life. He related an interesting coincidence, one of several premonitions which have subsequently come true. He dreamt that his hundredth Test wicket victim would be the Indian captain, Sunil Gavaskar. Ian was amazed to read in the Press, after it happened, that Sunil said he had also dreamt that he would be Ian's hundredth victim!

Superstition

Just over half, 53 per cent, said they were definitely not superstitious. Another 27 per cent said that they were a little bit, putting it down mostly to routine. One could see that a fixed and successful routine might become a superstition, and that it might be bad luck to change it. However, that aspect could have two other causes. Firstly why change a routine which has been successful as preparation for important competitions, and secondly, the fact that a routine is known and familiarity makes for a comfortable environment within which to base the calming thought of a forthcoming contest.

Within the group who felt that they had small quirks, a number cited associates who were very superstitious. John Havlicek said that he would never go onto the basketball floor with his shoe laces wrinkled; they had to be absolutely flat. He added that his team manager Red Auerbach was extremely superstitious. Indeed, Red had asked him to do two successful 'layups' as the last thing before the game started. If the other team went and took a shot at the same basket before the start, then Red asked John to go out and do it again. He also recalled that before the seventh and final game of one championships, Red called the team back to the locker room after the warm-up. They thought that they were going to get a rousing speech but all Red did was to ask their brilliant centre Bill Russell whether he had thrown up, something Bill did before every pressure game. When Bill replied that he had not, Red sent him in to complete the ritual while the team were forced to sit around and listen!

Billie Jean King said that she had her own peculiar routine to which she adhered. She also pointed out that Betty Stove would never step on a line on the court, something which the other players used to tease her about. Barry John said that he always put his right shoe on first. Heather McKay said she was not really superstitious but did admit to carrying around a four-leaf clover with her for the last twenty years, having replaced it many times. David Forbes wondered whether he was superstitious about not being superstitious!

Joan Benoit Samuelson, while not feeling that she was superstitious, did have two recurring dreams which happened before major marathon races; usually she found that was a good sign. 'If I don't have one of those recurring dreams before a big race then I kind of wonder if I'm going to perform well. One dream is a race that's held in a small European village or in a department store. I'm running up and down escalators and stairs, hallways and corridors, and I get lost and the race is going on and I can't find the rest of the course. The same thing happens in the village, I can't find the path. The other dream is where I'm running very fluidly and all of a sudden I can't run and I start to walk and from a walk I go to a crawl, from a crawl I go to trying to move myself on my belly and then at the last minute, I'm hanging off a cliff, trying to hold on for dear life . . . those dreams usually signal a good race.' The anxiety level is obviously high in both dreams. As a stable and easy-going person, Joan has experience of controlling her emotions before a big race. Dream analysts would no doubt have much to say about how personally important the coming race was to Joan. It certainly indicates that the arousal level was working subconsciously to prepare Joan for a good performance if she could maintain her personal control. She obviously did!

The remaining 20 per cent said that they were superstitious, some mentioning certain aspects. Rodney Pattisson said that he and most sailors would not have green on their boat. Marjorie Nelson referred to turning an old ring on her finger three times before she raced. Bryan Robson spoke of his shirt having to be number seven. Arnold Palmer said that he always had a new pair of shoes for a big competition. Gene Upshaw said, 'We would re-do what we did when we pulled it out and won.' J.P.R. Williams did not like the warm-up practice to go too well.

'It'll be all right on the night, you don't need all your best plays before the game starts.'

Lucinda Green spoke first of her superstitions and then of her view of being lucky, making that work for her by working hard on everything. 'I'm very superstitious. The same old shirt, same old socks, same old T-shirt, for the last seven yars and the number seven, although I don't really have an unlucky one because I'm a lucky person. I believe strongly that you get as much as you give and if you've just been a bit slack along the line, you won't get what you want. You put into it and often you don't get what you want out of it and you keep putting into it and you win in the end, and that is the thing I've learnt most, that when it seems that all the effort is to no avail, you are just being tested for that bit longer than you thought was possible.'

Luck

Do you consider yourself lucky to have been in the right place at the right time? Of the group, 87.5 per cent said they felt they had been very lucky to find their right sport and the people to help them. Some thought that they were in the right era while others said that it had been a fortunate coincidence of timing.

Margaret Court recognized a few of those elements in her life. 'My mum always said that I was born under a lucky star. I think I was fortunate that I had doors open at the right time because I think there probably are kids with talent for whom the doors don't open, and there aren't the right people to help. If I'd never had the opening with Frank Sedgman and different coaches in Melbourne, I wonder where I would have gone.'

Most of the athletes realized that they had been very fortunate but they also knew that they had contributed to their own good fortune. The proverb that God helps those who help themselves was in evidence. Billy Beaumont said, 'You make things happen for yourself.' Wayne Gretzky said, 'You make your own fate.' Rodney Pattisson and John Gilmour similarly said, 'You make your own luck.'

Duncan Goodhew had a view that each individual has talent and the lucky ones are those who find it. 'I think probability would show that almost everyone is good at something or has the possibility. I think you are lucky to discover it and are extremely lucky and may be shrewd to recognize it at the time and then the rest is the follow-through.' John Konrads's view was similar to Duncan's. 'The lucky people will seek out what they do best and pursue that.'

Herb Elliott knew that it was particularly lucky for him when he met his coach Percy Cerutty, but he also knew that there were many different routes to the top and that maybe it could have been done another way.

One who did not think that she was necessarily in the right place at the right time was Billie Jean King, saying that she wished that she was starting today. She equated herself with Arnold Palmer as pioneers in their sports and in spite of their years of playing, they have earned nowhere near the money of the stars of today. She also thought that she would have thrived on the tour set up of today. John Havlicek also mentioned financial reward saying that he felt lucky that he knew he was destined to do well. He thought he would earn up to $25,000 per year and play for ten years. 'I earned more than that and played for sixteen years.'

Ralph Doubell said, 'I'm not a great believer in luck. You've got to do it.' This statement correlates closely with Gary Player's now famous remark: 'It's funny, you know, the more I practise, the luckier I become!' O.J. Simpson used almost those words when he said, 'The harder you work the luckier you get.'

A couple of aspects stand out from these replies. There is a general recognition that ultimate success relies on proper timing and opportunity. Also it is necessary to consider how you can influence your own future fortunes by taking positive action. The recognition that timing and opportunity are vital for achievement makes one aware just how important it is to provide positive opportunities for aspiring youngsters.

PART 4

MORAL FACTORS

CHAPTER 19

GAMESMANSHIP

How a person ought to act on the sports field and what they indulge in, on and off the field, has become an increasingly important issue. Add this to serious drug problems both in social use and to enhance performance, verbal abuse of umpires and referees by players, racism, financial exploitation of athletes and athletes' exploitation of their sport – and it is easy to see that sport contains the same social and ethical issues which face society at large. Parents, teachers, administrators, coaches and participants are well advised to consider the issues which affect their sport. Coming to terms with the written and unwritten rules of sport may or may not alter one's moral or ethical development. However, sport is an arena where behaviour and codes of fair play are visible, and one can take a view about what is acceptable behaviour. It is my opinion that lessons can be learned and that the behaviour which is deemed acceptable will have a transferable value.

From a behaviour research viewpoint, sport has been described as a walking laboratory without dials. Much can be learnt from the level of behaviour which we find acceptable in sport. This is because it holds an unusual separateness from the outside world. The rules of sport do not change across social, economic, political or religious differences between people. With the option to participate open to almost all, there is the possibility for a study of behaviour and ethics. Violence erupts only where there is intensity of emotion. Drug-taking to enhance performance only takes place through an intense desire to be competitive. Sport provides the necessary testing ground to create the environment, and the test is whether the participants can learn to control their emotions and their competitiveness – to channel them into enhanced performance rather than the debasement of the individual.

Did you ever employ gamesmanship, and if so where would you draw the line? A moral decision has to be made as to where a competitor draws the line in trying to win or gain an advantage. Many individuals have become disenchanted by the ready acceptance of the 'professional foul'. For example, holding a faster player's shirt when marking them, or intentionally bringing down a player who has made a breakaway and could be about to score.

In a book written by Peter McIntosh entitled *Fair Play*,[31] he tackled many of the issues which face individuals in connection with the ethics and morality of sport. A study cited in McIntosh's text was carried out in 1970 by Professor Heinila of the University of Jyvaskyla in Finland. He surveyed soccer players from Sweden, Finland and England. The statistics on the English teams separated amateur and professional clubs. A very rough summary of the findings showed that some forms of cheating and dishonesty were accepted practice for more than half the players! Approximately 70 per cent of the English professionals accepted behaviour such as a player handling a ball when the referee had not seen it or gaining a penalty kick for his team by acting as if he had been badly fouled. Their amateur counterparts' answers averaged approximately 58 per cent acceptance of such behaviour. The average response for the Swedes was 52 per cent acceptance of such behaviour and 46 per cent acceptance from the Finns.

My study of the highest achieving athletes did not use multiple questions on this topic and therefore was not as specific. Nevertheless, it still elicited a variety of illustrations and reasons why the athletes would or would not employ such tactics. However, the response from this group of achievers was that 60 per cent did not employ gamesmanship and it would be fair to say that the majority of those who said that they did, drew the line at cheating, intentional fouling or trying to con the referee, umpire or official. I have tried to find a reason why the very best should have higher standards than the average good player. Two thoughts occur. Firstly, these athletes have consistently been honest with themselves in putting in the work, and that perhaps this resulted in carrying over the honesty factor when dealing with others. Secondly, they had combined a fair degree of aptitude with a great deal of consistent and solid preparation; perhaps the confidence in their ability allowed them to feel that they did not have to cheat in order to get an edge. It is also worth noting that in this study there was practically no difference between the responses of amateurs and professionals. The percentage from the amateurs was 40 per cent, and 38 per cent of the professionals said that they employed what they considered to be gamesmanship. (Professional athletes constituted 40 per cent of the total number of athletes interviewed.)

Conning or cheating

Gamesmanship can be considered healthy within the rules of the game but it has come to mean more than that. In this first area, conning the opponent, the initial illustrations could not be termed cheating but there were grey areas. Gene Upshaw said, 'You have to employ a tremendous amount in American football. If he hits you and hurts you, you don't want to let him know. You get up as if you weren't hurt, you get back in the huddle and you just die but you come back out ready to go again. I would draw the line at doing something illegal or dirty.' Billy Beaumont said that he was prepared to do everything within the laws, then added, 'I might bend them slightly but I'd draw the line at cheating. If I can hurt a player with a fair tackle that's okay but if he had his back to me, I'd never kick him in the back of the head or hit him because that doesn't appeal to me – it's a question of the ethics of the game really.'

Des Drummond said that his form of gamesmanship had been to appear to be tired, puffing heavily or acting disinterested and catching the opposition off guard, so that when the ball came to him, he was gone. He did not like the dirty play after a tackle where mud was rubbed in his face or a rabbit punch given, just to try to get him angry enough to concentrate on getting back the other fellow. 'If you're concentrating on getting the other player back, the centre is running past you on the inside. I don't like the kicking and stamping on hands and legs, trying to put a player out of the game. I've had fights because you can only take so much but I wouldn't initiate the violence. I was suspended for five weeks for defending myself in 1983. A fellow was trying to scratch my face and had his fingers in my mouth, so my instinctive reaction was to bite his finger. A punch up followed and I was suspended for five matches and he got three! . . . The crowds come to watch a good game – but they also like a good fight.'

Barry John said that he saw gamesmanship in terms of faking the other player, such as pretending to pass and not doing so, which was part of the game, but he did not consider this extended to faking or conning the referee. He gave an example which was also mentioned by Gareth Edwards and J.P.R. Williams, so the feelings of injustice obviously ran deep. An incident happened during the 1978 rugby match with the New Zealand All Blacks. The game was close and with two minutes remaining, Wales led 10–9. Then during a line out, as the ball was being put into play, Andy Hayden and Frank Oliver, two of the New Zealand players, ejected themselves from the line, each acting as if he had been shoved or hit when in fact, film replay showed that no body contact had been made. However, a penalty kick was awarded and because of it, New Zealand won the game 12–10. Gareth Edwards felt grieved to discover that the incident had been a premeditated plan to cheat. 'It might be splitting hairs because it might still be cheating, but I would say that if someone takes it on themselves to do a "Hollywood" in the heat of the moment, I can understand that, but I was really disappointed to read in Graham

Mourie's book *Captain*,[42] that he said it had been decided that if things were going bad for them, this was a tactic they would employ. It was preconceived and as much as I liked the man and admired him as a player, he'd gone down in my estimation for saying that. Now I might be naive but I never remember being on a team where anything like that was discussed. We would always talk about what we'd be trying to do on ability alone.'

Gareth was one of those who said that he did occasionally employ his own forms of gamesmanship. He said it was never premeditated but that at international level rather than sit back, he met fire with fire including conning the referee. He said in the cold light of day it may be called cheating, but he would collude in a con of the opposition in an attempt to cause his opponent to commit a penalty offence. He would tell his scrum hooker to wait for the ball and he would make a gesture, slapping the ball as if it was being put into play and cause the opponent to lift his foot early and thereby receive a penalty. Gareth added, 'You don't necessarily have to do it to succeed but you have to be very much aware of it.'

In track and field athletics where contact is rare, Steve Ovett said that he saw a race like a game of chess. 'Gamesmanship, if it's in the mind, is beautiful in the sense that you can use your mind and body in conjunction. You are using them in the same way as you can imagine chess – your body is the piece and your mind the player; if you can use that when you're under par or in a difficult situation, then all the better. I think I draw the line when it comes to physically damaging someone else in a sport.'

Intimidation

Those in favour of intimidation tactics aim to upset the confidence and concentration of the opponent. The form can be verbal, visual, physical, or psychological intimidation. Greg Chappell referred to visual intimidation, employing a stare, verbal undermining and also the threat of injury in the use of the bouncer. 'I suppose that gamesmanship is often a subconscious thing. Australia has been accused of using a lot of gamesmanship and I'm sure, at times, we've been guilty of utilizing it to try to gain an advantage, but I don't think we've gone anywhere near what we've been accused of doing, and I don't feel that I've been responsible for much of it. With someone like Viv Richards, you wouldn't bother with gamesmanship because that might just inspire him to want to smack you all over the place. It's probably with the up and coming young player, not an outstanding player, I might try a little bit of intimidation in some form. It might be a case of just walking past him and talking to someone about him, making sure that he could hear it, letting it be known that you think perhaps the bloke's not good enough to withstand the attack that Dennis Lillee or Jeff Thomson is firing in at him . . . I'm a frustrated bowler because I know that I'm not good enough to get good players out consistently. I'd probably glare at a batsman, try to upset his concentration a little bit. Let him think I'm angry with him or that you don't think he can bat on the off chance that it might have him thinking about that rather than what he should be thinking about . . . in small ways like that. I don't think it does any harm. It's all part of the competitive edge of the thing but I don't think it should ever get to the stage where you're continually haranguing a bloke verbally. It's difficult in cricket to get any physical intimidation except as a fast bowler by continuing to bowl short – that can be overdone as well. There have been times when I've felt it's been overdone and as captain I've stepped in and told the bloke exactly what I thought.'

Ian Botham also accepted that he used both verbal and eye contact to attempt to intimidate and also just an aggressive, threatening demeanour directed towards the opposition. 'I'll give as good as I take and at times I'll instigate it verbally. I'm a great believer in when in Rome do as the Romans. For instance, if I play against the West Indies, there's no gamesmanship because that's the way they play, whereas against Australia, gamesmanship is important. You can also do it by appearing aggressive or showing your aggression, just letting it flow through – the odd stare doesn't hurt, things of that order. The Australians are past masters at it and I can say that I'm one of the few Englishmen that have hardly ever been slagged off on the cricket field by an Australian because they have a love–hate relationship with me. They know that it will fire me up; it's not going to detract from my performance, it's only going to improve it and that can also rub off on the rest of the team. Where I would draw the line is that I would never blatantly cheat. Oh, I'll go after an lbw appeal that I think is close enough for a shout and I'll have a jolly good shout . . . When I say I would never cheat, that's not true because when the Australians play this game they have this great belief that if you nick the ball, you stand and let the umpire make the decision and I think if that's good enough for them, that's good enough for me; but if you do that, you've got to be prepared to take the bad decisions with the good . . . I think there's no point in cheating and then complaining when you get a bad decision against you, so I think you've got to take the rough with the smooth.'

Mike Wenden saw gamesmanship in terms of putting the others off by exuding confidence. He also used to talk to his opponents in an attempt to upset their concentration. Mike referred to an incident at the 1970 Commonwealth Games trials. He was not in his best shape for the 200m and had to swim flat out to scrape into the final. He was therefore relegated to an outside lane of the pool. Just prior to the final, someone threw a dye bomb into the pool. Mike worked on his opponents' minds and managed to talk them into lodging a protest. Meanwhile the dye was spreading and Mike continued quite earnestly: 'You know it's really not fair, my lane's completely clear!' He said that once the race got under way, they all watched him swim slowly for three laps, then he outkicked them to win.

John Konrads was not averse to directing attention onto the weak spot of an opponent. If he knew that someone had a sore shoulder, he might say, 'How's your shoulder?' However, he pointed out, 'The object was to get an edge but I think it's also a personal deconcentrator and in that respect it's negative. I'd never go beyond what I'd call fair play and sportsmanship.'

Duncan Goodhew said that for him the gamesmanship line was drawn when the whistle was blown. 'If someone tried to intimidate me after the whistle blew, I became nasty. I mean, in America, when you're under starter's orders and they'd try to break your concentration by coming to shake hands and wish you good luck, I'd swear at them. It was something I would never have said in any other situation – they were cheating and I told them where to get off.' About his own form of intimidation Duncan said, 'There was a chap called Graham Smith who was the most aggressive person I ever met. Nobody went close to him before a race, he used to break chairs and beat things. When I tried to mimic that, I found that it didn't work for me but I did find that it had an effect on other people. So what I started doing was ignoring people, making a conscious effort to ignore people and act as if I was getting aggressive and it became a kind of routine, ritual almost, and I found it was really affecting people because they'd start looking at me and not at themselves. I think that's one of the reasons I won the Olympics because I intimidated the Russians even before I got there. I'd swum so fast throughout the year they saw that I didn't have a weak spot. They tightened the thumbscrews by saying that I was the only guy who was going to win the 100m breaststroke, hoping that the pressure would get to me but it all seemed to work for me – they were totally intimidated by being ignored.'

Jonah Barrington used to eye his opponent. 'When I went to serve after a particularly long rally, I would give him what is known as the stare, which in itself would probably reduce some people to a moan but did put quite a few people at a disadvantage. They were aware that I was dominating them and in a clinical fashion assessing how well they were at that point. I would definitely draw the line at cheating. If I knew that the ball bounced twice I would never, ever, play on because I considered that was cheating. I also feel that in a game where the interpretation of the rules is so difficult, there is a terrific responsibility on each player to play fairly. For example, it's in the rules that a player must make every effort to keep the game flowing and these days a growing number of players make no effort and in a premeditated fashion bring the game to a grinding halt.' Jonah cited the tactics used on him. He had based his game on ultra fitness and usually wore his opponents down. He said that his opponents intentionally broke the rule which says that play must be continuous. In order to get inside his head, they would obstruct him continually and give themselves a breather.

Geoff Hunt said, 'It was very rare that I'd ever talk on court. Just occasionally, if my opponent hit the tin and he was winning at the time, I'd say "Right, that'll cost you the game" and then I'd change the tactics and try really hard for a few rallies. The fact that I won a couple of those rallies was because I'd changed my tactics and applied myself.'

John Newcombe used the element of surprise to intimidate the opponent on an important second serve. 'If you do it all the time, it loses its psychological force. I had a very strong forehand. Say we've been playing for two hours and on a big point the guy misses his first serve, goes back to serve the second, looks up and sees me standing in the alley [tramlines]. He knows I'm going to hit a forehand and that he can't reach my backhand. I'd call that gamesmanship. It's subtle because you've actually chosen the moment to use that tactic. I never consciously went on to the court wondering how I'd psyche the guy out there.'

J.P.R. Williams said that he would drop the odd comment when changing ends in tennis, such as, 'You're going to serve a few doubles soon'. He added, 'I always looked on that as fair psychological warfare. In rugby there's a lot of talk that goes on on the field, but I think that's an acceptable part of the game really. I think I draw the line with physical intimidation. There's a very fine line in rugby. I think it's fair comment to hit somebody as hard as possible and try to hurt them when they are coming towards you; but if they haven't got the ball, then it's not fair play. So it's playing as flat out as you can, both physically and mentally, but within the rules.'

Peter Snell recalled his coach inviting Tom O'Hara, one of his main Olympic 1500m opponents, to run in an 800m time trial. Peter ran 1 min 47.8 sec and believed it psychologically shattered Tom. 'He didn't even make the final. He ran about 1 min 52 sec which is okay for a time trial.'

Torvill and Dean's form of intimidation was that each time they practised at the competition site, they skated right through their programme, as if they were in competition giving an exhibition. They were not going to stop and start, publically repeating any fragmented image or giving any impression that it was anything short of complete but skate as close to perfection as was humanly possible. Chris said, 'In the week prior to competition, all the judges are there and other competitors can go in and watch. Our gamesmanship would involve going onto the ice very well dressed, as if it was the actual competition rather than just a practice session. Psychologically, the other competitors would see that and think, "Gosh, they're well prepared".'

Bob Cousy said initially that he never used gamesmanship in his basketball days but now enjoys using it in a jocular way with golf. 'If a guy's been putting well all day and on a crucial putt at the sixteenth he's got another short one, I might say, "Damn it. You haven't missed one of those all day!" or "That one's a sure-fire winner!" And invariably he'll miss it. Thinking back, I do remember saying something similar when the shooter was at the foul line. Not to him. I was too polite in those days, but I'd say it across the lane to a team-mate: "Hey, you know this guy hasn't missed tonight!" What it does is break the concentration of the opponent. You are trying to get him to think about something else.'

Only two achievers, Wayne Gretzky and Bryan Robson, said they would employ the 'professional foul'. Wayne Gretzky said, 'Usually I'm the one being held; it's part of the game, it goes with the territory I guess, but when I was younger I didn't like it at all. Now I believe you do anything to win. If you have to grab a guy from behind to stop him from scoring, you've got to do it, but I'd never try to injure somebody.' Bryan Robson held the same view. He has openly and obviously gone against the rules in dire situations, but he said that he would not intentionally injure anybody or cheat behind the referee's back. 'In open play I don't think I'd use gamesmanship, but if someone went through with just the goal-keeper to beat and I could catch him by bringing him down, I'd bring him down. If I didn't, I'd feel I'd let my team-mates and my fans down . . . I've never been a player where the ref's back's turned that I'd kick somebody or elbow somebody because they're to get an advantage on me. I'd never do that.'

There are, in my view, four levels of gamesmanship. The first level includes those who could not, under any definition, be considered breaking any rules of the game. For example, Gene Upshaw who was conning his opponents through not showing them that they had hurt him. The second level includes all those who were willing, to a certain extent, to indulge in conning the referee and they condoned that action by others if it was done in the heat of the moment. Gareth Edwards used the illustration of the All Blacks' game to denote where he drew the line. There is an understandable difference between a player's action in the heat of the moment and the pre-meditated cheating referred to before. However, in the eyes of the law, the only difference would be in the degree of wrongdoing. The rules exist to make the game as fair and equal as possible. Any rele infringement lessens the status of the individual and the game. The third level is in the open field, as referred to by Wayne

Gretsky and Bryan Robson, and involves the professional foul. Both of these men are a credit to their sport and play more cleanly than the average professional in their respective sports. However, both said that if they could, they would bring down a player who had made a breakaway and only had the goal-keeper to beat. My personal belief is that Steele Bishop was right when he said, 'If you can't win fairly, you don't deserve to win'. Once the rules have been broken, even by only a small margin, the game has been changed. The line has to be drawn somewhere. If the rules are wrong, have them changed for everyone, but while they exist they make the game all that it is. If it became known that a politician cheated on his taxes, then the average man in the street would feel more justified in doing the same. It is my belief that the athletes who are right at the top of their sport have to set the best example possible because it is absolutely certain that the youngsters of tomorrow will be following and copying every move made today. The fourth level, I am pleased to say, did not include any of this study's achievers. I refer to those athletes who foul with the *intent* of ending another player's career. It serves no purpose to give gruesome illustrations of the injuries which have ended great athletes' careers. The people who indulge in that type of intentional, premeditated action should not be allowed to return to the competitive sports field. Their actions are criminal and have no place in sport.

Can gamesmanship, therefore, be avoided? Nearly 60 per cent of all these high achieving athletes were against any form of gamesmanship. David Forbes recalled attempting gamesmanship once and that was enough to change his mind. 'There were sixty or seventy boats and I intentionally got on someone's air. It's within the rules. I've only done it once and I regretted it. I was very unhappy about it at the time and I've never done it since. No, I don't think gamesmanship comes into it as far as I'm concerned. I think that some people see that the rules are there to be used to win and they sail the rules and not the boat. They occasionally do well and they've got a lot of ability. They're mentally capable but they've got this little twist, they believe that it's part of the sailing scene – they just view it differently. They're quite entitled to their attitude but most times those people don't win consistently. They win occasionally. They have a lot of disasters because they make a lot of errors while they're thinking of how they can cheat somebody else.'

David Bryant pointed out that intent was an important issue. For example, was the intent in doing something to bring yourself on or to put your opponent off? 'You have to be honest with yourself in order to make it to the top. I want what's mine. I don't want what's not mine and my good name is worth more to me than any result. In my opinion it comes down to having confidence in your own ability and not having to stoop to gamesmanship.' A similar sentiment was expressed by Billie Jean King when she replied to this question. 'No, you've got to get your own act together to be the greatest.' Rod Laver would never employ gamesmanship and was direct in his approach. 'I wanted to beat them at their best and I let my racket do the talking.'

Carl Lewis was only too aware of the gamesmanship which was employed on him. In most books it would simply be called bad sportsmanship or cheating, because time and again he would find that the other high school competitors had moved the marker from where he would start his long jump approach. His own approach was not to get involved with that, but he added a very mature philosophical approach to competitive sport. 'Winning is not the aim, only a part of the whole. You have talent, you work within that talent and that's it. We're not out here to win, we're out here just to do our best and winning is a part of it, so let them do their best.'

Pete Rose was concerned about players damaging their sport through the use of gamesmanship. 'I learned a long time ago. I don't believe in ever knocking your sport or knocking another player in my sport because if you knock a player in your sport, you hurt your sport.'

Margaret Court spoke of her reaction to other people's gamesmanship on court. 'I believed that with my athletic ability, I didn't have to do that. I could play well enough that I didn't have to talk people out of it or carry on. I'd go quiet. I wasn't one to yell on court or say things. I'd just let them go over and I'd know that they'd calm down. I wouldn't say anything if someone else was saying something.'

O.J. Simpson was aware of the potential added consequences of gamesmanship. 'Being a professional athlete, everybody's so oblivious to it all . . . and being the running back, you're pretty much the target . . . you normally wouldn't attempt it because you wouldn't want to give them any more stimuli than they already had!' John Havlicek had a very similar objective to O.J.: do not give your opponents any additional ammunition. John said, 'I never used anything. I respected every opponent and I knew that you had to face them more than once and I never wanted them to be given a reminder of a situation which would get them up a little more or a particular challenge. I think I more or less patted them on the back and told them what a great job they did rather than try to infuriate them.' John must have known that a heightened performance is possible when someone becomes aggressively stimulated. Lynn Davies agreed with the other point which O.J. Simpson had made. Apart from not believing in the use of gamesmanship, Lynn said, 'I just don't believe that at the highest level, the kind of guys you're competing against are susceptible to gamesmanship. I think the main gamesmanship is trying to convince yourself that you can do it.'

Peter Sterling said that he had changed his views. 'In my early days, I used to try to put my opponents off their game, saying things like, "I didn't know you were still on" or "Look at the score" – something silly, but as I came into contact with better coaches, it was explained to me by a person I knew and respected that it was also putting me off my game because my mind wasn't where it should have been.'

Bobby Charlton said that he would not personally employ gamesmanship but could understand it in some cases. 'I never accepted anyone pulling my shirt. If you run past a defender and beat them fairly for pace and they just stand in front of you and catch you, that I can't forgive, but if I'd beaten a lad for pace and he tried to chase me and realized he couldn't do it and he'd maybe pulled me down, I could half forgive that because he could have stopped me unfairly in the first place and it was a last resort. Everyone's in the game to make a living and I don't think it's unforgivable. Nobody is perfect. Personally, I wouldn't do it but it's not in my make up. My philosophy is live and let live, but I was not a defender or a hard tackler and I think the game needs them just the same.'

Clive Lloyd spoke of his opposition to intimidation. He was against the use of gamesmanship and said that he thought that players had over-used it. His concern was the name calling by opponents to get their team psyched up. 'Comments like, "Come on, let's get this black bastard" are just plain abuse. I'm not saying that I can't take it but it's been over-used. I don't think being abusive to other players is right.'

CHAPTER 20

DRUGS

The subject of drug-taking to improve athletic performance is one which increasingly must be faced by those who aspire to fulfil their potential. Several sports list substances which athletes are not permitted to take because it is considered that these would artificially assist their performance level. However, the whole subject is not quite so cut and dried. There are many different substances which can affect a human being chemically. Many use them without even thinking that they are drugs. We are all familiar with items such as aspirin for easing the pain of a headache, and caffeine which acts as a stimulant and is found in coffee, tea and chocolate.

Society today accepts as normal a certain level of drug-taking; for example, decongestants to relieve symptoms of colds; and valium to calm the system when under stress. Alcohol can either be a stimulant or depressant. Everyone is conscious of the harmful aspects of cigarette smoking, and many who have attempted to give it up are only too aware of the addictive property of nicotine.

The medical profession makes a decision as to which drugs can be sold without prescription. The ones deemed to be potentially harmful, unless carefully monitored, are only available on prescription. Medical advisors also ally with the law in coming to terms with the social and hard drug scene. Statistics are frightening and public concern is increasing over the growing use and availability of all types of drugs to junior school age children and upwards.

The sports world is often said to mirror society, so one should not be surprised to find drug-taking in its midst. In the United States, steps have been taken to monitor and reduce the spread of hard drugs in professional sport. The administrators realize that the image which these individuals project can be a strong role model for the young. They also realize that a tarnished image is going to be bad for business.

Medical advisors have been used to make judgements on behalf of the sports world, in terms of performance-enhancing drugs. They and the governing bodies of organized sport have had to resolve the question:

what is considered to be beyond the norm for health purposes? The list of banned drugs for Olympic competitors grows almost daily. It was to this aspect of drug-taking which the high-achieving athletes were asked to address themselves.

What are your thoughts on the current drug scene in sport, specifically the use of performance-enhancing drugs? Have you ever experimented or been encouraged to experiment with them? As the latter question was asking whether the athletes had broken the rules which could ban their future participation in their sport, a denial of any such usage would be expected. Nevertheless, the additional supportive evidence tended to lead one to believe that in almost all cases their answers were honest. There was almost universal condemnation of drug usage. A few athletes expressed understanding of the pressures and temptations and felt that the decision whether or not to get involved had to be left to an individual's morality. All saw the potential which drug-taking had for wrecking their sport if it was used. All but one denied ever having experimented with performance-enhancing drugs.

In many sports the use of performance-enhancing drugs is virtually unknown – cricket, rugby union, yachting, ice skating and squash are just a few. The athletes who were competing before the mid-1950s would rarely have heard of drugs in sport. The advent of anabolic steroids came about through their use during the Second World War when patients were given these steroids to speed up the process of rehabilitation. Where the patient was weak, the drug would assist their body in putting on weight and generally stimulate the recuperative powers of the human system. The follow on thoughts of some were, if it could do this for the sick, how much might it assist the healthy to perform enhanced feats. In about 20 per cent of cases, the side effects produced serious damage to the organs which were excreting the substance from the system, for example, the liver, kidneys and urinary tract. The latest evidence identifies that in males, the prostate is the most lastingly affected area.

In the 1960s, the heavyweight activities were the most common areas of use – weightlifters, track and field athletics throwers, and American football players to name but a few. The premise was that whatever muscles were used they would be developed at a faster rate than normal, the key being that more work could be done because the steroid was assisting the recovery rate. In those early days, little emphasis was placed on the amount being taken, and as testosterone is produced in the male reproductive system, ingesting large quantities from outside the system supplanted the function of the body producing its own and as a result many males became impotent. This and other noticeable side effects apparently disappeared a short time after the users came off the drug. By the early 1970s, the pressure of competition moved the usage of this drug into the explosive running and jumping events as well as the endurance ones. In the 1980s, one advance, if it can possibly be referred to as that, is referred to as human growth hormone. This is a stimulant to the pituitary gland which promotes growth and is therefore irreversible.

Some of the athletes interviewed understood the temptation facing today's athletes. The ambition to win and at times the potential for substantial financial gain blinds them to either the potential physical damage or the moral issues of cheating or genetic interference.

Lynn Davies has been the British team manager for track and field athletics in recent years. Although he was competing before the advent of widespread drug-taking in the sport, he expressed his understanding of the motivation to take drugs. 'I was competing in the early 1960s and we didn't experience drugs. We didn't even talk about them . . . I'm sympathetic to some extent to the whole approach to them because they are perceived to be a highly significant factor in winning in present day sport, not just track and field athletics. I think it's far more widespread than people think. I was never pressurized to take drugs and never wanted to take them because they just weren't part of the scene then, but what one gleans from conversations now with athletes and others, is the pressures they feel if they are not taking them, the need to explore the possibility. To some extent, I think British athletes have felt second-class in terms of support services and the gap seems to be widening at an ever-increasing rate when you compare the success rate of Eastern Europe on athletes in various sports. This was most marked at the World Championships in Helsinki, this feeling of helplessness in terms of medical support and scientific monitoring of performance. As we fall further behind, I feel sympathy for athletes who are still tremendously dedicated and feel very frustrated that they haven't got very good support services.' Having said that, Lynn added, 'I would like to see it wiped out'.

Al Oerter talked openly about his experimentations with the anabolic steroid testosterone before it became a banned substance. He recalled the problems which he experienced and illustrated the dangers of the human growth hormone. 'I found that with anabolic steroids I retained so much body weight, water weight primarily, that my blood pressure went through the ceiling. I thought I'd get off that before I killed myself. I also found no real difference in performance. It's a drug that increases your aggression. It almost levelled everything off for me because in competition I was always fairly aggressive, but when I became equally aggressive in my daily life, I found that very uncomfortable. It just wasn't me. I had to be able to relax and enjoy the 99.9 per cent of my life when I wasn't in the discus ring in competition.'

Oerter continued, 'The nature of the athlete today is quite different.

It's instant gratification which is required today and if it's their belief that a drug can help them gain immediate recognition they're going to take those drugs. The rewards are there. Previously, the reward was strictly recognition, and came out of long periods of work rather than short bursts of high chemicals. I still think that virtually the same level is attainable naturally but it takes a longer period of time to reach it.'

Al expressed particular concern about human growth hormone. 'Those drugs are so damn dangerous. They began by using an extract from the rhesus monkey and some athletes began to develop the properties of the monkey, protruding forehead, expanding jaw and problems such as a perfectly functioning ball and socket joint which would somehow get out of shape and create a long term arthritic condition. Now they're taking it out of human cadavers [corpses], so those particular problems are gone, but the doctors I've talked to say that the athletes who are on these things are still experiencing tremendous growth. Even with mature people the bones start growing again. The first problem that they're seeing is that the athlete's heart is expanding. I don't know whether the heart muscle will go back later on. I suspect that they're going to have long-term difficulties with it. . . . they're really messing around with nature. Male hormones or something like that might make you more aggressive, but once you are off them, you return to your normal personality and size, but with human growth hormone the long-term effects are absurd. Your body just doesn't return to where it was. The athletes are looking at this risk–reward ratio much, much differently than they did in the past. They are saying, in effect, forget the risk because the rewards are there.'

Certainly the comments from these two athletes might lead one to believe that today's champions are all producing exceptional performances courtesy of their local chemist. There is no doubt that some of the top athletes have been taking drugs to assist the amount of training they can undertake; however, it is also the case that many others are not. It is interesting to see the athletes' performances in relation to the important games where they will be drug-tested. It was quite common to see performances in certain events substantially drop off. Athletes must get off their detectable drugs some weeks prior to the tests in order for these drugs not to show up. In that time some of the anabolic steroid effects will have reduced and the performances slip.

Perhaps the track and field athlete who would be most likely to take ergogenic aids would be the decathlete; he is, after all, cited as the man who has the greatest all-round ability. Daley Thompson has won the last two Olympic titles and the World Championships in that event, each time producing personal best performances. He is known to be against taking even an aspirin, and in a sense is a crusader against drugs, volunteering to make himself available at any time when, in 1984, there was talk of a drug-testing flying squad who would come in and test, unannounced, on training sessions or small meets. He expressed his feelings as follows: 'I think it's terrible. It's bad for the sport in general. It's bad for the kids coming into the sport because they feel that the only way they can get on is by taking all the drugs that they suppose most of the people are taking, especially here in the US [where Daley trains]. I must admit I understand why people take the stuff. They want to win almost as badly as I do, so I mean, I can understand. That's why I'm glad I don't have to do anything like that. I don't need to. You see, most of those things enable you to work harder – I don't want to work any harder. I can understand that if I wasn't as good, I might, but I have no need to, so it never occurs to me. I feel sorry for those who have to go that far . . . most of those taking it are not quite good enough – they're fifth or sixth or tenth in their country or the world.'

Apart from Daley, several other athletes gave their opinion when referring to their dislike of any form of drugs right down to aspirin. Steele Bishop said, 'It's terrible and totally unnecessary. I've proved that. I have a very clean diet and clean way of living, and train very hard. When I was competing in Europe, some Europeans said, "You should try this!" I've proved I can beat them without it. I've raced them when they were taking drugs and beaten them. So when the World Championships came and they were not allowed to take them, I'd got it all over them – mentally they'd had it.'

This clean approach was also expressed by John Havlicek and Wayne Gretzky. John said that he even stopped drinking Coke for a year because someone told him that it might affect his wind! Wayne said that he refused to allow DMSO (dimethyl sulphur oxide, a liquid which is rapidly absorbed into the body's tissue and is claimed to have assisted in numerous medical cases from soft tissue injury to rheumatism) to be administered to the shoulder injury which kept him out of action for three weeks, because the Canadian Medical Association were not yet sure whether there were any side effects.

J.P.R. Williams is a medical doctor and gave his medical, as well as personal, opinion. 'Talking as a doctor now, we should let the athletes know what are the side effects and potential consequences of anabolic steroids and leave it to the athletes themselves to decide whether they are going to take them. The interesting thing is that most of them will still take the chances. You know how single-minded athletes are in particular; they don't care about the future if they can get a gold medal. I don't know what the answer is because I don't believe in drugs, but on the other hand I don't believe in hypocrisy and if you can't test for some of them and the Eastern Europeans are using them, then that's not fair. The anabolic steroids have not been proved to increase strength but what they do is to allow you to train more times a day and harder. In other words you are enhancing your ability to train harder . . . I don't agree with them. I would never take them myself because I know the potential problems. A lot of them at the moment are thought to be reversible, like high blood pressure and liver problems. It's very frightening . . . I'll never prescribe them to anyone but you know this is going on.'

Three of the points made by J.P.R. Williams were brought out by other athletes. Firstly, the dangers are there and should be heeded. A second point made by J.P.R. was that these drugs simply allow one to train harder. Many athletes pointed out that they achieved their success without drugs simply by working hard over a long period of time. Ed Moses and Steve Ovett both referred to the time factor. Ed said, 'I hung in long enough to reach this level. At Moorehouse State, we barely had a set of weights. No one ever offered steroids to me until I came to California. [After his 1976 Olympic victory.] I'm all against it. I know that hard work has got me to where I am and I will never consider it, never have considered it and never had any urge to experiment or try it or anything. I know it's dangerous from the doctors . . . I have high school students asking me what they should do. People are trying to get them to take them. I just tell them that I've never tried it; that it's dangerous, you never know what's going to happen, and if you're thinking about a scholarship to an educational institution and they are approaching you now, just think what will happen when you get there and you don't want to do it.' Steve Ovett referred to the third point made by J.P.R.: that it is up to each individual to decide. Steve said, 'It's solely and purely up to the individual. I don't think you can enforce rulings on drug-taking, it's been done outside sport in narcotics and the results are disastrous. I believe that if an individual feels he needs to take a drug to succeed then that individual is the one who has to live with it at the end of the day. If he walks off at the end of the day with three gold medals round his neck and he knows he's got them because of X, Y and Z drugs, then he's the one that's got to live with that. It's never really interested me and I've never been encouraged to try them because I've been successful without things like that.'

Carl Lewis was another who was of the opinion that it was up to each individual's conscience but that there should be a constructive programme to try to rid sport of it. 'People are taking drugs. We know that. It's more prevalent now than it was but I don't think as many people take it as everyone thinks. You don't really necessarily have to take them to be the best; Edwin's [Moses] not, I'm not. But who am I to tell somebody that they can't take drugs to be the best they can be? If they're doing what they think is right to be the best, then that's right because it comes from within inside. But of course, there are rules so you can't do it . . . I shouldn't be running around saying you shouldn't take steroids, what I'm trying to do is help support the programmes that are against it and that's the only way we're going to fight the problem. We're not going to fight it finger pointing. We've got to say, let's start a programme against steroids and start making appearances, start being tested, so we can show the kids in particular that you don't have to take them to be a great athlete. I don't take them. And I'd test everyone. I've always said I think everyone who sets a world record or national record should be tested the day they set the record. We need to get people involved.'

Gene Upshaw saw the whole drug problem related to society. 'You have a cross section of society in sport. Whatever we do in sport we should deal with through education and rehabilitation and not punishment.' He said that a new rule had recently come into the NFL (National Football League) making the use of anabolic steroids an offence. O.J. Simpson said that the change of emphasis in American football had altered the amount of steroids used. 'Ten years ago,' he said, 'steroids were big for the smaller guy who was motivated because he was not big enough. Because of the nature of the game going to speed, you find most of the big guys are trying to get smaller. Uppers or bennys are used but less than in individual sports.' (O.J. is referring to the use of amphetamines, such as Benzedrine, which stimulate the central nervous system, increasing alertness in physical activities and decreasing fatigue.[38])

Ken Read felt strongly about drugs and saw it as an issue of cheating. 'An element that gets forgotten is that it's cheating. It's not a question of physical enhancement. It's unhealthy and it's against the rules. It's totally unacceptable.' The same word was used by Rob de Castella. 'Pretty simple, I think it's just cheating. I like to think an individual is competing on his own merit rather than on some drug company's merit. I have a similar attitude to blood doping for distance runners. [The process of removing, a few weeks before an event, some of the athlete's own blood. The plasma is taken away, leaving the red oxygen-carrying cells. Before race time, when the individual has fully rebuilt his or her quota, the extra red cells are reintroduced for additional oxygen-carrying capacity.] As far as I'm concerned it's cheating. I wouldn't recommend it or be happy with anyone who I knew to be doing it.'

Steve Cram was indignant that not enough was being done to put a stop to drug-taking. 'Until they start giving out life bans that are real life bans then it will continue. [Currently in track and field athletics, the International Federation has allowed banned drug offenders back into the sport within a year to eighteen months of the offence.] It's a ridiculous situation to have. The problem is, as certain people are allowed to do it, then the pressure on everyone else is for them to do it. I've purposely never been involved.' Duncan Goodhew also saw the need for wider testing and more harsh rule enforcement. 'My current feeling is, I think we're going to have to take drug testing to small meets, unexpectedly and try and clobber as many people as possible. "Banned for life" should be totally irrevocable. To have somebody back who has been on steroids is a disgrace. No, in swimming, when I was competing, I took the attitude of "let others take it"; it's a weakness and if you feel you have to take drugs, you are at a psychological disadvantage.'

Peter Sterling said that the Australian sporting public were aware of steroids but that he had never seen anybody in his club take drugs. 'I would never do it, I'd be disappointed in myself if I ever had to resort to that. It's probably a sign that you haven't got much further to go.' John Konrads also viewed the decision to take drugs as a sign of weakness. 'I don't know enough about the modern drugs to have an opinion as to whether they would help. I was anti-drugs based on the premise that a superbly conditioned athlete cannot be improved on and the risk is that in taking drugs you can undo what you have done right. It can become a crutch if you have to say, "Well I'm not sure of winning unless I rely on drugs".'

Jonah Barrington was personally against it but realized the dilemma for coaches with gifted young athletes. 'I think it's dreadful. I'm appalled by it. A journalist once asked me, "If I had a drug I could take which would win me another British Open Championship, would I take it?" I said, "No, because I would know that I had cheated." It's not a goody-goody thing. What I did was sheer hard work; blindly at times but increasingly systematic; hard work without having needles stuck into me or taking pills. It would be very difficult for me as a coach to know whether I would continue with someone who I felt had the ability to get to very near the top, but wasn't actually going to make it unless they took drugs.' Jonah also expressed great concern over the young Tour de France cyclists who were being pushed exceptionally hard while still in their teens and at a crucial stage in bone development. This concern has been expressed by many medical practitioners in all high stress sports, either in endurance, such as ultra long-distance running; or intensity, such as weight-lifting; or hyper-extension, as in back extension in gymnastics. A number of serious and permanent injuries have occurred in each area.

A further drug concern was the puberty-retarding drugs, which have been attributed to some Eastern European competitors. The premise being that since the time of Olga Korbut, the image required to win in that sport changed to one of pre-pubescence. Genetic engineering research continues outside of sport. I fear that it will not be long before the 'created body' will be another vehicle of propaganda. It is pleasing to hear from these athletes that the mind, will and dedication of the person plays just as large, if not a larger part, than purely physical talent. It is to be hoped that a combination of education and sensible rule enforcement will allow sport to live with itself in the future. Sport must retain elements of enjoyment and human dignity. Drug-taking and other forms of cheating could so easily ruin sport, causing individuals and organizations to self-destruct. Sport, at its best, is a human endeavour which can enhance the view we have of ourselves and our potential.

CHAPTER 21

Religious and Moral Standards

From the statements in the last two chapters, it is apparent that the standards and values of these achievers were generally high. It seems as though the teachings of their parents did have some effect because 93 per cent stressed fair play and keeping within the rules. This code of ethics has some basis in religious instruction, although many countries in the Western world pay only lip service to formal religion. Printed on each US coin are the words, 'In God we trust', and it is known that a few of the professional American football teams pray before 'going into battle'. Many sports followers will have seen the film *Chariots of Fire* and some, myself included, will have identified with the feelings of Eric Liddell in believing that God-given talent is there to be developed to the best of our abilities.

Did religious values, either through going to church, prayer, meditation or other non-formal religious aspects, ever have any influence on your sporting life? This was a broad question, leaving the door open for comment across the spectrum of what could hold religious connotations. Of these achievers, 60 per cent did not think that religion in any form affected their sporting life. Several individuals in this group held some form of personal religious beliefs but felt that their sport was in no way mixed with that belief. Others were quite forcefully opposed to the mixing of sport and religion and a few were opposed to religion in general. In the 40 per cent who did find some assisting influence from religious belief, there was also a spectrum from those who referred to being on the right path for their life, to one or two others who were begging for assistance in a time of need!

Duncan Goodhew was one who strongly objected to those who prayed for divine intervention to help them to win. 'To me competing to win is the ultimate self-interest, although I believe it is sacrilege not to do it if you're good because that's an insult to your talent. But to pray to God for success or to say when you lose, "Well, God didn't mean me to win this time . . ." It makes me cringe because it's you praying to somebody for victory. That means you are praying to beat somebody, asking for divine intervention and to me that's wrong.' Al Oerter was very much of the same thinking. 'I find it difficult with some athletes, boxers in particular, if they win the match, a microphone is stuck under their nose and the first thing they say is, "I want to thank God Almighty for helping me to beat my opponent". If there is a God, why would he or she or whatever not treat everyone equally? Why would the Deity help somebody to beat up on some other creature on earth? I find it difficult to understand . . . I know there is a God. I know there is something out there guiding me because every once in a while I feel that I've been nudged in a direction, but I don't have an appreciation of my religious life.'

Pat O'Callaghan felt that religion in sport was just a crutch: 'You're missing something within yourself.'

Bob Cousy said that religion played no serious part in his preparation but that he remembered saying, 'Oh God, please help us to win this one', but he added, 'It's empty and insecure. Obviously you don't expect God to be listening and helping but it's the next best thing, other than having the opportunity of doing something yourself, you implore the Deity . . . It's presumptuous to think that Jesus, Allah or whoever is watching, and thinking I'll give you a little help and not you. I mean, if there is a Deity, he set the whole thing in motion and I am sure he went out and played golf. I don't think religious belief plays a role in the competition itself. I think it plays a role in your overall life and your approach to problems, and, in a sense, prepares you better mentally; perhaps develops better confidence in yourself, more self-respect as a whole.'

Bobby Charlton was another who did not think the two areas mixed but said that although he did not go to church regularly, he had attended church when he was younger and knew what religion meant. 'Whether you believe in God or not, the Ten Commandments are good rules to stand by.' Greg Chappell was another who saw value in the Christian ethic and lived by that but did not see it integrating with his sporting life. Steve Cram referred to the indirect application of one's values. He had a reasonably strict moral code – basically Christian principles and values without going to church.

Daley Thompson and Torvill and Dean said that they believed in God, but neither asked for help nor did they think that it had any influence on them.

If the response was that values had not been taken from religion into their sport, a further question was asked: *Where did you think your values had been taken from?* In most cases, it was from the home. Steve Ovett referred to working class values, Heather McKay spoke of home and Ken Read referred to the family.

Religious values were certainly not the criteria on which to judge standards of fair play. Geoff Hunt, for example, said that he had strictly scientific beliefs and was cited by Jonah Barrington as having the highest ethical standards of any player he knew. 'Just because the referee and marker had not called the ball down, he [Geoff] was so fair that at 7–7 in the fifth set he would call his ball down if he thought it was down.' Geoff said, 'My philosophy was, "I wanted to win and win fairly on the court". No one would even know, probably, that I won within myself and I didn't cheat on the court and I didn't give myself second bounces, even though my opponent may have done. I'd have more satisfaction in coming off the court having won. I'd get a bit cross at times when I saw them do it but it made me more determined to win and say, "Right, you couldn't even beat me with your cheating". That's the way I used to tackle it anyway.'

Rod Laver was not sure where the thought came from. He said he didn't think it was religious but he said, 'When I was down by two sets to one and by four games to one against Emerson at Wimbledon in 1962, the thought came to me that I was going to win the match! How does that get into your head? I don't necessarily put that down to religion. I put it down to your attitude of accepting where you are and if destiny says you should win the Grand Slam in 1962, then given the chance it will happen – as long as you want to work hard. You're not fated to it and you're not going to do it without an effort, but given all those combinations together, you can do it.'

Mike Wenden spoke of another non-religious aspect. 'I did a little bit of yoga for a while. It started off my internalization – my self-concentration on what I had to do.'

Valeriy Borzov said that for him the State had the higher purpose. At the time of the Olympic final, his first thought was of himself, but later his feelings were for his country, for their training and support. This type of national patriotism was not limited to the 'State' athlete. Marjorie Nelson had mentioned this fact when describing her feelings for Australia. At times that greater cause can help one's perspective and motivation.

Ann Brightwell said that she did not think that religion had had any influence on her sporting life, but referred to the enormous strength of spirit of Betty Cuthbert. Betty now has multiple sclerosis. In 1964, Ann won the 800m at the Tokyo Olympics but finished second to Betty in the 400m. Ann said, 'When I spoke to her years afterwards, I realized that I wouldn't know if I could ever have won that race. She is a mystical girl with very strong religious beliefs. I call her mystical because she has an inner understanding of herself which would be very difficult for anyone else to touch and I just felt that she had a stronger belief in herself than I had. She has a very strong character and many, many setbacks have motivated her tremendously. Her depths of reserve enable her to keep coming back – that sort of spirit would be very hard to beat.'

Almost all of the individuals interviewed who felt that they did gain benefit from their religious beliefs, saw it in the light of a larger perspective on life and within themselves. They were not usually asking for direct intervention, so objected to those who saw it as a crutch or sacrilege. O.J. Simpson said, 'Religion is the foundation of who I am and what I believe. Whether it's the philosophy of Jesus or the philosophy of Muhammad – you do unto others, treat others, as you would want to be treated.' Clive Lloyd felt that his faith had a calming influence on him. 'My personal belief in Christ helped me quite a lot – as a human being, you tend not to get too annoyed. You can weigh up situations . . . and as they say, engage brain before putting mouth in motion.' Carl Lewis said that it gave him a perspective on life. 'It keeps me pretty level-headed because I realize that this is a God-given talent, like everybody else has and by having a religion and needing it, I believe that's what I have.'

In earlier discussions on personal sacrifice, reference was made by Herb Elliott to the connection he felt to striving for a higher cause. 'There was a certain connection with the mystics and Jesus and people who suffered as a result of their religion. I guess it was a way in which you could relate your suffering to a higher cause than just winning races . . . I did feel some sort of association with the Almighty God through my running. I felt in contact there. I think it helped. It gave a sort of total sense, a justification for what I was doing.'

Joan Benoit Samuelson also referred to her feeling of being closer to God while running. 'I consider myself to be a religious person. I have a great deal of faith in God. I don't spout it off or try to push my religion or faith in God on anyone. I have respect for anybody regardless of their religious preferences. I feel that God has been very good to me and my family and I think prayer and things like that have certainly helped. I go to church every Sunday but I think I've been closer to God in races and on training runs than I have in church. Prior to a race, my prayer is just to be at peace with myself and make myself happy and satisfied and those who are expecting good things of me. It's not to win, nor to set a record, it's just to run as well as I possibly can at that time and try to keep calm, tranquil and peaceful.'

John Havlicek referred to his faith and in particular to a booklet which has helped him to cope with the practical issues of life. 'I've prayed to be able to cope with particular situations. It made me more settled in myself. Everyday, for the last twenty to twenty-five years, I've read a booklet called *The Upper Room*,[55] which gives you a scripture, a thought or message for the day and a prayer. In one instance, after going to the 1960 Olympic trials, I had missed a week of classes at university. When I came back, I was overwhelmed with the work at hand and contemplated dropping out of school. The message that day was: no matter how overwhelming things may seem, give it a try, give it a shot. You'd be surprised what you can do if you apply yourself. Little hints and influences like that have been very common throughout my life.'

Lucinda Green never prays to win, just to do her best and not hurt her horse. 'It's one of those things which keeps me on an even keel. I wouldn't go round preaching but it's one thing I have got to hang on to and say "Help".'

Gareth Edwards said that at times the prayers did become appeals. 'Please God help us to win this one and we won't ask for any more – hoping he was Welsh or British! It was really asking to be given a break, not making a deal. Give us the opportunity to show what we're made of.' He added that his religious beliefs did give him an inner strength. He also said that for five minutes before the start of the British Lions matches, the captain, Willie John McBride, would tell them, 'Now go and make peace with yourselves' and there would be five minutes of quiet in which everyone settled themselves.

Steele Bishop's belief paralleled the thought that God helps those who help themselves – as long as one is on the right path with one's life. 'I believe in self and God. He'll look after you if you do the right thing.'

Billie Jean King had a good deal of religious involvement as a child and also in her teens, although that is not a part of her life now. She said that a significant influence on her had been a passage from the Bible about the need for faith to be combined with hard work in order to succeed.

Jackie Stewart spoke of the religious experience which took place at the time that he decided to end his motor-racing career. Part of his religious understanding came at the time of the violent and tragic death of his team-mate, François Cevert. 'When I made my decision to retire I didn't tell anybody. I made it in April but agreed to race through to October. My wife Helen had become very religious. I had never seen the value, never seen the results, if you like, of that strength. About a month after I'd made the decision to retire, I suddenly wondered if I could handle everything. I started to become very nervous about it – I'd been cocooned by the sport so completely, literally smothered with generosity, it was then that I ran into a situation where religion came to me. An Anglican priest in Indiannapolis asked me if I'd ever been confirmed. I said, "No", and he said, "Would you like to be because maybe you can be helped?". I knelt on the floor of the motel room and he confirmed me and it was like somebody had saved me from drowning. I felt myself pulling out of it and I just knew categorically then that I was going to retire, that I was going to be happy, that I was going to get through . . . I felt totally comfortable. It didn't give me a recklessness but I had a very calm knowledge. On the day before my final race, the US Grand Prix, which was my hundredth, my team-mate was killed in practice. We were fastest and second fastest qualifying. It couldn't have hurt me in a more profound way had it been a member of my own family. He was killed right in front of me and I had to stop and go to him. It said to me, "Hey, never take anything for granted". Still nobody knew that I was retiring – it was the week after that I announced it. The whole thing – understanding of life, a comprehension of energy and power, a being there – was unaccountable. It was part of a basis of religious understanding or belief that hadn't made itself evident to me previously. I've really felt that communication exists.'

Another deep response relating to death came from Marjorie Nelson. She feels that her athletic success has given her the fame to truly be of use in fund raising for cancer research. 'I believed in God. Values were taught when young – the Ten Commandments, that's what life was like then. Then with my husband Peter's illness, I couldn't believe in a God who would let anyone suffer like that. I nursed him for the last ten days of his life and he could hardly talk with all the ulcers in his mouth and he only weighed five stone (70 lb). He just said, "Don't blame God for what man made" and I thought, "How could he believe that after two years suffering?" . . . He bled to death in my arms . . . and I felt an uncanny peace all around me. I felt another presence in the room. I had a dead body in my arms and I felt God all around me and that I'd left him but he'd never left me. I just said, "Well, I've asked you why for two years and you've never told me – what do you want me to do?" That's when my whole life changed, when I stopped asking "why" and said "what". I stopped thinking about myself and my whole life changed. I found a meaning in life. I think I believe more in God now than ever before in my life.'

There is an unwritten rule that in polite conversation, one does not mention politics or religion. I had wondered whether it was inappropriate to include in my questioning an enquiry into whether religious belief had had any influence on the athletes' sporting lives. I decided that I should because I felt that it had been helpful for me. I had been brought up in a family who valued the teachings of Jesus. Over the years I have continued reading, reflecting and discussing religion, attempting to integrate my thinking and beliefs with a perspective on life, in its practical and physical reality. Each individual will have his or her own understanding of what God means to them, but I have valued the feelings of connection, particularly in difficult times, praying for guidance. I believe that there is a right path for everyone's life. We are each learning from the experiences in this life. We continually have choices as to our direction and actions and at any point in that decision-making, we can move away from the best direction for our lives. However, the next decision also gives us the option to move onto the next right path for our inner growth and development. Abraham Maslow did not overtly put religion or spiritual aspects into his hierarchy of human needs, but he did refer to the development of each individual with the central theme being one of transcendence. This hierarchy of human needs moves from physical through social into psychological aspects and culminates with the open-ended fifth stage, referring to the development of the ideals in human values. These include items such as justice, honesty, being alive, integration, wholeness, uniqueness, simplicity, effortlessness, playfulness, self-sufficiency and many others. The most logical extension, in my perspective, is that the spiritual overview is the ultimate step in the sequence. The 'need drives' are constantly drawing the individual through experiences by which the spirit evolves. The body and mind are the vehicles for the travels and growth of the spirit.

At the Mexico Olympics, I felt very much on the right path for my life at that time. I was not praying that I be allowed to win but I prayed that I be enabled to do my best. I was feeling a great deal of stress and I found that prayer gave me a connection with some ultimate life force, which was very settling. It gave me a sense of peace and an almost tangible inner strength. This question on religion was prompted because, for me, it was not possible to separate the assistance I felt in understanding and dealing with life in general, from the development of talent and personal growth through my sport experiences. It was all part of the same experience and dealt with through my philosophy of life, and as such, it could not be omitted from discussion.

Conclusions

One can never fully understand human motivation and what makes someone perform or act in a certain way. Part of the enjoyment of competition is its very unpredictability. Why then pursue this study? There were at least two reasons. The first was that by nature, humans are inquisitive and some questions refused to leave my mind. What makes a winner? Are there factors which winners have in common? Are there any aspects which unite the diversity of human beings who compete in different sports? Are we looking at human endeavour which transcends the outcome of a contest? The second reason for wanting to discover the factors which made these athletes winners, was my belief that each person has their own gold medal level. Perhaps there were some aspects which could be learned from the very best, that would allow each performer the chance to raise his or her own level, bringing them closer to fulfilling themselves and their potential.

When I was reflecting on this study at my coach, Billy Smith's home, his wife Jean came up with a reflection which may well assist in explaining why there are similarities and yet crucial differences in each area. I had referred to the fact that I was not the fastest nor the strongest in my Olympic final. She said, 'You may not have had 100 per cent of any one thing but maybe you had 95 per cent of everything.' In reflecting on the results of this study, her comment may be close to a perfect summary answer. In each area a few athletes are an exception to the rule but they were not the same few athletes in each case. All of them have most of the attributes in common. This means that being different or missing out on an aspect or two does not rule a person out from fulfilling their promise or reaching their goal.

As this is a summary section and I am drawing conclusions, it is necessary to generalize. There are exceptions in virtually every area, so the following represents the predominant trends. Most of the athletes had started out as shy, sometimes self-conscious, introverts. In several cases, sport provided an avenue through which they became far more outgoing; their sporting success strengthened their self-image and in many cases diminished their shyness. Obviously, because of their notoriety, the majority have a learned public exterior. Nevertheless, many still identify themselves as being quite shy, introverted people today. In my comparative study of double achievers,[24] those individuals who achieved an international level in sport and then went on to become successful in another area showed a marked difference in this characteristic. Most of the double achievers considered that they were extroverts. By contrast, the sports achievers often voiced the fact that they did not mind the solitude of personal preparation. The saying, 'it's lonely at the top', held no threat for this group. Their early introverted tendencies allowed them to be quite at home in their 'known' training environment. They did not consider that they were sacrificing the 'high life' because this had not been their choice of activity.

Very few of the group saw themselves as aggressive outside of the competitive arena. While most were assertive, one-third viewed themselves as neither aggressive nor assertive. On the field, however, it was a different proposition. Competitive sport is not play. Once a sporting contest has emotionally involved the contestants, effort is intense and the outcome is deadly serious. It is during competition that assertiveness and, at times, aggressiveness, is apparent. Some channel their aggression in on themselves, which intensifies their personal efforts. Others direct it into their play. In these highly competitive athletes, there is a degree and quality of intensity which not only can be seen but felt. However, in almost all cases, they maintain total control of themselves. It is this quality of maintaining a calm and controlled approach while 'fired up', that allows them to perform at their best under the most intense competitive fire.

Almost universally, their upbringing was stable, secure, happy and predictable. They were well nurtured. Even though there was no excess of material goods, each athlete was provided with support, physically and emotionally, usually through parents or by a strongly supportive surrogate parent. Physical support, and safety and security are the first two building blocks in Maslow's hierarchy of human needs, the ladder to fulfilling an individual's potential. The role of the parents should not be underestimated. The qualities which the athletes cited as the main attributes of their parents added together to provide a profile which exemplified the qualities of the elite athletes. In many cases the parents were excellent role models: they stressed fair play and keeping within the rules as part of their system of values. In practice, they were hard working, dedicated, honest, humorous and caring individuals. I recall school-friends saying that they wished they had parents like mine; I valued my parents' interest, support and friendship. The vast majority of these achievers expressed similar feelings regarding the worth of their parents, and valued their close-knit family relationship. Maslow's third level of love and a sense of belonging would strongly assist such home life.

Discipline from parents was mostly verbal and the closest parent–child relationships existed where physical punishment had not taken place. In the few cases where priority had been given to physical discipline, the adult parent–offspring relationships had badly broken down. The birth order in the family provided a disproportionate frequency of second born, but the largest groupings overall were those who were second from youngest. The reasons for this were not readily apparent.

Most athletes were introduced to a variety of sports and in their early years, enjoyed playing them. Sound fundamental technique was introduced early on, in many cases by their fathers. However, in a great proportion of cases, these achievers did not specialize until quite late on in their sporting life. Their parents had not attempted to live through them; encouragement and support were given in every area of interest, but they were not pushed. The obvious advantage was that the athletes' bodies and minds were allowed to mature. Specialization could take place when the athlete was ready to make his or her commitment to their sport. If the personal desire did not come from inside the athlete, no amount of external pushing was going to help. Once these achievers had made their decision to specialize, they usually had the help of a coach or some other significant person or group. As mature individuals, they chose to seek personal improvement by pushing themselves. The work ethic was very highly evolved. Nevertheless, these athletes were not kicking against the work load. Quite the opposite, the work was being done by choice because they enjoyed their efforts and their results. In some sports, discomfort in training was an accepted part of getting the best from themselves and was understood to be the route to improvement.

Apart from intensity, duration of training was a factor. The old saying, 'Rome was not built in a day', is equally relevant to sporting success. These athletes developed their abilities over *years* of consistent training and competition. In many cases they did not even realize the level to which they could aspire. It was a step-by-step progression. This highlighted two valuable points. Personal goal-setting must establish a challenging yet realistic target. Set too high and the impossibility of the task can kill enthusiasm, the goal being unrealistic. Set too low, and the goal produces no challenge or incentive. The second point is that high achievers set new goals each time they fulfil a task. For the high achievers in sport, these goals are usually highly visible. Maslow's fourth level of human need fulfilment is self-esteem and recognition from others. Public sporting success provides a strong fulfilling ingredient in this respect.

Nearly 90 per cent separated themselves from average through their growth and maturity pattern. Two-thirds identified themselves as late developers and nearly one-quarter as early. The conclusion which might be drawn from this is that the early developers are often singled out to be team leaders or in some way are given more responsibility simply because of their early maturity. Those who were late developers would have often struggled to prove that there was more to them than others saw on the surface. Sport is one area where it is possible to demonstrate acceptability almost regardless of size. Most of these late developers said that they acquired good skill levels early on. Once maturity produced size, they moved into contention with the best.

Almost all of these achievers found humour an invaluable part of life, seeing it as a tension reliever. Humour is a good ice-breaker and shared humour can bring individuals and groups together. In an environment of high intensity, humour can be a life-saver. A few athletes pointed out that their training time was serious throughout. For almost all, competition was serious – hence the need between times to lighten the mood.

Another characteristic of these achievers was their determination not to give up. They had been competitive from as early as they could remember and they would compete hard until time ran out. If they did lose they would usually try to establish why and see if there was any way of avoiding that in the future.

Most found injury upsetting, but it was accepted as a challenge and rehabilitation was pursued with the intention of getting back as quickly as possible. Generally, they did not see their training requirements and life styles as imbalanced nor, in most cases, did they think that they had sacrificed anything. The athletes enjoyed pursuing their personal quest, believing that they were lucky to have been in the right place at the right time.

Having the right support systems for their individual needs provided these achievers with the opportunity to progress. The support systems were important, whether it was mother's home-cooking, a ride to the game, or the opportunity to train provided by a sponsor, be that a club, an educational institution or a benefactor. Facilities were important but meeting the right person at the right time was invaluable.

Where there was a significant coach–athlete relationship, it carried a tremendous amount of influence. The intensity of relationships varied greatly, but the majority used coaching assistance. The largest proportion were lucky enough to establish one very meaningful relationship with a gifted coach. The second largest group took advice from several coaches in relationships which were more that of a teacher–student than anything else. Fathers introduced the basics to a number of them, and in four cases became the coach. The few remaining achievers either had no coaching or simply referred to advisors as and when they wanted them. Coaching styles varied in accordance with the personalities of the individuals. The old adage, 'horses for courses', appeared most relevant.

In a good coach–athlete relationship, there was mutual and matching aims with respect and commitment on each side. The coaches were knowledgeable and very effective communicators. These coaches identified with the athletes' desire to achieve but they were humble enough to have the athletes' ambitions as a higher priority than their own. 70 per cent of the athletes believed that they would not have reached the level they did without the assistance of their coach. If it was not a coach who inspired or assisted them, then the athlete often identified a significant other person who had helped them. These people were either role models or had somehow assisted the athlete either with advice, guidance, financial backing, emotional support or physical rehibilitation.

Most of the achievers believed, to a large extent, that they controlled their own destiny. This is reflected in the fact that they took responsibility for their actions. A physical example of this is that they would usually keep themselves away from distraction prior to important competitions. Mentally, they would take control of the outcome of the coming event. The mental aspect of visualization was one of the most determining factors in how these athletes performed. They rehearsed the successful performance of their sport, usually in great sensory detail. This provided familiarity with the coming situation and a positive mental picture of themselves as winners. It is understood that these individuals had a good amount of basic physical ability, but this should not be over-estimated. They picked up physical skills fast, then worked extremely hard and creatively over many years to perfect their performance.

The mental aspects in this study provided confirmation that this is the area for further exploration. We become what we think ourselves to be. Virgil wrote, 'They can because they think they can.' These athletes pictured themselves succeeding in high-risk situations. During the competition, their concentration was total. Their confidence level was high because they had successfully combined mental rehearsal with full physical preparation. Most believed that they were getting an edge by working harder or doing more than their opponents. They had prepared as soundly and fully as possible. These athletes were honest with themselves and that carried through their preparation, their competition and their lives. Knowledge that the work had been done to the best of their ability gave a strong sense of confidence and provided a sense of calm; all that could have been done had been done. This belief, coupled with a strong sense of fair play, made the majority of the athletes avoid any form of gamesmanship. The actions to intentionally foul or harm another contestant were, in most cases, considered unacceptable and unnecessary. This avoidance of cheating reinforced by a strong moral code of values also accounted for the forceful condemnation of the use of drugs in sport.

Money was not a determining factor in performance levels once the contest had started. The general response was, 'I couldn't have tried any harder'. This is simply another indication that the athletes internal commitment and levels of intensity were 100 per cent.

This group of achievers saw courage and risk-taking as part of their job. No great effort was necessary to overcome fear. In high risk sports, these individuals did not consider that they were gambling with life. Risks taken were calculated, but at the same time actions which were bound to produce physical punishment were simply accepted as part of the game.

To an extent, the specialization that helps the athlete reach the top in their sport can make an individual quite self-indulgent. However, in their quest for self-improvement, these high achievers have managed to discover an integration and balance within themselves. They have faced life and their weaknesses realistically and have taken up its challenges.

There was a Dutch philosopher who said that your religion is your attitude towards life. 40 per cent of these achievers felt that their attitudes and values in sport were tied to their view that man has a spirit and a higher purpose. They see the parable of the talents as a working example of fulfilling oneself. The remainder of the group do not put it in those words, but they live life the same way with the same degree of passion, conscientiousness and honesty.

Billie Jean King said, 'Have you ever noticed that the individuals who are your highest achievers are very together? They have tremendous self-understanding.' O.J. Simpson also referred to the people at the top being well-integrated and getting on with all types of people. Although I did not spend long with each of them, my impression was that they were all very balanced individuals and also possessed a positive view on life. They were almost never pushy. In no case did I find that success had gone to their heads. Quite simply, they were human beings with a talent for sport, who were striving for excellence and learning much about life on the way.

In discovering some of the factors which these achievers had in common, I discovered some of the essence of human endeavour. It need not have been sport about which these achievers were speaking; sport just happened to be their medium. Each person is individual and unique, yet at the same time there are common human traits. In searching for the best, I was allowed to see some of the characteristics, attributes and actions which brought them to the vanguard of human achievement. They were all trying to fulfil their potential. Their vehicle was visible for all to see through their success in sport. They tell us all something about ourselves and what we may be capable of achieving, if we dream and make the commitment to work hard towards that vision.

STATISTICAL SUMMARY

Stastical Summary of Findings

(Percentages have been rounded up or down)

PART 1: PHYSICAL FACTORS

Specialization	
Average age	16 years old
Training	
Believed intensity made a significant difference	97%
Consistently trained hard	97%
'Reading' the Body	
Read it well	82%
Improved during career	5%
Gave it no thought	5%
Didn't read it well	8%
Physical Development	
Late	66%
Average	12%
Early	22%
Courage and Risk-taking	
Accepted with no concern	78%
Not a factor in their sport	22%

PART II: SOCIAL FACTORS

Class	
Working	26%
Poor	22%
Lower Middle	3%
Middle	44%
Upper Middle	3%
Affluent	0%

Home Life	
Stable	98%
Secure	94%
Happy	93%
Relationship with Parents	
Close	70%
Respect for both	7%
Good with mother but not father	9%
Not close or friction	14%
Childhood Discipline	
Verbal	66%
Verbal and physical	20%
Primarily physical	8%
Neither	6%
Relationship with Parents related to Discipline	
Verbal:	
close	97%
not close	3%
Verbal and Physical:	
close	55%
respect	27%
not close	18%
Primarily Physical:	
strife	75%
not close	25%
Religion important to parents	55%
Fair-play and keeping within the rules stressed	93%
Parents considered to be competitive people	45%
Parental Expectations	
None	53%
For education only	27%
In general	20%
Sports Background of Parents	
Both played	32%
Only father played	50%
Only mother played	6%
Neither played	12%
Parental Behaviour	
Consistent	100%
Supportive and encouraging	92%
Not pushing	95%

Competitiveness with Siblings

No sibling rivalry	55%

(The majority of those who were competitive with their siblings were born approximately two years apart. More than three years age difference usually evoked no competitiveness.)

Social Characteristics

Initially shy and introverted	89%
Middle of the road	5%
Extroverted	6%
Assertive but not aggressive	55%
Neither assertive nor aggressive	35%
Assertive and aggressive	10%

Emotional Development

Late	56%
Average	18%
Early	25%

Coaching

One significant coach	40%
Several coaches	34%
Father coached or taught basics	15%
No coach (maybe occasional advisor)	11%

(68% felt they could not have reached the top without a coach)

Social Life

Did *not* feel it had been sacrificed	64%
Did *not* consider life to be imbalanced	80%
Got on well with everyone	78%

Social Attitudes

Importance of humour in everday life	89%
Felt it was important what others thought of you	88%
Wanted to please others	92%

PART III: PSYCHOLOGICAL FACTORS

Commitment

Mind totally involved in playing your sport	100%

Goal-setting

Always thought they would reach high level	57%
Situation gradually evolved	15%
Never thought they would reach high level	28%

(60% at some point set their goal of making the top.)

Visualization

Considered a great asset	80%

Learning

Fast learners of sporting skills	90%

Concentration and Control

Absolute or very high concentration	97%
Emotional intensity plus control required	100%

Pre-competition

Avoided involvement	73%
Ability to shut out problems	77%
Adaptability to sudden change	92%

Competitiveness

Competitive against themselves	92%
Had trouble passing up a challenge	83%

Aim in Competition

To win	53%
To avoid losing	37%
To do their best	10%

Effect of Increased Finance

Wouldn't alter performance	88%
Not sure	8%
Would alter performance	4%

Performance

Confident of producing their best	87%
Concentrated on their own performance	50%
Thought about others	50%

Destiny

Felt in control of their own destiny	89%
Considered themselves lucky	88%

Superstitions

Not superstitious	53%
Slightly superstitious	27%
Very superstitious	20%

PART IV: MORAL FACTORS

Gamesmanship

Would not employ it	60%

Drugs

Would like to see drugs have no part in sport	100%

Religion

Beliefs affected sporting performance	40%

ATHLETES' BIOGRAPHIES

Apart from a brief review of the athletes' career highlights, they each responded to the following questions:

- What was your most memorable event or win?
- What was your best example of holding together well under stress?
- How would you want to be remembered, as an athlete and as a person?

Jonah Barrington

Squash

Born 29 April 1941: Morwenstow, Cornwall
Specialized: 23 years old
Career highlights:
British Open winner 1966, 1967, 1969–72
British Amateur winner 1966–68
Australian Amateur winner 1968
Turned professional 1969

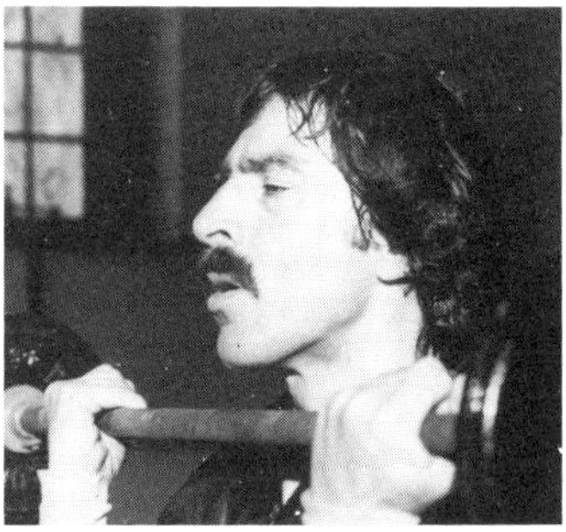

Jonah described himself as a 'compulsive exerciser'. Where the rules read that the game will be based on continuous play, Jonah based his training on becoming the fittest player in the game. He carried a 'never say die' attitude and had the reputation of being able to fight his way back from being the underdog to winning most tournaments.

For Jonah, his most memorable win and best example of holding together under stress was one and the same. He recalled the match in 1966 against the Egyptian, Abu Taleb. Jonah said, 'He had been unbeaten for four years. He was a bit of a braggard, considerably charismatic and possibly the most brilliant player I played in my career. He had a most invincible aura about him. This match was the quarter finals of the British Open. In the knock-up he never hit the ball to me. He kept hitting the ball to himself, playing trick shots, between the legs and behind the back. I'd only been in the sport for just over two years and I'd never played at a high level in front of the general public and it was a cauldron. In a very rugged match he not only tried to beat me with his racket, he tried to beat me with the ball. He drilled me thirteen times with the ball – I think he drew blood in seven areas, which is pretty good. Twice he took time out, the first saying he'd split his shorts and disappeared for ten minutes and later he claimed that his racket had broken. I beat him . . . It was a breakthrough win and it produced a surge of confidence that continued into the semi-final and the final and became a stepping-stone through the next period.

'I would like to be remembered as a great player and as a sportsman with it. Geoff Hunt is possibly the best player of all time; he was always the fairest player I ever played against. I talk about him that way and would always like people to talk about me in the same way.'

Billy Beaumont
Rugby Union *(Lock forward)*
Born 9 March 1952: Preston, Lancashire
Specialized: 17 years old
Career highlights:
International career 1975–82
In 1980 under Beaumont's captaincy, England won the Triple Crown, the International Championship and the Grand Slam.
He played lock forward thirty-four times for England and was captain on a record twenty-two occasions.

At 6 ft 3 in and 15 st (210 lb), Billy was a hard man on the field. In spite of injuries during the 1981–82 season causing severe headaches and several concussions, he did not miss a county game between 1973 and 1982. The diagnosis of a neck injury finally put an end to his playing days in 1982.

His most memorable game was captaining a regional side from the north of England to victory against the All Blacks. He said, 'We beat them 21–7 and that's the highest defeat that the All Blacks have ever had in this country. The preparation and the homework was superb . . . and everything that happened out on the field we'd prepared for. That was the most satisfying, not just because we won, but it was a great game of rugby and all the hard work had been worthwhile.'

Billy was a team man and made a good captain, leading by example and having the ability to get on well with people. He was also versatile enough to be able to treat players differently.

He would want to be remembered as, 'A good player who always gave 100 per cent on the field. As a person, I'd like to think my team-mates would say, "Well he was a good lad, Bill, we enjoyed playing under his captaincy and we had a good time, enjoying ourselves as well." A pretty easy going sort of guy who gets on well with others.' And that he was.

Steele Bishop

Pursuit Cycling

Born 29 April 1953: Perth, Western Australia
Specialized: 15 years old
Career highlights:
1968 Won State schoolboy title at 15 years old
1973 Turned professional at 21
1983 Won the World title and was made Australia's Sportsman of the Year
Personal best for the 5000m pursuit, 5 min 51 sec
Steele Bishop was a professional for ten years, during which time he won thirteen Australian professional championships and nearly thirty State amateur and professional titles

His most memorable moment was the World Championships in 1983. 'It was great to stand up there and have the world shirt put on you and the gold medal and then the Australian flag and anthem being played. That was really great.

'Besides that, my most memorable win would be Westeral [25 March 1984 in Midland, in front of his home crowd], the last race I rode in my career . . . not only because it was my last race but I won it in really good style. Over 3km I had a 450m handicap in the heats. There should have been no hope of winning. In the final it was a 280m handicap and with 500m to go they were still about 100m ahead, yet I caught them and went ahead with 150m to go and sat up in the final straight saluting to the crowd. It was the same at the World Championships. I saw Robert Dill-bundi up the track and I knew that was the world title, fifty metres up the track . . . all I had to do was catch him. I just lifted. It's unbelievable what strength comes out. In this case being my last race and wanting to win so badly, I came from an impossible position and won and I just couldn't believe it. The crowd couldn't believe it.'

How would he want to be remembered? 'I like the title I have in the East – "the gentle giant". I'm always pretty fair and straight. I'd like to be remembered as retiring as world champion, undefeated. That was my big goal. That's what I set and I did it.'

Steele was possibly the most fully prepared of all the champions I spoke with, not simply in terms of the time he spent training which was awesome, but in surrounding himself with every possible assistance, from chiropractor to psychologist, from trainer to masseur. If he thought it would enhance his performance he would try it so long as it was within the rules. Steele kept learning and applying what he discovered. To him there were no barriers which he could not overcome.

Valeriy Borzov
***Athletics** (Sprint)*
Born 20 October 1949: Lvov, Ukraine
Specialized: 12 years old
Career highlights:
1968 European junior 100m and 200m winner
1969 European champion 100m
1970 European champion 60m indoors
1971 European champion 100m and 200m
1972 Munich Olympic champion 100m (10.14 sec) and 200m (20.00 sec)
Borzov is the only European athlete to have won the Olympic sprint double

Valeriy started by saying that the reason he ran was his name. In Russian, Borzov means 'speed'! Although the Soviet sports authorities said that Valeriy was made rather than born a sprinter, he believed that the natural gifts were in fact the most important component of success. 'First talent, second work and third control of the mind. The modern athlete should be intellectual.' Valeriy worked with scientists in Kiev to develop a programme of training based on a study of his capabilites. The resulting combination of power, smoothness and a relaxed action proved to be irrestible in 1972.

Valeriy said that his most memorable moments were winning the Munich Olympics 100m gold in 10.14 sec and setting a personal best in the heats of 10.07 sec. He said that he would like to be remembered for having left something in the sport.

Ian Botham

Cricket (*All-rounder*)
Born 24 November 1955: Heswall, Cheshire
Specialized: Never
Career highlights:
1974 Began first-class career with Somerset; captain in 1985
1977 Began England career: eighty-five consecutive games for England, 1977–1984; captain in 1980–81
Highest first-class innings 228 for Somerset v. Gloucestershire, 1980
Best bowling performance 8-34 for England v. Pakistan, Lord's 1978
1,000 runs and 100 wickets in record fewest Tests–21
2,000 runs and 200 wickets in record fewest Tests–42
Reached 350 Test wickets in April 1986 in the West Indies

Ian's most memorable moment and one which will live for ever in the minds of English cricket followers was his magical performance against Australia at Headingly in 1981. Ian simply said, 'We followed on and came back to beat them'. How it happened was staggering. England had followed on and were 105 for 5 when Ian came in, England still trailing by 122 runs. With the help of Graham Dilley who scored 56 runs to Ian's 149 not out, England moved from 135 for 7 on the arrival of Dilley, to a total of 356. Bob Willis took up the challenge and England won by 18 runs! Ian said that an equally enjoyable performance was playing for Somerset in the Gillette Cup. Middlesex had set them 220 runs to win. Somerset were 55 for 5 but a 98 not out score from Ian won the match.

How did he cope with stress? Ian will never admit defeat until the last ball has been bowled. He said, 'I'm a survivor . . . I believe that no situation is beyond repair . . . half the battle of stress is you think you're under stress.' He would like to be remembered as 'a sportsman – a person who was prepared to do anything within the rules and the bounds of the game to win it, but be the first guy to have a beer with afterwards. I played hard but enjoyed it and was still a friend afterwards. I'd also like to be remembered for my loyalty to my fellow pros.

'As a person, as I am really – just a big softy. I'm a soft touch for every charity. [Ian walked the length of Britain in October and November 1985, raising funds for leukaemia research.] At the end of the day I'd rather be known as a person rather than a cricketer. My real friends are because of Ian Botham, not Ian Botham the cricketer.'

Ann Brightwell (née Packer)
Athletics *(Sprint, Long jump and Middle-distance)*
Born 8 March 1942: Moulsford, Berkshire
Specialized: 19 years old
Career highlights:
1959 Won English Schools 100 yds
1960 Won WAAA long jump
1962 Finalist in European Championship 200m; finalist in the Commonwealth Games 80m hurdles
1964 Tokyo Olympics, silver medal in 400m in a European record of 52.2 sec; gold medal in 800m in 2 min 01.1 sec – a new world record

The variety of events above show Ann's versatility. One wonders what she could have done if she had not retired at twenty-two. Her most memorable win was, 'When I won my first All England Schools. That was quite on a par with the emotion of winning the Olympics.'

Her best example of holding together under stress was during the Tokyo Olympics. The schedule of events was such that on six consecutive days Ann had the heats, semi-final and final of the 400m and then the 800m. She said, 'I found it very difficult to get myself together for the heat of the 800m. It wasn't anything physical because I was strong. It was psychological stress as a result of failing to win the 400m. Losing the 400m was a major disappointment for me. If I'd gone out in the first round of the 800m, nobody would have been surprised.' She had only run the event twice in her life before the Olympics. Needless to say, David Coleman's commentary was alive with emotion as Ann raced from seventh to first place in the final 150m to her Olympic win.

Ann took a long time before speaking about how she would want to be remembered. 'Well, I know how I will be remembered because that is established, and because it is already there, it isn't important to me. I would like people to remember me for being altruistic along the way, to have been of a generous nature, not to have just been an athlete. The important thing when you're married and have a family is that you're there in your children and that you are remembered in them and that some sort of spirit of yourself will transfer to them. I don't mean athletic ability. I suppose even now, I just want to be remembered as a reasonable sort of person, a person that others could go to for help and advice.

David Bryant

Bowls

Born 27 October 1931: Bristol, Gloucestershire
Specialized: 16 years old
Career highlights:
International Masters 1978, 1979, 1982, 1984, 1985
Indoor English Singles 1964, 1965, 1967, 1969, 1971, 1972, 1977, 1979, 1983
Outdoor English Singles 1960, 1966, 1971–73, 1975
Indoor British Isles Singles 1967, 1969, 1977, 1979
Outdoor British Isles Singles 1960, 1971–73
United Kingdom Masters 1983
Granada Superbowl 1984
Commonwealth Games Champion 1962, (1966 not held), 1970, 1974, 1978
Embassy Indoor World Champion 1979–81
Outdoor World Champion 1966, 1980

David Bryant has been called 'the Bradman of bowls'. It was also said that if W.G. Grace was the first cricketer, then Bryant was the first bowler. He has played at international level for nearly thirty years and dominated the sport for a good part of that time.

The most memorable win for him was the Commonwealth Games in Perth in 1962. Beginning with the fours, he won all thirteen matches: it was the only time it has happened. For many years he was called the unofficial world champion because until 1979 there were no World Championships.

His best illustration of holding together under stress and 'raising his game' was being behind 17–20 twice in the World Championships, and winning both times. He said, 'When you're playing badly and you're behind, you have to have a plan to get out. You have to play conditions which suit you the most. Keep it as simple as possible. Don't be dictated to by opponents and be taken off your best hand. You must also learn from your previous bowls.'

As far as how he would want to be remembered, David said, 'As a sportsman, for my skill and playing in the right manner – with sportsmanship, not for what I won but as someone who was good for the game. As a person, as someone who was easy going – a friendly person – and easy to get on with.'

Greg Chappell

***Cricket** (Batsman)*

Born 7 August 1948: Unley, South Australia
Specialized: 19 years old

Career highlights:

Most Test runs by an Australian 7,110 in 87 Tests (average 53.86)
Most Test catches 122
Career batting 24,535 runs at 52.20
Career bowling 291 wickets at 29.96
Career catches 376
Australian captain from 1975–82, with breaks for World Series Cricket. Captained Australia on a record 48 occasions

After two seasons playing in England, Greg decided not to make cricket his full-time job. He said, 'I didn't want to do it as a job . . . I enjoyed playing cricket as a sport.'

Greg cited several memorable moments on tours. 'My first tour of England in 1972 to the home of cricket. We drew the series but we won two very memorable Test matches, one at Lord's and the other at The Oval – that was probably the turning point of Australian cricket at that stage.

'Then there was my first tour of the West Indies, where cricket is so popular. We weren't expected to win the series. We won and there was one particularly memorable Test match in Trinidad in 1973; also the Centenary Test match in Melbourne in 1977, and winning the Ashes back in Sydney in 1975 and then winning them again in 1982.

'As a batsman, to make a hundred runs, all the thrill is in getting there because of the anxiety, nervous tension, concentration and effort and when you've got there it's more an anti-climax . . . feeling it's a job well done but the more important thing is the next innings. The culmination of the season's efforts coming together in a great team performance, far outweighs any individual performance for me.'

Greg mentioned two occasions when he held together under stress. In both cases outside incidents were mentally put to one side. The first was when his wife was expecting their first child: he saw that she was not in her seat and knew that something must have been wrong. The other was in Brisbane in 1974 when he was told between innings that his home had been flooded. In both cases he said, 'There was nothing I could have done about it at the time,' and so decided he was better off concentrating on what he was doing and finding out about what had happened later.

How would Greg want to be remembered? 'I'd like to be remembered as someone who developed their talent and their potential to the fullest. But I don't want to be recognized or remembered only as somebody who had a sporting talent and developed it. I'd like to think that I can be successful in other areas – in business, as a successful father and a husband and somebody who leads a good life in the community and does things to help the community in general, rather than just for myself.'

Bobby Charlton
Soccer *(Inside forward)*
Born 11 October 1937: Ashington, Northumberland
Specialized: 15 years old
Career highlights:
644 Football League appearances, beginning in October 1956. He played his last game with Manchester United on 28 April 1973 having only received one 'booking' in all his appearances with them. He retired from Preston North End on 29 March 1975, having amassed a total of 206 League goals. He made 106 International appearances, scoring 49 goals.
With Manchester United he won League Championship medals in 1956–57, 1957–58 and 1966–67; the FA Cup in 1963; the European Cup in 1968. He was in the England team which won the World Cup in 1966, and was voted British and European Footballer of the Year in the same year.

Bobby's most memorable win was also cited as his best example of holding together under stress. 'We won the European Cup against Benfica and the World Cup against West Germany but my most significant win was against Real Madrid in the semi-final of the European Cup the year we won it [1968]. We had beaten them 1–0 at home, but in Madrid we were 3–1 down at half-time, so they were in the lead on aggregate and they'd annihilated us in the first half. In the second half, they'd slackened a little and it gave us a chance to get back into the game. We scored to make it 3–2 and equal on aggregate. Before we scored again to win the match, I remember the ball went out of play and there are no barriers in Madrid. A member of the public leaned over from his seat and picked up the ball. I thought if I dash to get the ball from him he might throw it away, which will take more time, so I said to myself, "Just stay calm" and I walked across and put my hand out for the ball and he put the ball in my hand and I took the throw-in. I thought if I had said, "Come on, give me the ball!" he might have thrown it down the touchline, which would be quite the norm, but he didn't and I thought, "You've done well there", because it was really a stress situation. But you make lots of decisions like that on the field when you're actually playing, saying to yourself, don't panic, take your time, have a rest, pass that one sideways not forward, it'll just give you that little bit of time to settle down and it'll give our players time to adjust their positions again.'

Asked how he would want to be remembered, Bobby replied, 'As a good player. I mean, people say nice things about me all the time and it is very nice, but if I wanted to be remembered, it's as a bloody good player, Bobby Charlton, that would please me a lot. I was a good player but sometimes I think that maybe I could have scored a few more goals, maybe been a bit more selfish and gone forward a bit more, but I wouldn't change what I did, really. I was very pleased with what we won and what we achieved. I was very lucky that I was with the greatest club in the country, Manchester United.'

Sebastian Coe
***Athletics** (Middle-distance)*
Born 29 September 1956: London
Specialized: 14 years old
Career highlights:
1978 European Championships, 800m bronze
1980 Moscow Olympics, 800m silver, 1500m gold
1982 European Championships, 800m silver
1984 Los Angeles Olympics, 800m silver, 1500m gold
World records: 800m 1 min 42.33 sec, 1979; 1 min 41.72 sec, 1981; 1000m 2 min 13.4 sec, 1980; 2 min 12.18 sec, 1981; 1500m 3 min 32.1 sec, 1979; mile 3 min 49.00 sec, 1979; 3 min 48.53 sec, 1981; 3 min 47.33 sec, 1981.
Coe is the only athlete to have retained the Olympic 1500m title

While saying that intensity made all the difference to his success, Seb gave an example of a session which he said was harder than any racing – and I can well believe it! The session illustration was the 1200m in 2 min 51/52 sec, two minutes later, 800m in 1 min 51 sec, then 600m in 1 min 18 sec and finally a 400m in 49/50 sec.

Seb said his most memorable moment was, 'The 1500m win in Los Angeles because it was the uniqueness of a second Olympic win at that distance and the fact that, other than close friends, nobody thought it was possible, six weeks beforehand.'

His best illustration of holding together well under stress was at the Moscow Olympics: 'Coming back after three days.' Seb had been labelled clear favourite for the 800m, which Ovett won with Seb in second place. The Press followed him on a distance run the following day and entitled a photo, "Seb's trail of shame!" Seb showed what he was made of by coming back to win the 1500m title.

How he would want to be remembered? 'As an athlete, as somebody who wasn't afraid to commit themselves to an idea, to an aim, to a system in athletics. It was a gamble that paid off and ultimately it is the way that most people are now training at 800m, marrying pure sprinting with the endurance work that's needed to run a very good 5000m. I'm proudest of all of being involved in the experiment that pioneered an approach to 800m racing. Also athletically as someone who has reacted very well under pressure, normally coming through with an element of success, and I hate to say it, with an element of dignity I suppose, in that I've managed to put it into perspective.'

As a person, he would like to be remembered as, 'Somebody who will be considered basically honest in what they stood for, who wasn't swayed too much by outside influences. Basically trustworthy to people and friends, within the confines of inordinate pressures from athletics as well.'

***Margaret Court** (née Smith)*
Tennis
Born 16 July 1942: Albury, New South Wales
Specialized: 14 years old
Career highlights:
Major Championship singles titles:
Wimbledon 1963, 1965, 1970
US 1962, 1965, 1968–70, 1973
French 1962, 1964, 1969, 1970, 1973
Italian 1962–64
German 1964–66
South African 1968
Australian 1960–66, 1969–71, 1973
Grand Slam 1970
No. 1 world ranking 1962–65, 1970

Margaret was the first Australian woman to win Wimbledon. The most memorable event in Margaret's tennis career was, 'The year I won the Grand Slam [1970] because I'd played at the top so long and twice previously I'd come so close.' In 1962 she had won the Australian and French championships but went out in the first round of Wimbledon. Margaret showed her will to win when she phoned home. Her mother had said, 'Well, I suppose you'll be coming home now.' Margaret said, 'I thought, no way, I'm going to show them all how to play and I went on to win the next thirteen or fourteen straight tournaments.'

How she would want to be remembered is tied closely with the fact that at the end of her playing days, Margaret became a 'Born Again Christian'. 'It's funny, I never look back on my playing career except when somebody comes along and asks about it. I wonder, sometimes, if I ever really did it. It's interesting because that door is closed and another is open to me. I think that winning souls for Jesus is more exciting to me today than winning Wimbledon. I only start to talk about that and I start crying. People are saved and my heart's there.'

Bob Cousy

***Basketball** (Play-making guard)*
Born 9 August 1928: Massachusetts
Specialized: 14 years old
Career highlights:
1950–63 Played for Boston Celtics
1969–70 Played for Cincinatti
Bob Cousy played a total of 924 games for the National Basketball Association, scoring 16,960 pts at an average of 18.4 per game
NBA Championship wins 1957, 1959, 1960–63
Played in 109 play-off games, averaging 18.5 per game
NBA Most Valuable Player 1957
Elected to the NBA Hall of Fame 1970

His most memorable win or personal achievement was, 'Winning the National Championships for the first time. We'd done six years in the pro's without winning it. Obviously the longer you go towards a particular goal the more meaningful it becomes when you achieve it. I was around for five more championship wins. Whenever it happened it was meaningful, special, but the first one, that's the most important.'

His best example of holding together under stress was, 'That four overtime game we played against Syracuse in 1953. Everyone literally collapsed, it was a hot afternoon – Syracuse ended up with only four men on the floor, I scored fifty points, made thirty out of thirty-two free throws and all of them in the overtime. It was the first time we'd ever made it into the play-offs. Syracuse was a bitter rival at the time. It was very dramatic, four overtimes, everyone fouling out, a pressure-packed game. I guess that's the personal highlight of my life; I often said it was my claim to fame. I scored 50 points in that game – one game with four overtimes, the same that Wilt Chamberlain [a 7 ft 4 in centre for Los Angeles Lakers] averaged in one year!

'Given my cynicism, I really don't care how I am remembered. I'm a present person. I hang those medals in the cellar and I seldom look at them. I take a certain pride in terms of accomplishing something. I've established an identity in the world, even though it's a child's game. I'd be lying if I denied that I get a certain amount of pleasure out of it but I don't worry about the past at all. I know my image is a positive one, I think, and fine, I'd rather have that than be thought of as someone who won using gamesmanship or who was a bully out there. I'd rather be remembered in a kindly way but there are so many more important things . . . I've rearranged the priorities at this point in my life.'

To an earlier question, Bob had spoken of the great impact sport can have in psychological and social terms when a youngster is growing up. 'I tell kids now, I think you do absorb a lot of everyday beneficial lessons through participation in sport that you can apply to life. All the things we're aware of, the dedication, sacrifice, working with other people, taking instructions, how to be a good loser and a humble winner.'

Steve Cram
***Athletics** (Middle-distance)*
Born 14 October 1960: Gateshead, Northumberland
Specialized: 13 years old
Career highlights:
1982 Commonwealth Games, 1500m gold
1982 European Championships, 1500m gold
1983 European Championships, 1500m gold
1983 World Championships, 1500m gold
1984 Los Angeles Olympics, 1500m silver
World records: 1500m 3min 29.67sec, 1985; Mile 3min 46.31sec, 1985; 2000m 4min 51.39sec, 1985

Steve's most memorable moment to date has been the World Championships in 1983. 'I like surprising myself. That's what I look for. The biggest kick, the most personal satisfaction came from running 1 min 43.6sec in the 800m after my World Championship win in Helsinki in 1983. The World Championships were very important and it meant a lot but any athlete worth his salt would have half expected it. When you think you're going to win, it's a bit of a relief when you do. But to go and run 1 min 43.6sec surprised me . . . more than winning a normal championship race.'

Steve said that there are so many races which he knows he is going to win, that he sets challenges for himself. 'I like to try something different like running the last 400m in 52 seconds.'

His best illustration of holding together under stress was at the European Championships in 1982. 'For the first time in my life I was favourite in a major championships and I felt the pressure a lot, from media people saying, "No problem". I knew I should win but I still had to go out there and do it, plus getting out in front with so far to go and then starting to tire and holding on. So I suppose that was holding it together in that sense.'

How would he want to be remembered? 'As someone that could always be relied on to give 100 per cent and was a good and fair competitor. Not someone who'd go through the motions but someone who'd try to give it a little bit extra. It would be nice to finish up with some world records, but that isn't as important as running to achieve what I want to achieve . . . no more world records wouldn't bother me but it might bother me if I never win the Olympic title.'

Steve had been interviewed prior to his record breaking 1985 season. I asked him at the end of that year whether he would change his most memorable moment, having broken three world records and also run 1 min 42.88sec for 800m. He said, 'Not really. The training and early season competitions indicated that I was capable of faster times. The 800m time in 1983 was special because it was an unexpected break-through.'

How would he want to be remembered? 'Easy going and fun to be with. I prefer to have an easy life and enjoy things rather than get too serious about anything. I like to feel I always have the option to stop. At present I'm enjoying it.'

Lynn Davies

***Athletics** (Long jump)*

Born 20 May 1942: Nantymoel, Glamorgan
Specialized: 18 years old
Career highlights:
1964 Tokyo Olympics, gold
1966 Commonwealth Games, gold
1966 European Championships, gold
1970 Commonwealth Games, gold
Lynn raised the UK record by almost two feet during his career; he jumped over 26 ft on 67 occasions.
Personal bests: 100m 10.4 sec; 200m 21.2 sec; long jump 27 ft 0 in; triple jump 50 ft 7 in

His most memorable moment was in the Tokyo Olympics in 1964. 'I was going to make the Olympic final if things went well, possibly even the bronze; in fact coach Ron Pickering's last words to me at the warm-up were, "You can get the bronze". Half-way through the competition, I perceived that the weather conditions were bad and I suddenly realized that I could win. It was like a sudden insight, no one had jumped over 26 ft [7.88m] and I knew that I could jump eight metres in those conditions. It was purely psychological but I snatched the opportunity.' Lynn jumped 8.07m (26 ft $5\frac{3}{4}$ in) and the others responded but could not catch him.

What made Lynn different from others with similar natural gifts? 'I wanted to be the best. Others thought they did but it was reflected in the amount of training I did and the importance I placed on it within my life style. It wasn't so important in the others' lives and they did other things. I loved physical activity and was a physical fitness fanatic. One person might say, "Well, I'm here, I've made the Olympic final." Another will perceive it as a life and death situation. I was going to try to win and in those critical seconds or minutes prior to the start of the next jump, it was the ability to place enormous pressure on oneself to do it. Certainly in the Olympic final the one who wants to win most will win. The margin of physical ability isn't that great. Generally the eight people in a final have similar physical ability, it's what the person feels and thinks that is critical.'

How would he want to be remembered? 'Just basically as a competitive athlete and Olympic gold medallist – the Olympic gold medal representing the pinnacle of any athlete's life I suppose.' And as a person? 'Somewhat as a contrast, as a reasonable guy yet a competitive athlete. It is possible to have a separate personality in a competitive situation and in your normal life. A lot of people seem to expect that you'll be highly competitive in everything you do. I don't try to be the centre of attention or the funniest in the group, whereas some others are like that.'

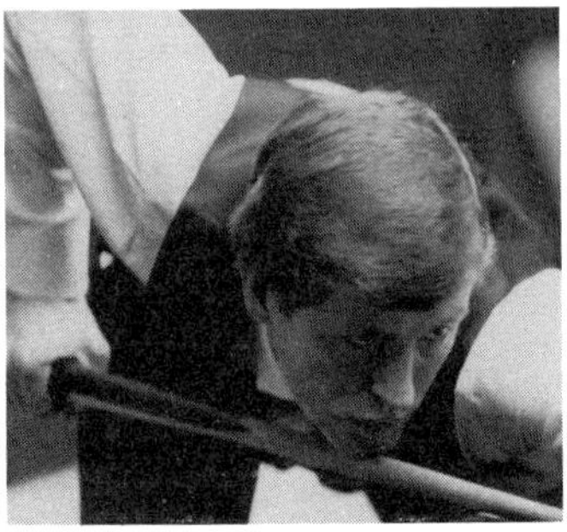

Steve Davis

Snooker

Born 22 August 1957: Plumstead, London
Specialized: 16 years old
Career highlights:
Major Tournament wins:
Coral U.K. 1980, 1981, 1984, 1985
Dulux British Open 1986
Embassy World Professional 1981, 1983, 1984
Yamaha International Masters 1981, 1982
Tolly Cobbold English Professional 1981, 1985
Jameson International 1981, 1983, 1984
State Express World Team 1981, 1983, 1984; Pot Black 1982, 1983
Benson and Hedges Masters 1982; Scottish Masters 1982–84
Hofmeister World Doubles 1982–85
Benson and Hedges Irish Masters 1983, 1984; Rothmans Grand Prix 1985

Steve pointed out the requirement in top sportsmen is for emotional intensity to be coupled with control. That self-control has been clearly demonstrated by Steve in several championships. He cited the 1981 World Championship semi-final match with Cliff Thorburn as both his most memorable win and his best illustration of holding together under stress. 'The reason why it meant so much to me was that I went through a very bad patch of losing four frames on the trot and from being 6–4 in front I went to 8–6 behind and, up to that stage, when I got behind in matches, I'd always sort of crumbled. I was okay as long as I was in front all the time. I didn't pot a black for an hour, I was in agony in the chair, but you've just got to sit there, there's nothing you can do. It was the first time I had come from behind. I actually came out at night completely changed. In a way I was putting on an act but I just didn't move a muscle when I was sitting in the chair. The fact that I was capable of putting on an act meant that I was in control of myself and that changed the whole swing of the game.' Steve won that best of thirty-one games 16–10.

How would he want to be remembered? 'As a player, the greatest player that has ever held a cue, a tough thing to do because it's a different era, or the greatest player of my era. As an individual inside the game, as a sportsman, a fair player, a winner who puts on a good show. I don't particularly want to be liked by my fellow professionals, but as long as I'm respected as a player and as a person, that's all you can hope for.'

Steve quoted a line from the film *Whose Life Is It Anyway*. The scene shows a sculptor who was paralyzed through a road accident; he was asked why he did not want to write or teach. Steve said, 'I can identify with his reply which was, "It's the doing of it, not the result, that matters."'

Robert de Castella
***Athletics** (Marathon)*
Born 27 February 1957: Melbourne, Victoria
Specialized: 15 years old
Career highlights:
1979 Victoria Marathon champion; Australian Marathon champion
1980 Moscow Olympics, tenth
1981 Fukuoka Invitational Marathon, winner
1982 Brisbane Commonwealth Games, gold
1983 Rotterdam Marathon, winner
1983 World Championships, gold
1984 Los Angeles Olympics, fifth

Rob's most memorable win was, 'Certainly from a competitive point of view, Rotterdam 1983 against Salazaar and Lopes because it was such a tough and close one. It was great to beat him [Salazaar, who had been undefeated and held the world best time] but it would have been more satisfying if he'd been in 100 per cent shape. [Salazaar finished fifth. Lopes, the 1984 Olympic winner, was just two seconds behind Rob's time of 2 hr 08 min 37 sec.] From an athletic prestige point of view, the 1983 World Championships in Helsinki and from a personal and emotional point of view, the 1982 Commonwealth Games because it was in Australia and because it was my first big international and I felt I had a fair bit to prove.'

How would he like to be remembered? 'As an athlete who was extremely successful and dominated the event for a period of time. To be remembered out of the era you competed in. It takes an outstanding athlete to be remembered by youngsters coming up. Off the track – as an honest, sincere person, competent, determined but not ruthless.'

Shirley de la Hunty *(née Strickland)*
Athletics *(Hurdles and Sprint)*
Born 18 July 1925:
Guildford, Australia
Specialized: 21 years old
Career highlights:
1948 London Olympics, 100m bronze; 80m hurdles bronze; 4 × 100m relay silver
1950 Commonwealth Games, three gold and two silver medals
1952 Helsinki Olympics, 100m bronze; 80m hurdles gold (in a world and Olympic record of 10.9 sec)
1956 Melbourne Olympics, 80m hurdles gold (in a world and Olympic record of 10.7 sec); 4 × 100m gold (world record of 44.5 sec)
Additional world records 80m hurdles 10.7 sec; 100m 11.3 sec in 1955 – a record which stood for nine years

Shirley's most memorable win was, 'The first gold medal in Helsinki [1952 Olympics] in the hurdles. It was a dream-like place, in a foreign country where the crowds were tremendous. It was a beautiful day. I didn't feel equal to the task but I knew I was committed. I had been injured beforehand and I think I kept that quiet, but I didn't know how much that had taken from me. I was still taking this big gamble that Professor Cotton had talked me into doing and that was to take a week off before competing. I remember nothing about the race, just the wind in my eyes and then going through the tape and the unbelievable feeling that I had actually won. It was so unbelievable I didn't know what to do to express the feeling. I just remember this corner where there was a small group of Australians going mad and I will never forget the moment, it's imprinted on my brain.'

Shirley said that her best illustration of handling stress was the 11.3 sec 100m world record in 1955. It was the self-imposed mental stress to execute what had been repeatedly, mentally rehearsed and it took intense concentration. Shirley took half a second off her previous best time.

'I would like to be remembered for things other than athletics, for compassion perhaps . . . if people remember me. As a compassionate person who cared about other people, standards and the land. I don't want to be remembered as a crank. There's a certain stigma attached if you're a conservationist, a greeny! But I'm proud to be a greeny all the same . . . As a person who leaves this world a little better for having been in it and that's as much as I could expect. Some of the feelings I have about the world I would class as religion though not in the formal sense. Relationships of people and the relationship of the human race to the world. I have strong feelings about the world, the evolution of the human race and it's influence on the world and conservation. I love the land.'

Ralph Doubell

***Athletics** (Middle-distance)*
Born 11 February 1945: Melbourne, Victoria
Specialized: 17 years old
Career highlights:
1967 World Student Games, 800m gold
1968 Mexico City Olympics, 800m gold equalling Peter Snell's world record of 1 min 44.3 sec
1970 World best indoor 1000 yds 2 min 5.5 sec

Ralph's most valued win was the Mexico Olympics in 1968. 'With sixty yards to go I passed the favourite, Kenyan Wilson Kiprugut and I thought, "I'm going to win it, I'm going to win it, I'm going to win it" – and I did in 1 min 44.3 sec. For forty yards we had been together and there was a physical or psychological break with 50 to 60 yards to go. Just that extra push and I felt I had broken contact and all I had to do was finish it – that was my most satisfying sporting moment.'

Other than the Mexico Games, Ralph's best example of holding together under stress was given as the time at the World University Games in 1967. Franz-Joseph Kemper was the European record holder and European champion. Ralph was virtually unknown but managed to beat him in those Games, giving a good indication of things to come in the 1968 Olympics.

How would he like to be remembered? 'As an athlete, a person who could win a major championship in a classic way, and the 1968 Olympic 800m was a classic confrontation of the front runner versus the kicker and it was a finish where the kicker won. As a person, as someone who achieved his potential in whatever field. I don't think I'll ever be remembered as an overly aggressive or overly flamboyant type of person but basically a person who can achieve what he sets out to achieve.'

Des Drummond

***Rugby League** (Wing)*

Born 17 June 1958: Westmorland, Jamaica
Specialized: 16 years old
Career highlights:
1976 Signed professional for Leigh
1979–80 International debut
1980 Scored two tries in the historic British win (10–2) in New Zealand
1980–81, 1981–82 Truman's Young Player of the Year
1982 Runner-up in British Superstars and fifth in the World Superstars in Hong Kong
1984–85 Member of Great Britain touring team to Australia, New Zealand and Papua New Guinea

The most memorable game or personal performance that Des recalled was one derby match, Leigh against Wigan in 1982. 'I got the ball on our twenty-five and I went down the middle and beat a few players and scored under the sticks. That was one of the best tries I've ever scored and I really enjoyed that. Plus, it added to it because it was away and a derby match.'

Des said that his best example of holding together under stress was while playing for Leigh in the quarter-finals of the Challenge Cup against Hull Kingston Rovers. 'The lead kept changing, four or five times, and we ended up winning. It was a tough game and they were a good team, but we held out. We were back and forth across the pit. It was played at such a fast pace. Our team was playing well, and I was playing well, tackling and running.'

Part of Des's character is illustrated when he said, 'If I miss a tackle, I'm mad at myself but my head doesn't drop. I say to myself, next time, I have to do better.'

How would he want to be remembered? 'In the same way as Billy Boston, who played for Wigan and Great Britain, as a nice bloke. I'd want to be remembered as greater, but from a different era.' And as a person? 'As a kind person and a fun-loving person. I don't bother anyone unless they bother me. I get on with anybody as long as they're truthful and not trying to exploit me.'

Gareth Edwards

***Rugby Union** (Scrum-half)*

Born 12 July 1947: Gwaen-cae-Gurwen, Wales
Specialized: 18 years old

Career highlights:

1967 International debut, aged nineteen.
Named captain before he was twenty-one
Fifty-three international appearances, scoring 20 tries (a Welsh record)
Grand Slam 1976, 1978; Triple Crown 1969, 1971, 1976–78
International Championship 1969–72, 1975, 1976, 1978
Ten Test appearances with the British Lions

What was Gareth's most memorable event or win? 'I've never been able to pinpoint it over the years because there is no pinnacle like winning an Olympics. There have been many particularly joyous moments but you can't say it was the pinnacle. To be picked for Wales for the first time and then the fiftieth timc were both memorable moments for me, but they were only achievements and they go no further than that.There were also great team achievements winning abroad with the Lions in New Zealand in 1971 and in South Africa in 1974 which meant I'd won in both recognized World Championship countries. To win the Triple Crown three times in succession with Wales has to be a yardstick of achievement but I can't say that one was more important than the other.'

Regarding holding together under stress, Gareth said, 'Against, for example, the All Blacks, you might be behind 13–0 at half-time or you've used the wind and you're up 13–0 and hanging on in the second half, tackling everybody and absorbing pressure. It's pushing yourself when it hurts and not wanting to lose. This I think is the difference between champions and "also rans". In rugby the pressure is absorbed physically. Half-way through one game for Cardiff versus Llanelli a chap got on my back and I went down with a hamstring. I was sick – I knew there was a match the next Saturday against Ireland. I thought that was it. I turned up at training on the Sunday and told the selectors but they said, "Don't tell anybody, don't make a hasty decision, we'll get it tested, but don't pull out." So I went for treatment and it felt a bit better. I went to training on Thursday and they said, "Strap it up". The coach said, "It's important that you play – for you and for the team, for everybody." That I call pressure because I had to go on and play a restricted game. I was criticized for it because there were opportunities which I couldn't take and the Press didn't know that.' That incident occurred after ten consecutive years of international representation by Gareth.

How would he want to be remembered as a player? 'As having brought a lot of entertainment to people. I find one of the nicest things I get is to be stopped by someone who says, "Thank you for the amount of pleasure you gave me whilst you played".' And as an individual outside of sport? 'In life, as a nice bloke. I don't want to be the richest man in the world or anything materially. With my friends, being happy and still being identified with the game.'

Herb Elliott

***Athletics** (Middle-distance)*
Born 25 February 1938: Perth, Western Australia
Specialized: 18 years old
Career highlights:
1954–60 Unbeaten in his 44 races over 1500m and mile
1958 Commonwealth Games, 880 yds and mile gold
1960 Rome Olympics, 1500m gold
World records: 1500m 3min 36.0sec, 1958; 3min 35.6sec, 1960; mile 3min 54.5sec, 1958

What was Herb Elliott's most memorable win or valued event? 'The Olympic Games in 1960, I'd have to say. It was just that so much pressure was on me for that particular race – for all sorts of reasons, even just the sense of relief once I had actually done it. It would have to be the most significant thing that happened in my athletic career.'

His best illustration of holding together under stress was: 'Every race! I can't really pick any one out.' Herb placed tremendous pressure on himself in training and competition. He was known for his intensity in those areas and stated that he believed his training was totally useless until it started to hurt.

How would he want to be remembered as an athlete? 'I guess the way I am remembered as an athlete, I'm happy with whatever that was. Something a bit different, someone who could be relied on to produce a bloody good performance every time that I performed.' [Herb's record of being undefeated over the premier track distances for six years is unique.] And as a person, 'I think probably as a reasonable, decent sort of person. I think I'd like to be seen in that way.'

David Forbes

***Yachting** (Star class)*

Born 26 January 1934: Sydney, New South Wales

Specialized: 14 years old

Career highlights:

1968 Mexico Olympics, Star class, sixth

1972 World Championships, International 5.5 class, gold

1972 Munich Olympics, Star class, gold

1975 World Championships, Soling class, second

Four Admirals Cups; Five Sydney to Hobart races

What was David Forbes's most memorable event or win? 'The gold medal has to be the most valued but it wasn't the most difficult win. In Olympic yachting, there's only one from each country racing. The fleet is smaller, so I don't think it's as hard to win the actual race itself, but it's mentally harder to win because there's a lot more pressure on you. The pre-Olympic regatta in Canada was the best I ever did. We had about eighty Soling racers and we won without having to sail the last heat, but that was probably the toughest regatta from a competitive point of view.'

What was his best illustration of holding together under stress? 'There were many. I've sailed with some top yachtsmen, holding on when things were equal; not giving up over time, steering the boat to gain one foot on him over a wave and keeping on doing that until I've got him. It may go on for five minutes. It's not an explosive sport at all. It's a matter of constant concentration and perseverence, gradually grinding past somebody.'

How would he like to be remembered? 'As someone who hasn't trodden on people too much to get where I'm going – or where I've come from. I wouldn't like to think that people would hold it against me because I've been selfish in achieving my goals – in sport or whatever else I do. I think people should understand that to be successful you have to be fairly ruthless in how you handle yourself, but if that doesn't happen then I can't do anything about it because you won't win unless you have this attitude. I believe it's very important. You can't be such a person who looks after everybody's feelings and still win. You've got to tread on some toes. I'd like to be remembered as someone who hasn't been totally ruthless in their treatment of human beings . . . I don't think I've been successful enough for people to remember me for any great period anyway.'

John Gilmour
***Athletics** (Long-distance)*
Born 3 May 1919: Ayr, Scotland
Now resident in Australia
Specialized: 26 years old
Career highlights:
1937 Started competing aged 18
Post-war, following three and a half years as a POW, John won the State ten mile title. He became blind as a result of malnutrition as a POW, but can see enough to identify the curb of the track.
1956 Aged 37, won the Western Australian Marathon
1970 Aged 51, started veterans career
1971 Won 5000m and 10,000m at World Veteran Championships
1983 Aged 64, World Veterans Championships, Hanover; within five days won the 800m, 1500m, 5000m, 10,000m and marathon
1985 Aged 66, following months off due to a ruptured Achilles tendon, he ran 1500m in 4 min 49 sec; 5000m in 17 min 25 sec; 10,000m in 36 min 25 sec; and the marathon in 3 hr 10 min

It was reported that Herb Elliott called John the greatest track and field athlete in Australia. His record is impressive not only because he has won so many titles but he has shown that advancing age need not be as much of a disadvantage as most people allow themselves to think. His times alter little with age.

John's most memorable moment was, 'Winning all the races at Hanover in the sixty to sixty-four age category [at 800m, 1500m, 5000m, 10,000m and marathon]. Also running the Olympic qualifying time at aged fifty-nine! At thirty-seven I had won the Western Australian Marathon in 3 hr 4 min. Aged fifty-nine, in the Australian Open, the Olympic qualifying time was 2 hr 40 min and I ran 2 hr 38 min.'

How would he like to be remembered? 'As a good sport, who enjoyed being with people, made a lot of friends through sport, lifetime friends and who got on well with other athletes. Athletics has been really good to me. I've had a good life out of it. I would like to be remembered as an example of what can be achieved by the older sportsman, especially in relation to running, fitness and health.'

Duncan Goodhew

***Swimming** (100m breaststroke)*
Born 27 May 1957: London
Specialized: 17 years old
Career highlights:
1976 Montreal Olympics, 100m breaststroke, seventh (he set an Olympic record in the heats of 65.0 sec)
1978–80 British swimming team captain
1980 Moscow Olympics, 100m breaststroke, gold
1980 World Invitational Masters, winner (set a World best for 110 yds)
1981 European Championships, two-man bobsleigh team
1982 World Masters, five gold medals

Duncan's most memorable moment was, 'My first International, which was the Montreal Olympics. The heat was in the morning. I walked down the side of the pool for the first time for Britain and the Queen walked in. I got on the block and swam the two lengths and broke the Olympic record swimming 65.0 sec and got to the Olympic semi-final aged nineteen. It was a very special time.'

Duncan's best illustration of holding together under stress was his win at the 1980 Olympic Games. 'I dived in and as I'd had trouble with my stroke rate because of my injury, I tried a new technique and I tried building into it, because water rips, if you pull too hard it bubbles and you spin a bit like an outboard. I built it up and worked at it for 25m and I felt as though I was going backwards. I realized then that I was going to have to start getting pretty aggressive so I hit the turn very hard. In fact I won on my dive and my turn. I came out of my turn and made my second mistake. I rushed my first stroke and I spun, which meant that with 25m to go I was in trouble and I remember saying to myself, "Duncan, if you don't do something right now you're not going to win, and that's totally absurd". The next 25m was nothing, I mean everything was right and it was that 25m where I really concentrated.'

How would he like to be remembered? 'I suppose as someone who has got time. Having gone through a bit as a kid, I'm a great believer that adversity makes or breaks, and people with adversity need time. I like to think that I would give it and, what's more, I like giving it. I do clinics and speak at conferences and my feeling is that if I do clinics and get through to one kid, then I've succeeded.'

How would he like to be remembered as an athlete? 'One thing that upsets me is that I never came through to break a world record. I set a world best time for 110 yds, some six months after the Olympic Games and I hadn't trained. I'd built myself up to the Olympics and then there were all the flings after the Games; then I swam David Wilkie up in Scotland in December and went 62.2 sec for 110 yds. As I said at the time, it's the only time when I have been truly shocked at my performance because it was as near as damn it to the time of my Olympic win.'

Lucinda Green *(née Prior-Palmer)*
Equestrianism *(Three-day eventing)*
Born 7 November 1953: London
Specialized: 18 years old
Career highlights:
1971 European Junior Championships, team gold
Winner of Badminton Horse Trials on six different horses: 1973 on Be Fair; 1976 on Wideawake; 1977 on George; 1979 on Killaire; 1983 on Regal Realm; 1984 on Beagle Bay. She was also runner-up in 1978 and 1980
1975 European Championships, individual winner on Be Fair; team runner-up
1977 European Championships, individual winner on George; team winner
1982 World Championships, individual winner on Regal Realm, team winner
1984 Olympics team captain; team silver on Regal Realm

What was Lucinda's most valued win? 'I think, the first time I won Badminton. It was like being in fairy-tale land. It sounds corny to say it but I stood there in front of the Queen with every single other person in the field behind me, and the national anthem playing because of me. I was only nineteen so I was really nothing and I suddenly thought, "It's happening to me and it can't happen to me because I was never going to be able to do this sort of thing – that was somebody else's luck." That feeling, it was such a long time ago now, I don't think it could ever be bettered. It was a wonderful feeling on the Olympic rostrum and all that but it had been seen before. It's the first time that can never ever be over-shadowed.'

Her best illustration of holding together under stress was the World Championships in 1982. 'We were one point behind the German team and half a point behind the American team which in our game is incredibly close, with twenty or thirty points difference being the norm. I was to go third which is not normally my team starting position. We'd done all the steeplechase and had ten minutes break before we set out for the cross-country and the *chef de mission* just sat down and said, "Right, no beating about the bush, if we're going to win this competition you've got to go fast and clear." Only two people had been inside the time the whole of the day. I suppose that was about as tall an order as I ever had, and I did end up winning.'

How she would want to be remembered? 'Frightful question! . . . I'd like to be remembered as not being foul, I think.' And as a sports person? 'Being decent to my horses. I think a lot of people think that horse sports are cruel. I don't think they are because I think if a horse doesn't want to do it, you can't make him. Some people have ways of being able to get him to do more than he may want to, and I would like to be remembered as not being one of them.'

Wayne Gretzky
***Ice hockey** (Centre)*
Born 26 January 1961: Brantford, Ontario
Specialized: 14 years old
Career highlights:
1978 Signed first professional contract, aged 17, joining the Edmonton Oilers
1981–82 National Hockey League record scoring 92 goals in one season
1982–83 NHL record scoring in 51 consecutive games
Since 1981 selected to the All-Star first team
1983 Won the Stanley Cup with the Edmonton Oilers
The eighteenth player in NHL history to reach the 1,000 point plateau. The average time taken by the others to reach that total was sixteen and a half years. Wayne reached the total in five and a half!

Put on skates from the age of two, Wayne was competing in hockey from the age of six. He remained in other sports though winning the Ontario schools 800m, 1500m and cross-country titles at the age of eleven. It has been said of Wayne that he displays a unique calmness under pressure. A fellow player commented: 'If there was a fire in Wayne's home, he'd be there quietly gathering up the valuables.'

What was his most memorable win? 'Stanley Cup 1983. There's no question, that's the greatest feeling that I've ever had.'

His best illustration of holding together under stress was, 'In 1984 when we lost to the New York Islanders in the final of the Stanley Cup. I received a lot of heat, that I didn't play well. I'm a big believer in, "you win as a team and you lose as a team", but I seem to take a lot more heat, although it doesn't bother me. We came back in 1985 and played the same team again and I thought I played very well and the team played outstandingly well, and we beat the same team which beat us the previous year.'

How would he like to be remembered as a player? 'I want to be remembered as a Canook who worked his rear end off to help contribute to winning every game. As someone who played fairly and came to play every night consistently.' And as a person? 'As a good father and a good grandfather [laughing] . . . It's the only thing I could think of! My parents taught me to treat people properly and I try to do that, to the best of my ability – be fair to people and try to help contribute to those who are less fortunate.'

John Havlicek

***Basketball** (Guard)*

Born 8 April 1940: Martins Ferry, Ohio
Specialized: 18 years old
Career highlights:
1962 All-American at Ohio State
1963–79 Played with Boston Celtics
Eight times on the National Basketball Association World Championship team
Boston Celtics all-time leading scorer with 26,395 points (ranks fifth in the NBA)
Only player in League history to score at least 1000 points in sixteen straight seasons
NBA record most play-off games 172 scoring 3776 points
1974 Play-off Most Valuable Player award

'My most exciting moment was in 1976, a triple overtime against Phoenix. I'd scored a basket that everyone thought had won the game and we were in the locker room, half undressed and the officials decided there was one second to be played. We came back out onto the floor leading by two points. They inbounded the ball to the most unlikely shooter on the team. He let fly and scored! That sent it into the third overtime. At the end of regulation time and at the end of the first overtime we thought we'd won it – a real emotional roller-coaster. We won it with three starters and the first two off the bench had fouled out!'

What was his best illustration of holding together under stress? 'What you fear under stress is making a mistake. You don't want to make a mistake.' John added to his illustration above by saying that another most memorable and pressure-filled moment was in the 1965 play-offs when he stole the ball on an inbound's pass in the last seconds of the game. The moment has now been immortalized by the Johnny Most record, 'And Havlicek stole the ball!'

John cited one further situation of holding together under physical stress when he played in a game with a torn *plantar fascia* in his arch, for fifty-eight out of sixty-three minutes.

And how would he like to be remembered? 'As an individual coming from an obscure background and fairly common or lower class, to be a person who worked hard to achieve a high standard and becoming a person who never let that affect the values of what he had when just coming up and not allowing himself to think he's more than he is. I think I'm a humble person, who is not flamboyant or extreme in any area to gain attention. I just let my actions speak louder than my words.'

Geoff Hunt

Squash

Born 11 March 1947: Melbourne, Victoria
Specialized: 12 years old
Career highlights:
Won three World Amateur Titles 1967–69
Won a record four World Open Titles 1976, 1977, 1979, 1980
Won his record eighth British Open title in 1981

Geoff Hunt's most memorable moment was, 'My eighth British Open [1981 against Jahangir Kahn, then only seventeen] which was the record, even though I'd won the first ever World Amateur Championship and the first ever World Open Title. Probably that is because it's the most recent of all the major achievements. I was thirty-four and the underdog as far as the media were concerned. My father was there, my wife was there, which was very important, and my son was in the gallery and a couple of friends from overseas were there as well. It was a close game and it was a record length of time for a British Open final [two and a quarter hours]. I have never been more exhausted in my life than when I played at the end of that match. Winning under those circumstances makes it even more memorable.'

What was his best illustration of holding together under stress? 'I think when you're down at squash, you've got a lot of time. It's not as if things are running away from you quickly and therefore you can think about what you're doing, where you're falling down and you can try and change it, so you change your pattern of play. That might not work, then you try something else. You've got to go through the process. There's not much point in going on playing in the same old way unless you know what you're doing will eventually allow you to win, but it's very rare that it happens like that, in my experience, anyway.'

How he would want to be remembered? 'I'd like to be remembered as someone who played fair and square and was as tough as nails on court. I know it might be a contradiction but I want them to think that it's as hard as bloody hell to play squash against me but they knew I was going to do it in a fair way.' And as a person? 'Well, as a fair person, basically. Obviously you want to be reasonably well liked but it doesn't worry me if people don't agree with me in everything. I suppose most people would prefer to be liked, though, if they had the choice.'

***Shane Innes** (née Gould)*
***Swimming** (Freestyle)*
Born 25 October 1956: Sydney, New South Wales
Specialized: 13 years old
Career highlights:
Shortly after her fifteenth birthday, Shane held every freestyle world record: 100m, 200m, 400m, 800m, and 1500m
1972 Munich Olympics, 100m freestyle bronze; 200m freestyle gold in a new world record of 2 min 03.56 sec; 400m freestyle gold in a new world record of 4 min 19.04 sec; 800m freestyle silver; 200m individual medley gold in a new world record of 2 min 23.07 sec

Shane Innes's most memorable event was also her best example of holding together under stress – the 100m freestyle world record in the New South Wales Championships in Sydney in 1972. 'In November and December, I broke the world record three weeks in a row. [Shane already held the 200m and 400m world records.] I was in full training – anyhow I broke the 800m and 1500m freestyle records and because I was in such a peak it was predicted that I was going to try to break Dawn Fraser's world record which she had held for eight years. My Dad helped to set a goal to break it. On the door of my bedroom he put up a little sign saying "58.5 club" and the record was 58.9. There was a lot of media publicity and build-up to it and the North Sydney swimming pool was packed out, and there were people lined up on the Harbour Bridge to see it and there was live TV coverage of it too. I can still feel the butterflies and the adrenalin but that's the only time I think I had to perform, that I felt I really had to pull something out of the bag. The others were just chance and a matter of course but this one had to be a real performance. I did a 58.5 . . . I nearly missed the race because in the marshalling area I'd retreated to a room to psych up. The race was called and because of the pumps I didn't hear and everyone else was undressing and the officials came and said, "Where have you been, everyone's getting on their box!" I raced out crying by that stage and falling apart inside, the adrenalin was pumping so much when I got on the blocks.'

How would she like to be remembered? 'I'd like to be remembered as a person who swam well and enjoyed it rather than a person out there to win medals. Just as a person who did well because I wanted to do well but not to beat others. That I enjoyed the physical exhilaration but the rewards didn't seem that important to me, it was more the moment – the process and the moment. My Dad was always saying, "That's history now". At the family meal time we'd have a discussion of what each of us did in the day and if I'd report, "Well, I'd broken a world record", my younger sister would say, "Well, I did this drawing", and my older sister would say, "Well, I passed my exams but only with a B+" . . . each of those things was treated as equally terrific.'

Barry John

Rugby Union *(Fly-half)*
Born 6 January 1945: Cefneithen, Glamorgan
Specialized: Never
Career highlights:
Twenty-five internationals for Wales, scoring 90 pts
Two Lions tours 1968 to South Africa; 1971 to New Zealand where he scored a record 180 pts
Triple Crown 1969, 1971
International Championship 1969–72

Barry was known to defuse pressure situations with humour. His attitude is typified in the story which Gareth Edwards relates when they were first picked to represent Wales. Gareth phoned Barry to discuss tactics and training. Barry's response was, 'Don't worry, you throw it, I'll catch it!'

His most memorable moment was in 1971 when Wales won the Grand Slam, beating the French in Paris 9–5. 'Both teams played well. Both had the ball enough and both played brilliant attacking rugby. In defence there was a bit of last minute tackling by us and there'd be last minute tackling by them and it's rare to get two sides playing wonderfully well on the same day. As it happens we came out winners 9–5 but what a game! Everyone on the field played well . . . talk about being knackered, but everybody had a chance to contribute that day and the nice thing about it was at dinner that night, as we came in, and we'd just won the Grand Slam, the French team and administrators of the French Federation stood up and applauded. The French President in his speech said that he was proud of his team, it was one of the best teams he'd seen play and to have been beaten, you boys must be a good side to beat us. It was a lovely compliment.'

And his best illustration of holding together under pressure? Barry again cited the 1971 game in Paris saying that he had been 'able to sneak in for a try'. He said that he was always looking to make things happen adding that it had to do with his temperament and inner belief. He said, 'I couldn't panic to save my life. If somebody called "Fire", I'd count to three and work it out. When all the options were gone then I'd panic, but I would have to go through stages. It would be a controlled panic!'

How would he like to be remembered as an athlete? 'For the New Zealand tour – a record number of points for the Lions, 180 in sixteen matches, all against good teams. As one of the great kickers, and I hope I'll be remembered for my style of play – Passing off the other foot! Generally, as a thinking and skilful player.' And as a person? 'That's up to others . . . a bloke with some common sense and not bad company!'

***Billie Jean King** (née Moffitt)*
Tennis
Born 22 November 1943: Long Beach, California
Specialized: 11 years old
Career highlights:
Major Championship singles titles:
Wimbledon 1966–72, 1973, 1975
US 1967, 1971, 1972, 1974
Australian 1968; French 1972; Italian 1970; German 1971; South African 1966, 1967, 1969
Billie Jean King also holds the record number of Wimbledon singles and doubles titles – 20

Billie Jean's most memorable win was the 1974 US Open against Evonne Goolagong. 'I wasn't going to enter it. I'd played team tennis all summer and was just tired. I was down the whole match. I don't know how I won. I swear a guardian angel came down and played the match fo me. To this day I don't know how I won. It was a packed stadium, standing room only, people on the side of the court, I just remember this unbelievable ambience. I think the whole occasion was the reason I won probably, the idea of being in the finals. I loved playing Evonne Goolagong because it was never boring.'

What was your best illustration of holding together under stress? '20 September 1973, playing against Bobby Riggs. I felt the pressure because everyone was giving it to me. He'd asked me to play him for three years and I never would. But Margaret Court was persuaded. I asked her why she wanted to play him and she said the money was unbelievable – $10,000. When she decided to go ahead I said, "Please beat him!" She lost to him 6–1, 6–2! I was getting on a plane from Japan to Honolulu when I heard the result on the radio. I thought, "Oh no! I'm going to kill her! Now I'm going to have to play him. She set it up. I'm going to have to play him now!" I said to Larry my husband, "You have no idea how important this match is to me. It's not only about winning when people get that emotional about something." For six weeks before, it felt like life and death. I'd never seen him play and I was trying to visualize what it would be like to play him. We didn't have any footage of Bobby Riggs to look at. I saw a tape of the Margaret Court–Bobby Riggs match the night before I played him and took it all in.' In front of over thirty thousand in the Houston Astrodome, with fifty million more watching on television, Billie Jean beat the 1939 triple Wimbledon champion and self-promoted male chauvinist, 6–4, 6–3 6–3.

How would she like to be remembered? 'It doesn't really matter, because I'm gone then! It's what I can do with my life today and tomorrow. But I hope each person feels fulfilled in what they do. I wish the youngsters would understand that if you're not number one it doesn't mean that you're a loser. Winning for each person is different. Their goals are different in life at different times. You have to keep re-evaluating but it's important that if you're not number one it doesn't mean you're a loser. I just know that's what I wanted and it made me very fulfilled but it's not for everybody.'

John Konrads

***Swimming** (Freestyle)*
Born 21 May 1942: Riga, Latvia
Now resident in Australia
Specialized: 11 years old
Career highlights:
In January 1958 he broke six world records–200m and 220 yds, 400m and 440 yds, 800m and 880 yds
By January 1960 he held eight world records from 220 yds to 1650 yds.
1960 Rome Olympics, 1500m freestyle gold in an Olympic record of 17 min 19.6 sec; 400m freestyle bronze; 4 × 200m relay bronze

John's most memorable moment was the 1500m gold in Rome – 'Partly because of the fact that the Olympics is only once every four years and not every world record holder is an Olympic gold medallist. It's a rare event and it's recognized by one's peers as being the pinnacle and it is – no doubt about that whatsoever.'

What was his best illustration of holding together under stress? 'In Rome the 400m preceded the 1500m. It was a question of getting back onto the track having just got off it. It was saying, "Here's where you went wrong. Let's forget about that now. Here's what you're going to do to avoid that happening again." Get back into the preconceived notion, because when you don't succeed it's because you've done something wrong.'

How would he want to be remembered? 'It's probably how I will be remembered anyway, being one of the pioneers of young swimmers, who developed or brought about an era when records were broken by large margins and to a certain extent revolutionizing the sport. I was one of that party with my sister Ilsa, when I was fifteen and she was thirteen, we broke world records within days of each other, in January 1958.' And as a person? 'Apart from the usual ones of being a nice guy, having made a contribution to the sport and continuing to contribute as much as one can, having set a good example.'

Rod Laver

Tennis

Born 9 August 1938: Langdale, Queensland
Specialized: 16 years old
Career highlights:
1956 US Junior champion
Wimbledon singles champion 1961, 1962, 1968, 1969
Australian singles champion 1960, 1962, 1969
French singles champion 1962, 1969
US singles champion 1962, 1969
The middle six years of his career from 1962 to 1968 Rod played in the National Tennis League, the professional circuit, until tennis went 'open' in 1968. He is the only player to have twice won the Grand Slam – Wimbledon, Australian, French and US Championships, all in the same year

Rod's most memorable win was, 'The very first time I won the Australian Championships, when I shouldn't have won. My parents were down and they very rarely saw me play on the main circuit as an older person. As a kid, yes, because they were taking me. I beat Neil Fraser 8–6 in the fifth set after three and a half hours . . . Wimbledon 1961 was another highlight – it's the first time of anything.'

Rod reflected on the different situations which can cause stress, for example, an argument with your partner, someone close to you is sick or dies unexpectedly, personal sickness or injury, all can increase pressure and stress. 'Sometimes that sort of thing can give you a great desire to do something or it can just make you quit because it's too much to grasp. If things aren't going right, rather than go out there and say, "Look everybody, feel sorry for me", you go out and say, "Well, I've got to try and wipe this all out of my mind and go ahead and play, then I'll continue to worry about it after I've got through . . ."'

Rod related a story of how he won Wimbledon in 1968 with a bruised thumb and sprained wrist. 'I used to put a match box on each side and played with it stiff so I couldn't feel it as much. No one knew I had the sprain and my wife couldn't understand why I was doing it, I had to go and bandage up my wrist in the telephone box while nobody was watching. I knew that if people knew I was injured, they would make me play shots I didn't want to hit. As it turned out I got through the first week and after that it was better.'

How does he want to be remembered? 'I'd like to think I was emotionally free on a tennis court. I wouldn't want to be recognized for being bad tempered. Your record or your performance does all the talking. Inwardly I feel good about what I've accomplished but I don't want to push that on others if they don't want it. It's only a matter of whatever your reputation is and if you've been fair with your competition and fair with your fellow man, I think that's all that counts.' And as an individual? 'Not to be put on a pedestal, I think. It's nerve-racking enough if you're self-confident, but if you feel like you're quiet and shy to a point, you don't want to be put out there on a high pedestal. I guess that means I'm a fairly private person.'

Carl Lewis

***Athletics** (Sprint and Long jump)*

Born 1 July 1961: Selma, Alabama

Specialized: 16 years old

Career highlights:

1981 World Cup, long jump gold

1983 World Championships, 100m gold; long jump gold; 4 × 100m gold

1984 Los Angeles Olympics, 100m gold; 200m gold; long jump gold; 4 × 100m relay gold (in a world record of 37.83 sec)

World best non-altitude performances: 100m 9.97 sec; 200m 19.75 sec; long jump 8.79m

In answer to my question about coping with stress, Carl pointed out that it was actually easier running a final of the World Championships or the Olympics than a US trial because in the former there are only two other American sprinters!

'My first memorable moment was in 1978 when I was seventeen. I made my first international splash when competing in the Age Group National Championships winning the long jump, the first time over 25 ft and I came second in the sprint. The second was the 1979 TAC Championships where I set the high school national record and made the Pan-American Games team. The third was being at the Pan-American Games, because it gave me experience of competition, meeting people from outside the US and going through a difficult time of almost being disqualified, through a mix-up with the American team officials. Fourth and foremost has to be the 1984 Olympic Games. It made all the other times I went through important because they were stepping stones for the most memorable moment of my life.

'My best illustration of performing under stress was without question the 1984 Olympic Games. I had the whole world staring at me, judging me and focussing in on everything you can imagine. People were saying I was going to do this or do that, but I was able to hold together under that, including some family trials and tribulations concerning the Olympics. Under all that stress I was able to hold together and win the gold medals I said I was going to.

'I would like to be remembered as an athlete who took chances and never let anyone tell him that what he thought he could do was not possible. I've always believed that if you work hard at whatever you want to do, you can make it. Making it doesn't mean doing "the best", it means doing "the best you can".

'I want to be remembered as a person who was an innovator in sports, as an athlete and as a black person. I've always felt that I've crossed barriers, in terms of being a person who looked at everything as being equal and even. I feel that a person who sets goals in life can set high standards. I want to be remembered as a leader of his time. I'd like to be remembered as someone who could be looked up to as a person who set goals and made them. Whatever you want to do, you can always do, as long as you work hard, and whatever you want in life you can get it. I want to be remembered as a family man and most of all as my own man.'

Chris Evert Lloyd

Tennis

Born 21 December 1954: Fort Lauderdale, Florida

Specialized: 9 years old

Career highlights:

Major Championship singles titles:
Wimbledon 1974, 1976, 1981
US 1975–78, 1980, 1982
Italian 1974, 1975, 1980–82
French 1974, 1975, 1979, 1980, 1983, 1985
Australian 1982, 1984
Ranked world number one 1974–78, 1980, 1981
A.P. Female Athlete of the Year 1974, 1975, 1977, 1980

'My most memorable moment would have to be when I beat Margaret Court as a fifteen-year-old. She had won the Grand Slam in 1970 and I was pretty unknown at that time as I was still an amateur.'

Chris said that it was difficult to pick out her best performance under stress, as she placed a great deal of stress on herself to perform well in every match. 'That's a tough one, but two come to mind. The French Open in 1985 against Martina Navratilova because it was such a see-saw match. I would have a lead and Martina would catch up; I would have another lead and then Martina would catch up again. So the end result was, who was going to hang in there mentally? [Chris beat Martina for the first time in a couple of seasons.] The other would be in '76 when I beat Evonne Cawley at Wimbledon, 11–9 in the third set. That was also a see-saw match, which kept going back and forth – and in the final of a major tournament I think the strain is more magnified.

'I would like to be remembered for my longevity of being a champion, and the consistency of my career. Also as a good sport because I think that sportsmanship is important.' And off the field? 'To have personally contributed to women's tennis, by talking to the younger players a little bit; by doing things to sell the game a little bit and being able to handle success. I try to be down to earth about it and not get caught up with it.'

Clive Lloyd

***Cricket** (Batsman)*

Born 31 August 1944: Georgetown, Guyana
Specialized: 13 years old

Career highlights:

1963/64 Made his debut for Guyana
1969–1985 Captain of West Indies
1968 Began career with Lancashire. County Cap 1969; Benefit year 1977; Captain 1981–1983 and 1986–
Highest Test score 242* West Indies v India, Bombay 1974/75
Captained his country in 69 Tests
World Cup winning captain 1975, 1979
105 Test appearances; 18 Test 100s

What was his most memorable moment? 'The first World Cup we won in 1975. There will never be another first, and I thought, in the situation, it was an excellent day. So many people were proud of our achievement.'

His best illustration of the team holding together under pressure was, 'The World Cup in 1975 when the West Indies were 25 for 3 against the bowling of Australia's Jeff Thomson, and Rohan Kanhai saved the day. Also, the World Cup in 1979 where the score was 23 for 4 and we came back to score 290. After that, the Test against Australia when we were 30 for 4 and Viv Richards scored 189. We came out and fought back and brought out the full potential of the West Indies players – mentally and physically.'

How would he like to be remembered? 'As a sportsman – as someone who I hope epitomized everything that is good about sport, my sport or any other sport. I would hope that I have given enjoyment to quite a lot of people and that whatever I've done will always be remembered. I'm not saying that I will have pleased everyone but I'm hoping I will have pleased the majority.' And as a person? 'That they will always have found me someone very pleasant. Someone they can always come up and speak to. I hope that I will end up as a respected sort of individual.' He added, 'Being a West Indian – I have to speak for them. I hope I've left something for them to work towards. Cricket is only one part. I hope that in the future we can develop other sports as we have cricket, perhaps even West Indies at the Olympic Games under one banner.'

Heather McKay *(née Blundell)*
Squash & Racketball
Born 31 July 1941: Queanbeyan,
New South Wales
Specialized: 18 years old
Career highlights:
British Open Squash champion 1962–77 (considered then to be the unofficial world championships)
World champion (once that tournament had been established) 1976, 1979
Australian Squash champion 1960–73
New South Wales Squash champion 1961–73
US Women's Amateur Racketball champion 1979
US Women's Professional Racketball champion (recognized world champion) 1980, 1981, 1984
During her career from 1959 to 1979, she lost only two games, one in 1960 and the other in 1962

Heather's memorable moments were, 'The first Australian Squash Championships in 1960, because it was so unexpected . . . The first British title in 1962 because it's the biggest and unofficially was the world championship . . . Becoming the ABC Sports Person of the Year in 1967, because I'd been up for it at least five or six times before. I think I was up for it ten times altogether. I'm sure it was because I'd been named in the All-Australian women's hockey team the same year . . . And finally when I officially became World Champion in 1976.'

What was her best illustration of coping with stress? 'I always played better when I was behind. I tend to be very basic when I get under pressure. The last US National Racketball Championship I was up 2–0, lost the third one in a nip and tuck, then got absolutely creamed in the fourth, 21–13 and came back to win it quite comfortably in the fifth. You have to stay calm and also know what you can do and do that. Just stay calm and be patient. There's nothing worse than hearing someone tell a player what to do and you know it's not that person's game! They're telling them to do something that is not an automatic part of their game, so you know they're going to be down the tube anyway.'

How would Heather like to be remembered as an athlete? 'One of the greatest, if not the greatest in squash. Someone who gave everything, every time they went on the court – played hard but fairly.' And as a person? 'Genuine. I think I'm a genuine person. I don't make friends easily but I think people who know me know I'm fun loving and a person who enjoys life.'

Edwin Moses

Athletics (400m hurdles)
Born 31 August 1955: Dayton, Ohio
Specialized: 15 years old
Career highlights:
1976 Montreal Olympics, 400m hurdles gold in 47.64 sec (world record)
1977 World Cup, gold in 47.58 sec
1979 World Cup, gold in 47.53 sec
1981 World Cup, gold in 47.37 sec
1983 World Championships, gold in 47.50 sec
1984 Los Angeles Olympics, gold in 47.75 sec
World records in 400m hurdles: 47.64 sec, 1977; 47.45 sec, 1977; 47.13 sec, 1980; 47.02 sec, 1984
The 1984 Olympic final was his 105th consecutive win

What was Ed's most memorable win? 'The World Championships in Helsinki, 1983. I was out injured in 1982 and I had to listen to, "Can he come back? Will he be able to make it? Can he get back in condition?" And a couple of weeks after that I ran a world record, so 1983 was a good year. There was too much pressure in 1984 to say that it really meant more than anything else. It was more like a job – a big task that must be done. I enjoyed it much more in 1976. All the Press and politics! . . . One year at a time now. I have to create new incentives. I mix training up with something else. I'll allow myself to do something I want to do as long as I train first.'

What was Ed's best illustration of holding together under stress? 'The way I get the best out is by not expecting an easy race. It's easier when there's pressure. You get emotional and you go out and perform. The most pressured time was the Los Angeles Olympics. 103, 104, 105 in a row!'

How would he like to be remembered? 'People are saying I'm an extraordinary athlete – unparalleled, but when it's all over I want people to realize that I've really made a contribution to the sport and been relatively unselfish about it as well. Also trying to make a previously amateur sport more conducive to allow athletes to stay around for a longer time and helping other people with training and personal problems. I help a lot of people every year. They come with all sorts of problems. "What should I do?" or "This is what someone is offering me, what do you think?" or "I'm sick, who should I go to?"' And as a person? 'If people do remember me outside the sporting context that would be nice. Just as a nice guy who was more than an athlete. As a person who would help others who weren't athletes – just to help out.'

Marjorie Nelson *(née Jackson)*
Athletics *(Sprint)*
Born 13 September 1931: Lithgow, New South Wales
Specialized: 16 years old
Career highlights:
1950 Auckland Commonwealth Games, 100 yds gold; 220 yds gold; 4 × 110 yds gold; 3 × 220 yds gold
1952 Helsinki Olympics, 100m gold (11.5 sec); 200m gold (23.7 sec)
1954 Vancouver Commonwealth Games, 100 yds gold; 220 yds gold; 4 × 110 yds relay gold
World records: 100 yds: 10.7 sec, 1950; 10.4 sec, 1951; 100m: 11.5 sec, 1952; 11.4 sec, 1952; 220 yds: 23.6 sec, 1952; 23.4 sec, 1952

Marjorie's most memorable win was winning the Olympic 100m in 1952. 'It was a burden to carry. Once the gun had gone, I could heard the crowd, everything else was blank and all I could think of was getting to the tape. I can remember when I broke it, my grin must have swallowed the world. I was just so excited. I could never explain the feeling. Oh, it was a terrific moment for me. Then to stand on the dais and know that for fifty-six years you were the first one to put the flag up there. It was just a moment in time and I marvelled in it. It could never be taken away from me. I always felt that one was for Australia, the second one was for me. In the 220 yds semi-final I ran twelve yards faster than ever before, 23.4 sec which was pretty good for the tracks we had in those days and Peter [Nelson, her husband-to-be] was there for the run and it was the first time in my life that I felt like showing off!'

For her best illustration of control under pressure, Marjorie chose the time leading up to the 1952 Olympics. 'We had to compete out-of-season training for it during our winter. There were no races. We trained by the lights of a motor-car, in sleet and fog and snow. You hoped you were on the track and we ran towards what we thought was the light. The fog was too thick to see!'

How would she like to be remembered? 'To be thought of as an athlete, who just for a little while made Australia proud. I think we needed that at the time. We'd just come through a war and we didn't have much to hang on to. The Press built me up and were wonderful to me. I'm glad I had my feet on the ground because I don't think I ever got a swollen head.' And as a person? 'I'd like them to think of me as a nice person and that I have lived my life to the full. I just look at it that God's gift to us all is life. What we do with it is our gift back to him. I'd like to think that He's proud of me for what I've done with my life.'

Peter Nelson, Olympic cyclist for Australia, died in 1977 of leukaemia. Marjorie started the Peter Nelson Leukaemia Appeal. Six years later she was three-quarters of the way towards the million dollar target. She said, 'Peter showed so much courage, I felt that I had to show courage in another way. It meant commitment again. I feel God let me win for this. My name can be used to help somebody else.'

John Newcombe

Tennis

Born 23 May 1944: Sydney, New South Wales
Specialized: 11 years old
Career highlights:
Major Championship singles and doubles titles:
Wimbledon singles 1967, 1970, 1971; doubles 1965, 1966, 1968–70, 1974
US singles 1969, 1973; doubles 1967, 1971, 1973
Italian singles 1969
German singles 1968
French doubles 1967, 1969, 1973
Australian singles 1973, 1975; doubles 1965, 1967, 1971, 1973, 1976

John's most memorable win and his best illustration of holding together under stress was, 'Probably when I won Wimbledon the second time [in 1969] and I beat Ken Rosewall in the final, because in the first I beat Bungert and I was supposed to beat him. 1967 was the last amateur Wimbledon, and Laver and Rosewall weren't playing. But once I'd beaten Rosewall and won Wimbledon, I'd arrived at the top of the mountain. I was almost trying to finger my way up that last little bit and that was the jump up to the top. I went through a tremendous psychological thing that I had to beat in that match. I'm playing someone who at ten years of age I'd looked up to and the crowd were 90 per cent on his side. The whole aura of the occasion – he won the first set. Then I was blowing him off the court, 6–3, 6–2, 3–1 and the crowd got to me and they started clapping double faults and everything and I hadn't done a thing wrong and you know that Centre Court out there can be electric and I just got caught up emotionally in why they were against me and five games just went like that. Suddenly, it was 6–3 to him and the crowd went crazy and I had just sixty seconds changing ends to get my act into gear and I just said to myself, "How badly do you want to win this match?" The answer came back, "Well, I really want to win it, so you'd better put yourself into some sort of zone where you just see Rosewall and the tennis ball and that's it." Within that sixty seconds I put myself into a cocoon. I just thought – I had to do it. I was about to fall into the chasm if I didn't do something – it just had to be done. I played the fifth set and beat him 6–1 Everything he did, I knew he was going to do it before he did it.'

How would he want to be remembered? 'To the tennis world as someone who left a good impact on the game and played a positive part in developing the roots of the tree. Call the tree tennis and the roots the structure – the wider the roots go the more solid the game is going to be. So in that way, as someone who was one of the best tennis players but left a good mark on the game.' As a person, John would like to be remembered 'as someone who is a caring person, a nice guy who looked after his responsibilities and was a good friend to have. I believe very strongly in friendship and spend a lot of time cultivating friendships. I put a lot of effort into it because I think that in this world you really need good friends to get you through it happily. You could be pretty lonely without good friends.'

Dr Pat O'Callaghan

***Athletics** (Hammer)*

Born 24 January 1906: Kanturk, County Cork
Specialized: 26 years old

Career highlights:

1928 Amsterdam Olympics, gold, 168 ft 7 in (51.39m)
1931 European record, 56.06m (183 ft 11 in)
1932 Los Angeles Olympics, gold, 176 ft 11 in (53.92m)
1933 European record, 56.95m (186 ft 10 in)
1934 British AAA champion, 168 ft 9 in (51.44m)
1937 World record, 195 ft 5 in (59.56m)

Both a memorable moment and a good illustration of Dr Pat O'Callaghan holding together under stress was at the Los Angeles Games of 1932. He recalled that the throwing circle at the Games was solid and he had been used to throwing from grass with long, screw-in spikes in his shoes. He was the defending champion but found himself slipping as he attempted to throw. He tried to unscrew the spikes, only to discover that they were rusted in and extremely hard to remove! Between throws he managed to remove more and more spikes. He watched his team-mate Bob Tisdall win the 400m. hurdles and then Bob joined him, assisting him in removing the last few spikes. Remaining exceptionally cool under the circumstances, Pat finally removed the last spike before the fifth of his six throws, and this was all that was needed. He won the competition on his fifth throw! Everything was taken in his stride.

Self-reliance was a simple fact of life. He had no coach and taught himself the fundamentals of the event. He said, 'The mind, that's the big field.'

How would he like to be remembered? 'In a decent way – in the sense of being elevated, as people would elevate you, I think.' And as a person? 'As myself.'

Dr Pat is a man who has commanded respect all his life. He was an imposing 16 stone (224 lb) by the age of sixteen. His was the first medal for Ireland as a free state. He qualified as a veterinary doctor between Games and has been held in high esteem in Ireland throughout his life.

Al Oerter

Athletics (Discus)

Born 19 September 1936: Astoria, New York
Specialized: 16 years old
Career highlights:
1954 Set an American high school record, 184 ft 2 in. (56.14m.)
1956 Melbourne Olympics, gold, 184 ft 11 in (56.36m)
US National champion 1957, 1959, 1960, 1962, 1964, 1966
1960 Rome Olympics, gold, 194 ft 2 in (59.18m)
1964 Tokyo Olympics, gold, 200 ft 1 in (61.00m)
1968 Mexico City Olympics, gold, 212 ft 6 in (64.78m)
World records: 200 ft 5 in (61.10m), 1962; 204 ft 10 in (62.44m), 1962; 205 ft 5 in (62.62m), 1963; 206 ft 6 in (62.94m), 1964
In 1980, the US Olympic boyott prevented Al from going to Moscow whilst ranked second in the world. In 1984, injury prevented him from competing in Los Angeles, aged forty-seven.

His most memorable event or win was his return to sport in 1976. 'I was travelling with a friend through the Berkshires in Massachusetts and we saw an advertisement in the paper for an open meet at the Braintree High School. I had a discus in the back of the car so we decided to go and compete. We went there, and I threw 181 ft. It amazed me. I didn't think I'd throw 150 ft and that was the thing that really cemented my going back into sport. The Olympic medals were nice and they each had a different meaning to me. But I think I've never been more fulfilled in competition than I was with about half a dozen people in Braintree High School competing on a field that at that time had nothing but rocks on it!'

What was Al's best illustration of holding together under stress? 'I only felt stress when I had an injury and in 1964 I won a gold medal while severely injured – I mean badly injured, because I took apart a good deal of my rib cage, six or seven days before the Olympic finals in Tokyo. I was spinning in a wet ring from towel to towel of all the silly things to do. I just tripped and went down. I thought I'd hurt myself. I felt it – but I did it again and this time I tore a tremendous part of my rib cage. I can remember just before the Olymic finals, taking phials of Novocaine. They just kept pushing it into me until they had it frozen, then taped it . . . and *it hurt*! Then they gave me these ammonia capsules and said, "Here, take these if you feel nauseous or something." I had to go out to compete in the Olympic final, and I didn't think I could make it out to the door! . . . I threw over sixty metres for a new Olympic record. It was amazing. I kept breaking those capsules and smelling that stuff . . . I never want to go through that again but I was able to put up with the stress of an injury.'

And how would he like to be remembered? 'I never know how to answer that. I've been asked that a lot of times. Most things you might say about that sound so highfalutin, like "I'm a person who sought goals and achieved them", and all that kind of nonsense. So when I'm asked what I would like chiselled on my tombstone, I say, "The oldest person in this graveyard!" I like being alive.'

Steve Ovett

***Athletics** (Middle-distance)*

Born 9 October 1955: Brighton, Sussex
Specialized: 16 years old
Career highlights:
1971 English Schools Championships, 400m bronze
1972 All England Schools, 800m champion
1973 European Junior Championships, 800m champion
1974 European Championships, 800m silver
1975 European Cup Final, 800m gold
1977 European Cup Final, 1500m gold
1978 European Championships, 1500m gold; 800m silver
1980 Moscow Olympics, 800m gold; 1500m bronze
1980 World Cup, 1500m gold
World records: 1500m 3 min 32.11 sec, 1980; 3 min 31.36 sec, 1980; 3 min 30.77 sec, 1983; mile 3 min 48.8 sec, 1980; 3 min 48.40 sec, 1981; two miles 8 min. 13.5 sec, 1978

When asked what was his most memorable event or win, Steve said, 'I'm struggling to find one, I mean it's a question everyone asks me and I still haven't actually found one . . . I think that probably one of the nicest was the world 1500m record in 1983, because I wasn't really expecting to run well with the way that things were going and the poor weather conditions on the day. When it came, it was rewarding really because it filled a gap, it was rather a desperate season because of injury, and to do it in those circumstances was quite a good achievement, definitely.'

What was his best example of holding together under stress? 'I would say the Los Angeles Olympics, really, holding that together, when things were falling apart physically.' (Anyone who watched Steve pull himself back from the point of collapse to race again and qualify for both the Olympic 800m and 1500m finals could not question his choice here.)

How would he like to be remembered? 'I don't think I really want to be remembered. It's not something I set out to do . . . I'd prefer that I wasn't to be honest . . . As an athlete my personal life would never overshadow my athletic career. It's just there, isn't it? So it's very difficult for me to say, "Yes, I hope people remember me more as a person, but obviously they won't."' And if they were to remember you as a person, how would you want to be remembered? 'I suppose as a fairly level-headed bloke. Worth a good laugh . . . and someone who could be depended upon – that I could do a thing that was asked and do it the best I could.'

Arnold Palmer

Golf

Born 10 September 1929: Latrobe, Pennsylvania
Specialized: 17 years old
Career highlights:
1954 First major title – US Amateur
1955 Turned pro and won his first professional tournament, the Canadian Open
1955–73 Sixty-one US Tour wins
US Masters winner 1958, 1960, 1962, 1964
US Open winner 1960
British Open winner 1961, 1962
World Cup individual winner 1967
1970 Won the American Athlete of the Decade Award for his seven 'Big Four' wins, nineteen overseas tour wins and thirty-two Ryder Cup matches
1980 Joined the Seniors tour; won Canadian PGA
US Senior PGA winner 1980, 1981

Could Arnold identify his most valued win? 'I try not to do that because there are too many important ones. I've answered that question in various ways but the most common answer is that my life has just been a big winner, a tournament for me and I feel very fortunate that I've had the opportunity to do the things that I've done, and if I have a goal in playing golf and continuing it's to make sure that the young people who come along after me have the same opportunity.'

How does he hold together under stress? 'Every time I won, whether it was the walk up to the last hole with a big, big lead or walking up with only a one stroke lead, I was under stress to do what I thought was right. I've won ninety times as a professional, one way or another, so I suppose I must have coped with it pretty well.'

It was said that the common man could identify with Arnold Palmer because he'd go for broke and find himself in difficulty. He was admired because he would give it his best and, time after time, come through under pressure with brilliant putting.

How would he want to be remembered both as a player and as a person? 'That's a difficult question as I'm asked that a lot. I suppose as having made my contribution to the success of the sport, meaning I helped it. I didn't just take it all and not leave anything. Personally, as someone who's fair, not totally self-indulgent, willing to give as well as to take.'

Rodney Pattisson
Yachting
Born 5 August 1943:
Campbelltown, Scotland
Specialized: 13 years old
Career highlights:
1960 International Cadet Championships, winner
1968 European Championships, Flying Dutchman class, winner; Mexico City Olympics, Flying Dutchman class, gold
1969 Quarter-Ton World Championships, winner; World Championships, Flying Dutchman class, winner
1970 Australian World Soling, winner; World Championships, Flying Dutchman class, winner; European Championships, Flying Dutchman class, winner
1971 World Championships, Flying Dutchman class, winner
1972 Munich Olympics, Flying Dutchman class, gold; European Championships, Flying Dutchman class, winner
1975 European Championships, Flying Dutchman Class, winner
1976 Montreal Olympics, Flying Dutchman class, silver; Quarter-Ton World Championships, winner
1983 British America's Cup Challenge, co-skipper
1985 One Ton World Championships, winner

What was Rodney's most valued win? 'Winning cadet week was, at the time, the ultimate – very memorable at the time, but winning the gold in Mexico. It's the ultimate in one's sport and standing on the rostrum was special. It felt like being on top of the world. The others are not as memorable as the Olympic gold.'

His best example of holding together while under stress was in Mexico in 1968. 'During the first race, we had an incident with a Canadian. We unwrapped ourselves from the starting line and were last and I went through and won the race but then got disqualified at the protest afterwards. You're only allowed to drop one race. There are seven races and I had to race the next six knowing that I'd been disqualified in the first. Everybody was gunning for me because I was the favourite – especially starting last and winning, they knew they couldn't match me for boat speed. My only consolation was that I'd won various regattas that year without having to sail the final race. So I just thought to myself, "Well it's a slightly different situation, but I've lost my first race rather than not having to sail the last, I have to keep myself clean and not be involved in anything in the next six races" – and that was quite a difficult thing to live with.'

How would he like to be remembered? 'As one of the most, or one of the more successful yachting sailors of all time . . . In my old age I'd like to contribute something to the sport that would be remembered.'

Lester Piggott

Flat-racing

Born 5 November 1935: Wantage, Berkshire
Specialized: 12 years old
Career highlights:
Record twenty-nine English Classic victories
Nine Derby wins: 1954, 1957, 1960, 1968, 1970, 1972, 1976, 1977, 1983
Six Oaks wins: 1957, 1959, 1966, 1975, 1981, 1984
Eight St Leger wins: 1960, 1961, 1967, 1968, 1970, 1971, 1972, 1984
Two 1000 Guineas wins: 1970, 1981
Four 2000 Guineas wins: 1957, 1968, 1970, 1985
Eleven times Champion jockey: 1960, 1964–71, 1981, 1982
His final total of winners in Britain between 1948–1985 was an incredible 4,349

What was Lester's most memorable win? 'The big races, the Derbys have to be the most memorable ones. All the big ones . . . but I suppose The Minstrel, when he won the Derby in 1977. It was a close finish and he was a horse I always liked, coming up, and it was a very exciting race. I think that's the one that stands out. I think nobody really thought he could do it. A lot of people didn't think he could stay the distance. He was such a little horse, you know. I always had a lot of confidence in that horse and he did it.'

His best example under stress was, 'Probably the 1977 Derby, but it's different for someone like Steve Ovett. He'll tell you the Olympics . . . When you're racing every day, you get used to it.'

How would he like to be remembered? 'Really, as a good jockey. That's how people will remember me, you know. That's all really.' And as a person? 'Well, I think a lot of people argue – how life is a bummer . . . That type of person can't really do it and that's the reason why they don't succeed as much as others . . . they just haven't cottoned on. I'm a bit different, I suppose.'

Ken Read

***Skiing** (Downhill)*
Born 6 November 1955: Ann Arbor, Michigan
Canadian by nationality
Specialized: 11 years old
Career highlights:
1974–83 Represented Canada on World Cup tour
1975–80 Won five Canadian downhill titles
1975 Won the World Cup downhill, Val d'Isère, France
1978 Won World Cup downhill, Chamonix, France; won World Cup downhill, Schladming, Austria; Canadian combined title, slalom, giant slalom and downhill; Canadian World Championship team
1980 Won World Cup downhill, Kitzbühel, Austria; won World Cup downhill, Wengen, Switzerland

His most memorable event was, 'Winning Val d'Isere, 1975, at twenty. It was the first time a Canadian male had won a World Cup race. It was such a shock. I didn't fully appreciate it at the time. I was sort of overwhelmed by the whole thing . . . There was also Kitzbühel, 1980. We believe that's the pinnacle, the unofficial World Championships. It is the toughest and really if I were going to win at any course, that was the one to win at and I really built towards it. I hiked up the course twice, just to get a better feeling for the place. Over the course of several years, I'd discovered that if I went and hiked the downhill, I'd be more familiar with the surroundings. Snow tends to flatten a course slightly. So there was this building towards it . . . and when I did win it, I did savour that one. It was one I'd really looked forward to.'

His best example of holding together under stress is described in Chapter 5 on 'courage and risk-taking'. He referred to the extremely rough middle of the downhill at Kitzbühel where the pitch is a steep hillside taken at 70 m.p.h. For self-preservation, everything tells you to balance yourself with your arms but if you can hold your tuck all the way across, you can save fractions of seconds which could make all the difference. Ken said that it requires physical and mental toughness being rattled around, but when he conquered it and locked himself all the way across it, he won the event.

How would he like to be remembered? 'As an athlete who broke new ground for Canada, internationally, as well as the first non-Eastern Canadian trained athlete to win a downhill; and the first Canadian to win a World Cup downhill. What I would select as the most significant achievement out of all that was proving that the constant talk about our inferiority in Canada was garbage. I proved that, with the right amount of dedication and perseverance, you can succeed. And I proved it in a sport that was not one we thought we could win ten years ago.' And as a person? 'As someone who would always give 100 per cent, whatever he did, be it in sport or any other pursuit and that I said it and believed in it.'

Viv Richards

Cricket (Batsman)

Born 7 March 1952: St Johns, Antigua
Specialized: 17 years old
Career highlights:
1977 Cricketer of the Year
Most runs in a Test series 829 at an average of 118.42, West Indies v. England, 1976
Highest Test innings 291, West Indies v. England, 1976
Passed 6,000 runs in Test cricket in April 1986
Captain of West Indies 1985–
In 1985 for Somerset v Warwickshire, Viv scored 322 runs in 294 minutes off 258 balls and just 133 scoring strokes, including 42 fours and 8 sixes.
In 1986, he scored the fastest ever Test century off just 56 balls against England in the West Indies

What was Viv Richard's most memorable moment? 'I always wanted to be on a rostrum receiving an award, like an Olympian does, with the national anthem playing. The time arose in 1975 with the first World Cup. Running three batsmen out and in the end West Indies winning, that was my biggest highlight, I think.'

How did he cope with stress? 'I personally feel that one cannot perform best when nervous or anxious about things. I've tried not to get mixed up in chatting in the dressing room. I don't want to get myself heated or too emotional.'

And how would he like to be remembered? 'I'd like to be remembered for a certain amount of entertainment given. Probably by enjoying myself I may not have given the best that I know Viv Richards can. I'd like to be remembered for that – being an honest human being; a guy who went out there and did his job the way that he knew best. I'd like to be remembered as just a normal, down-to-earth person, who anyone could approach. There are certain ways and times where people do things because they've actually made it in their profession and become unapproachable, and I wouldn't want people to feel that way about me.'

Bryan Robson
Soccer *(Midfield)*
Born 11 January 1957: Chester-le-Street, Tyne & Wear
Specialized: 15 years old
Career highlights:
1975 Signed as a pro with West Bromwich Albion at the age of nineteen
1981 Transferred to Manchester United for a record fee of £1.5m
1983 and 1985, captained Manchester United to F.A. Cup victory
Currently captain of Manchester United and England

What was Bryan's most memorable moment? 'The first F.A. Cup Final. The whole day – the atmosphere, everything – the celebrations afterwards. It was just fantastic. It was great to captain the team. I scored two goals, and I was brought down for a penalty which gave us a third goal and we won 4–0 in the replay. The whole day was great, and then to pick up the Cup . . . the atmosphere within the ground. Our fans outnumbered the Brighton fans so that two-thirds of the stadium was Manchester United. The noise they made at the end of the game, I felt like jumping in with them. It was sort of a shaking feeling because I was so high.'

What was his best example of performing under pressure? 'One of the worst times was after I moved from West Brom. to United for £1.5m., which was then a record fee. I found that different from anything I'd had to cope with in football. Before, I could just go out and relax and play and just do my own thing on a Saturday, and nobody expected anything. Suddenly, people were saying, "One and a half million pounds, you've got to play and you've got to do well". At first I tried to justify the fee and do things I didn't used to do. Then I'd get letters and calls saying, "You're not worth this money and you're just a greedy bastard", and things like that. That was a difficult period at first.'

How would he like to be remembered? 'As a good player – having given a lot of people satisfaction, watching me do what I enjoyed doing.' And as a person? 'As a credit to my sport in the way I handled myself off the pitch as well. That I could always mix with anybody, whether it was the Royal family, who I've met, or somebody on the dole in a working man's club.'

Pete Rose
Baseball

Born 14 April 1941: Cincinnati, Ohio
Specialized: 19 years old
Career highlights:
1963 Major League Rookie of the Year
National League Batting titles 1968, 1969, 1973
1973 National League, Most Valuable Player
1975 World Series, Most Valuable Player
1978 Collected his 3000th career hit
Named to National League All-Star team sixteen times, including ten years in succession 1973 – 82. The only player in National League history to play over 500 games in each of five positions
1984 Became player–manager of Cincinnati Reds
1985 Collected his 4000th career hit

What were his most valued moments? 'My proudest possessions are my three World Series rings. They're from 1975, 1976 and 1980. We were runners-up in 1970, 1972 and 1983. The ultimate goal, I always thought, was to play in the big leagues. Then you play in the World Series and although we lost the first two times I played in it, I thought that was the ultimate goal. Then when we won, and I stood right up on the fountain there with 30,000 people in that square. Playing for my home town, and being the M.V.P. [Most Valuable Player] of that 1975 Series – that's got to be the ultimate.'

How does he cope under stress? 'The only pressure in baseball is the play-offs. But I never look at pressure. The World Series is fun . . . I just drive. It's like they're playing a machine. I'm not going to get tired. I'm not going to get bored. You have to have a lot more ability than I do to beat me – and then you have to go some. There's no way anybody with equal ability can beat me. I mean, they just can't do it. I'm just going to grind them into the ground.'

And how would he like to be remembered? 'I'd like to be remembered as a winner. I've played in more winning games than anybody in the history of baseball. That makes me the biggest winner in the history of sport. I play in 162 games a year. I've played in close to 2,000 winning games in the big leagues . . . I've played in more winning games than Joe di Maggio played in games.' And as a person? 'As a nice person . . . I think I'm a very considerate person, as far as always trying to help youngsters to become better players. I take a lot of time with young players. I don't worry about the sport. I don't think it needs to be worried about, but I'm always concerned about the sport as far as big contracts and different things, because it's given me so much and did so much for me that I'd hate to see the sport deteriorate. I don't think it will. I think this new commissioner [Peter Ueberroth] is going to be great for the sport. I hate to see guys cheat the sport, any sport. There's so much good that can come from it.'

Joan Benoit Samuelson

***Athletics** (Marathon and Long-distance)*

Born 16 May 1957: Cape Elizabeth, Maine
Specialized: 17 years old
Career highlights:
1983 Pan American Games, 3000m winner
1984 Los Angeles Olympics, marathon winner
World best times established on the roads: 10km 31 min 37 sec; 10 miles 51 min 38 sec; 25km 1 hr 25 min; half marathon 1 hr 08 min 23 sec; marathon 2 hr 22 min 43 sec (She lowered her personal best to 2 hr 21 min 21 sec winning in Chicago, 1985.)

Joan named her three memorable events. The top one was the Olympic trials in 1984, because of the difficulties overcome to win that race. Second was the Olympics themselves and third was the world best time established while winning the Boston Marathon in 1983.

Bob Sevene, Athletics West coach and advisor to Joan, said that she was the toughest athlete he had ever seen. Just seventeen days before her Olympic trials she underwent knee surgery. Her first words to Bob after waking from the anaesthetic were, 'Can I start tomorrow?'

Joan said that the trials and the time leading up to them were her best illustration of holding together under stress. She said, 'The trials were on 12 May and a week before them I couldn't even run. The ups and downs, it was just a nightmare. I didn't say, "Why me?" but I said, "Why the timing?" Things had been going so well and all of a sudden, "boom". I was stressed and I was questioning what was going on but I dealt with it and I just tried to find different things to keep me occupied and alternative exercises.' This included pedalling the exercise bike with her arms prior to clearance to do so with her legs!

As a runner, Joan said that she would like to be remembered as a person who faced challenges and overcame them; someone who set goals and succeeded. She has had many people tell her that she has been a great inspiration for them. She said, 'It's nice if my running has helped somebody else.' Outside of running, 'I would like to be known as a well-rounded person more than just Joan Benoit Samuelson, the runner. Running has been a means to help me become more balanced as a person.'

O. J. Simpson

***American Football** (Half-back)*

Born 9 July 1947: San Francisco, California
Specialized: 21 years old

Career highlights:

1967 USC track team, world record 440 yds relay 38.6 sec
1968 Heisman Trophy winner, College Athlete of the Year
1969–77 Played with Buffalo Bills
AFC Most Valuable Player 1972, 1973, 1975
1973 Individual season rushing record, 2 003 yds in fourteen games
1976 Season touchdown record, twenty-three
1978 Joined the San Francisco '49'ers'
One of the leading rushers in NFL history, running up a total of 11,236 yds
1983 Inducted to the College Hall of Fame
1985 Inducted to the Professional Football Hall of Fame

O.J.'s most memorable moment was also his best illustration of holding together under stress. 'We were known as the "cardiac kids" because in seven out of our eleven games we were either behind or tied in the fourth-quarter. Junior year, my first at USC. The last game of that year was against cross-town rival UCLA. It just so happened that we were the best two teams in the country that year. Not only that but Gary Beban of UCLA and I at USC were ranked as the two best players in the country. The winner of the game would be National Champions and Conference Champions and would represent the conference in the Rose Bowl. In the fourth quarter we were behind 20–14. I had a 64 yd touchdown run and with the conversion we won 21–20 . . . The second high was in 1973 going over 2000 yds in one season . . . The third would be the 440 yds relay world record.'

How would he like to be remembered as an athlete and as a person? 'Maybe almost the same. He was a good guy. He was fun to be with and he was a joy to compete against and play with.'

Peter Snell
***Athletics** (Middle-distance)*
Born 17 December 1938:
Okunake, New Zealand
Specialized: 19 years old
Career highlights:
1960 Rome Olympics, 800m gold in 1 min 46.3 sec
1962 Perth Commonwealth Games, 880 yds gold; mile gold
1964 Tokyo Olympics, 800m gold in 1 min 45.1 sec (Olympic record); 1500m gold in 3 min 38.1 sec
World records: 800m 1 min 44.3 sec, 1962; 880 yds 1 min 45.1 sec, 1962; mile 3 min 54.5 sec, 1962

What was his most memorable moment? 'The one I recall most clearly is the first – winning the gold in the 800m at the Rome Olympics because it was so unexpected. I was transformed from a nonentity into what I'd been working for, I suppose, but never in my wildest dreams did I think I would achieve number one status as an 800m runner and win the gold medal. The night before I knew I had a good chance but not before coming to the Games. I didn't see myself as an Olympic champion. I just didn't have any good reason to believe that I could do that. Setting a world record without really expecting to do that either, that was also memorable. Fulfilment was being able to repeat the 800m victory. It established that it was no fluke. I identify much better with the 800m I feel that's where I really earned my credentials, so to speak, more than in the mile. The fact that other people don't recognize that is beside the point. I recognize that I had a superiority in that event and that I was able to maintain that over a four-year period.'

What was his best illustration of holding together under stress? 'The big competitions were the most important. I always came through – the Olympic Games, the Commonwealth Games, the time I said I'd run under four minutes for a mile – and delivered on that. On three occasions I said I'd break the world record and I did. The recognition factor is extremely important to me and that had the effect of unlocking stuff that I normally couldn't pull out when it wasn't a big occasion.'

And how would he like to be remembered? 'The reason that I worked hard was for recognition. It was important for me to do something spectacular and good. I would like people to feel that at the time I was competing, I was indeed the best runner around. I am not concerned whether they consider me better than others that have come following or better than those that occurred previously. As long as they realize that at the time I was competing, that I was number one, that is how I would like to be remembered . . . and as someone who was able to win and lose in the right sort of way. Someone who competed with distinction and who responded conscientiously to social obligations that went with achieving that distinction.'

Peter Sterling
Rugby League (Scrum-half)
Born 16 June 1960: Toowoomba, Queensland
Specialized: 17 years old
Career highlights:
One of the world's best scrum-halves
1978–86 Played for Parramatta Club
Rugby League Grand Final winner 1981–83
Australian national side 1982–83
1983–85 Played in Britain for Hull; 1985 got through to the final of the Silk Cut Challenge Cup

Peter had no doubt as to his most memorable moment. 'Certainly, it was the 1983 Grand Final, which is the last game of our Australian season and is now a four-day competition. Most teams play twenty-four matches and then the top five sides play off in a semi-final series. Eventually you end up with the two teams that have got through, playing at the Sydney Cricket Ground. The reason that it was so important to me, and was probably equal to representing my country, was because it was the first time my club, Parramatta, had ever reached the Grand Final. They came into the competition in 1947 and really hadn't won anything. There had been plenty of bad times and coming up to 1981, they'd had good years when they'd been competitive all the way through and looked like winning but never did. To be part of the first ever winning side for that club and to know that nobody else was ever going to do it . . . You could honestly see what it meant to the people when we went back to the club. The scenes were just unbelievable. The Parramatta is the best supported club in Australia and it's a fanatical support. It's not an affluent society by any means. A lot of lives revolve around going to work on Monday and talking about how the football team went and you could see on the faces of those people just how much it meant. It made it worth more to us. And we won it again in 1982 and again the following year. It was great because we'd achieved what we set out to, ten months earlier but it was nothing compared with the first time.'

What was his best example under stress? 'I think it would just be the big games. After we won it in 1981, it was tougher in 1982 because you were the premier side and everybody was trying to knock you off, whether you were playing the top side or the bottom side. It was the Grand Final for them every week and there was a lot of stress then. Worse than that were the end of the season games, where ten months' work depended on the result. So I think it was staying together, playing in those games, when there was so much at stake.'

How would he like to be remembered as a player? 'As one of the greats, of which there are not that many in Australia. I want to be one of those.' And as a person? 'I'd like to be remembered in good ways, as a good friend, as somebody that you could rely upon and trust and as an honest person. Success has certainly changed me. I'm not the same person I would have been if I'd not been a good league player. But I'd like to be remembered by people who thought, "Well, he's had a lot of success but you can still talk to him".'

Jackie Stewart

Motor-Racing

Born 11 June 1939: Dumbarton, Scotland
Specialized: 23 years old
Career highlights:
1965 winner Italian Grand Prix
1966 winner Monaco Grand Prix
1968 winner Dutch, German and US Grand Prix; runner-up World Driving Championship
1969 winner British, Dutch, French, Italian, Spanish and South African Grand Prix; World Driving champion
1970 winner Spanish Grand Prix
1971 winner British, Canadian, French, German, Monaco and Spanish Grand Prix; World Driving champion
1972 winner Argentinian, Canadian, French and US Grand Prix
1973 winner Belgian, Dutch, German, Monaco and South African Grand Prix; World Driving champion

Jackie Stewart's most memorable win was in 1968 when he won the American Grand Prix. 'It was the year that Jim Clark died and I was put in as replacement, the other 'flying Scot'. I won it, totally controlling the race and it was the first time that had happened. I went slower, they went slower; I went faster, they went faster. It was the first time I twigged that I had control.'

What was his best illustration of holding together under stress? 'Jochen Rindt was killed on 6 September 1970. He was in practice for the Grand Prix of Italy. It was a Saturday. Jochen was one of my best friends at that time. I wasn't at the track when he had his accident but he was taken from the scene of the accident to a mobile hospital and he was pretty badly bumped about. I was told of his accident, so I ran over to see if I could help. I didn't know how serious it was. I recognized that he was dead and they were trying to bring him back to life as he lay in front of me. Then I had to collect his things, get his wife Nina sorted out and make sure my wife Helen was with her. These things are not normal, but all drivers have to go through this kind of thing. Finally, they didn't want to proclaim him dead on the track because if that happened an inquiry would take place and then they would have to close the circuit and the race was the next day.

They took him off in an ambulance and rushed him to Milan Hospital. I knew he was dead but nobody was prepared to commit to it. Then I had to go back out and practise. I had to go back in the car. Now to do that, to collect yourself and start your programme again, to get in and say, "Hang on now. Now you've got to apply yourself". At Monza it's very important to get a good practice time to establish a good grid position. I got back in the car and did four laps and I put the car into fourth position on the grid; it was the fastest lap I'd ever done at Monza, and I set a new lap record. When I got in the car, I was emotionally upset. I just had to channel my energies and my resources, and control everything, but when I got out of the car again, I make no excuses, I wept. But my drive had no relation to Jochen's accident and when I came to the bit of the track where he had crashed, obviously the tyre marks were still there and some of the engine too; that had to be cleared from your mind, and you have to be able to do that, to discipline yourself to do that. A journalist might say, "Ah, that's a sort of death-wish thing", but that's not how it was. It was calculated, calm, clinical, and emotionless. I was able to tuck away any feelings in one corner, while applying myself to do the job in hand. When I came out of the car, as I said, I cried. And the rest of the night I had to deal with Nina and Helen, and the fact that it was now clear that Jochen had died. The next day I had to drive in the race. I drove as hard as I could and finished second. Jochen was the first posthumous world champion. After the race, the media were very heavy because of our close friendship and that we lived next door to each other. That's an example of pressure if you like, but another kind of pressure.'

How would Jackie like to be remembered? 'As a driver, as a sportsman, I'd like to be remembered as the man who did it best in the complete sense. I don't just mean driving round the track but the total package – a racing driver, development engineer, bringing the car to racing level, driving the car to the best of its ability, handling the Press properly, doing the commercial side effectively, and projecting the sport positively. I think that's an enormous responsibility. Nowadays, there's a general lack of responsibility for the sport's future. I think that's a great weakness.' And as a person? 'I don't know, I hope not as a bad person. I think that would be it. Not as a bad person.'

Daley Thompson

Athletics *(Decathlon)*
Born 30 July 1958: London
Specialized: 16 years old
Career highlights:
1977 European Junior Championships, gold 8190 pts
1978 Edmonton Commonwealth Games, gold 8467 pts
European Championships, silver 8289 pts
1980 Moscow Olympics, gold 8495 pts; world record, 8622 pts
1982 Brisbane Commonwealth Games, gold 8410 pts; world record, 8702 pts; European Championships, gold 8743, (world record)
1983 World Championships, gold 8666 pts
1984 Los Angeles Olympics, gold 8797 pts

Daley's most memorable moment is always the last one. 'It's the most important because that's why I did it, but then the next I do will be the most important one to me. And after that, there's always the next one. I try not to live in the past. I always try to look forward. When I'm finished, in ten years, I can look back over the total thing and see actually where the greatest amount of pleasure occurred, but at the moment, it's always the one I've just finished and the one I've got to do tomorrow or whenever.'

His best example of holding together under stress was the 1983 World Championships where he carried a serious muscle injury right through the competition. 'That was when I was most stressed because even though I was only going from event to event, I still had my own goals to make every time. Even though I was injured, if I wasn't making the goals, that made it worse. Although I was achieving some goals, I wasn't achieving others. That was the most stress I've ever been in. But once I started, I was fine.'

How would he like to be remembered? 'By my friends, the people who know me, I'd like to be remembered as a nice, regular guy – no seriousness. By the people who don't know me, just as the best decathlete that there's ever been or whatever. You can't expect people who don't know you to think you're a nice guy because they don't know. But by my friends and people who know me, perhaps as a regular guy who happened to be good at something else . . . a nice fellow to have as a friend, that's all.'

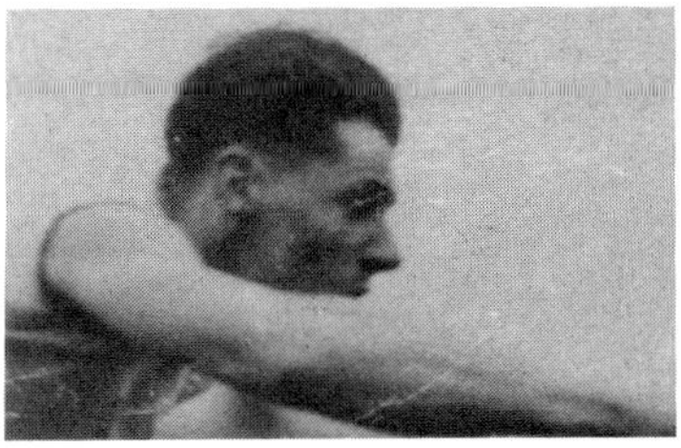

Bob Tisdall
***Athletics** (400m hurdles)*
Born 16 May 1907: Hatten, Sri Lanka
Now resident in Australia
Specialized: Never
Career highlights:
1931 Won four events for Cambridge in the varsity match – shot putting, high jump, low hurdles and quarter mile
1932 Los Angeles Olympics, 400m hurdles gold
His time of 51.7 sec was by far the best on record but not allowed as a world record as he clipped the last hurdle and the rules of the day read that no hurdle can be knocked down to qualify for a world record. He never raced another 400m hurdles

Bob said that he never did specialize. He said, 'I had a go at everything. I never had a coach. I was just a natural at sports.' His best time before the Olympics was 54.2 sec but as his friend Pat O'Callaghan pointed out, Bob was a novice in the event. Bob said, 'I had run a few flat quarter-mile races, but not in lanes!'

How did he cope under pressure? 'The mind is the master . . . and the bridge. All the instructions came through from the mind and everything you do physically, comes through the mind. Fear is mentally under control. The mind controls the fear but fear is a very important thing. It controls the adrenalin glands. Too much and you're scared stiff . . . If the mental pre-competition stress was getting on top of me, I'd go to bed, read Edgar Wallace and smoke my pipe.'

How would Bob like to be remembered? 'As a person who regarded sport as sport – as a game. When the game goes out of it, the sport goes out of it and everything goes out of it.'

Jayne Torvill and Christopher Dean
Ice Dancing

Jayne – born 7 October 1957: Nottingham
Chris – born 27 July 1958: Nottingham
Specialized: 18 years old

Career highlights:

1971 Torvill (with Michael Hutchinson), British Pairs champions
1974 Dean (with Sandra Elson), British Junior Ice Dance champions
1976 Torvill and Dean, British Northern Ice Dance champions
1978–84 British Ice Dance champions
1981 European Championships, gold; World Championships, gold
1982 European Championships, gold; World Championships, gold
1983 World Championships, gold
1984 European Championships, gold; World Championships, gold; Sarajevo Olympics, gold
1985 Embarked on professional career

What was their most memorable event or win? Chris's reply was similar to Daley Thompson's. 'The most recent is always the most enjoyable. There are many high points for us. The first time we won the Europeans and the Worlds [both in 1981].' Jayne added, 'I was going to say, the first time we won the Europeans was as memorable as winning the Olympics. It was just amazing. We couldn't believe it because this was the year we thought we might get the bronze medal. We were not confident by any means. It was really great.' Chris reflected, 'I think, most probably, there was a sigh of relief from us both by the end of the Olympics and Worlds, in 1984. We had set a goal four years ago and we managed to live up to that.' He continued, 'The pressure built up each year. We then had to win to top the previous year, until the 1984 Olympic year when we decided to retire from amateur skating.'

What was their best example of coping under stress? Chris explained first: 'Well, I think we know if something feels out of place or wrong. There have been one or two occasions. One was the first time that we did the Barnum routine, in November 1982 at the Nationals. We hadn't even had the opportunity to try the costumes on the ice before the actual competition, although we knew all the steps. Something was foreign. It was like a little thorn in the foot, not really painful, but irritating and then everything goes down to that thought and you can feel it.' Jayne continued: 'The first move that I did, the shoulder of the costume moved out. It didn't fall off but it felt like it was now off-the-shoulder!' Chris added, 'I knew that she felt awkward so all that time we were using each other to get through, just with eye contact. You've rehearsed everything so thoroughly in practice, you almost know when the other person breathes in the wrong place. It gets down to that fine tuning because you've done it so many times. I could sense that she was thinking about something and that threw my concentration as well.' Jayne gave another example, 'When we caught hands in the rock and roll routine, my dress bobbed up in the air and Chris took both my hand and the dress! I knew that if he tried to release it, it would fall down, but in keeping hold, he might have ripped the dress!' Chris took up the story: 'So I just held on. But we had this split second when we both looked at each other, she knew I'd got her dress and I knew I'd got her dress and our faces were a picture of horror.' Jayne continued, 'I was thinking, "What's he going to do?" In the end he held on to everything and the dress slipped away, rather than tore. But we both knew what was happening. In retrospect, I must admit, it was quite funny.'

How would they like to be remembered? Chris answered for them both: 'If you still remember us in ten or fifteen years time, you remember because of what we brought to the sport, what we've achieved. There are a lot of one-year wonders. If somebody has brought something to the sport, people generally tend to remember and we hope that we have brought something more to it.' And as a person? Jayne: 'As quite a nice person, not nasty or horrible in any way.' Chris: 'Just as normal people. Just Nellie from the Deli and that's it.'

This couple will certainly be remembered longer than most. They managed to integrate sport, art and entertainment. By the end of their amateur careers, in European, World and Olympic competitions, they were receiving perfect 6.0 scores from all the judges for artistic impression. The most lasting impression for most will be their free dance to Ravel's *Bolero*.

Mary Twomey *(née Rand)*
Athletics *(Long jump, Hurdles and Pentathlon)*
Born 10 February 1940: Wells, Somerset
Specialized: 17 years old
Career highlights:
1957 National record, pentathlon, 4046 pts
1958 Commonwealth Games, long jump silver
1962 European Championships, long jump bronze
1963 Share in world record 4 × 110 yd relay
1964 Tokyo Olympics, long jump gold in a world record of 22 ft 2 in (6.76m); pentathlon silver, 5035 pts, second best all-time record; 4 × 100m relay bronze
1966 Commonwealth Games, long jump gold

Mary had three memorable moments in her career. 'The first was when I competed in Belgrade in the 1962 European Championships, four months after giving birth to Alison. I went through hell all through pregnancy. I threw up all the time. I was quite young and didn't know anything about having children. I was in labour for twenty-four hours and it was horrendous. The Press were there hours after she was born asking, "Are you going to run again?" and I said, "I don't know if I'm ever going to walk!" I hadn't done any training and I didn't really want to compete, mainly because I wasn't fit. I got a bronze medal in the long jump in the European Championships and, for me, that was the most memorable thing. Then in 1959 I was competing in Russia as our second string hurdler behind Carol Quinton. She kept saying that it was wet out there and they had these great big old heavy hurdles. Carol kept saying, "I can't get my strides." I kept saying, "You'll be fine." We had to compete against Tamara Press, the world record holder. We went outside and the track was wet and heavy. We went from the blocks and at either the first or second hurdle, Carol fell. That's when the competitiveness came out. I'd been in Carol's shadow without being aware of it. I was the second string hurdler and that's what I was. I was going out there to do my best. When Carol fell, I felt I had to win. And I did. I received a standing ovation. The Russian people stood up, shouting my name, "Mary, Mary". I've never forgotten it. It probably meant more to me than the Olympics because I was nineteen. I think I was the only woman to receive an award for an outstanding win. Then obviously there's the Olympics. People have always said, "Well, what do you want, a gold medal or a world record?" I think I was one of the few who wanted a world record. I'd say, "I'd like the gold medal but I'd like to be the best in the world, just for a moment." I was fortunate that it happened together. That was a double bonus.'

For Mary, her best illustration of dealing with stress was, 'Just dealing with the competition. Probably going out four years later in Tokyo, knowing I was going to be the only one out there. There was no atmosphere and there was a lot on my shoulders. Four years before [in the Rome Olympics], everything had gone wrong. This time I was going out thinking, "Well, if I can win, it's going to really make a big difference. It's going to get the others thinking, gee, one of us did it, we can all do it." I was just concentrating on the one thing I was doing.'

How would she like to be remembered? 'As a likeable person and as a genuine person. Maybe that sounds corny. I don't know – not mainly for sport. Obviously I'm going to be remembered because of that but I feel although I did what I did, it was because of a whole bunch of people, who never will be known or get that recognition. If I could say anything to those people, it would be "thank you". I was fortunate enough to have met them. I was always honest. There are lots of people who don't really know us as people. They know us as athletes. It's like a film star. People read something and believe it. That's hard on the person, especially if they're sensitive to it. Some athletes don't want to be bothered with the Press but that's part of being an athlete. You have to be able to give the time to those people. They want to know about you. It's part of the package and a lot now think they're prima donnas. They say, "Speak to my agent". Well, forget the agent, because it's you they care about.'

Gene Upshaw
American Football *(Guard)*
Born 15 August 1945: Texas
Specialized: 18 years old
Career highlights:
Sixteen years, offensive guard, L.A. Raiders
Started in 217 straight games
Elected team captain for twelve years
Captained winning Superbowl team 1977, 1980
Executive Director, National Football League Players Association

What was Gene's most memorable moment? 'Winning the Superbowl in 1977, although the last one in 1980 was also important. What was memorable was the opportunity to play. It's nice to win but you forget about the wins; you don't forget the friends you make or the opportunities you have. To me the advantage I got out of competing in the National Football League is that I have a number of friends. Having the chance to meet people and the associations that you build up was more important than any win I had.'

What was his best illustration of holding together under stress? 'Pressure is self inflicted . . . For me the fifty-seven day strike in 1982, when 1600 players were out of work.' As Executive Director of the Players Association, Gene was shouldering most of the responsibility. He also spoke of the pressure situations on the field saying, 'We were always behind in the last minute and we always won. All you need is the will to win. Number one, you need to know what it's like to win and to know what it's like to lose. Number two, it's good for everyone and number three that's the only way they judge you in this society – you won!'

How would he like to be remembered as a player and as a person? 'Both in the same way, as a guy that believed in what he was doing; was willing to sacrifice to achieve it, not for himself but for someone else. I want it better for the kids who are coming up. I want the system better. I want to be thought of as a person who was fair and reasonable and not one that tried to force my ideas and my philosophy down anyone's throat. If you can be thought of as someone they trust and respect, that's all you need.'

Mike Wenden

***Swimming** (Freestyle)*
Born 17 November 1949: Sydney, New South Wales
Specialized: 13 years old
Career highlights:
1965 Australian Junior record 100m freestyle, 56.7 sec.
1966 Jamaica Commonwealth Games, 110 yds gold, 54.0 sec; 880 yds relay gold
1968 Mexico City Olympics, 100m gold 52.2 sec (world and Olympic record); 200m gold 1 min 55.2 sec (Olympic record); 400m relay bronze; 800m relay silver
1970 Edinburgh Commonwealth Games, 100m gold; 200m gold; 400m relay gold; 800m relay gold
1973 World Championships, 100m bronze
1974 Christchurch Commonwealth Games, 100m gold, 52.37 sec (Games record); 200m freestyle bronze; 800m relay gold

Mike Wenden's most memorable moment and his best illustration of holding together under stress was in 1973. 'The first World Championships, held in September in Belgrade. In October our second daughter was born and in November, I had my final University exams. So I was under quite a bit of stress! I was training myself as I was living too far from my coach and I came third in the World 100m freestyle, and I thought that was absolutely terrific! The important thing about that was that I finished the race and as I touched the wall, I felt that was a perfect swim for me. The mental approach and preparation couldn't be improved upon. The starting technique, the stroking and the pacing were excellent all the way through, then the beautiful turn and one of those finishes where you reach out and just tip the end of the pool. It was the perfect swim and I was pleased as punch. Of course you get out of the pool and the bloody Press say, "What happened, you only came third . . . You were the Olympic gold medallist five years ago, you still should win!" I would class that swim above winning the Olympics.'

How would he be liked to be remembered? 'It's very difficult in terms of being remembered as an athlete, as there are so many other athletes. To be remembered is probably the important thing! It doesn't matter what you're remembered for.' And as a person? 'As someone who was reasonably honest, and fitted into a community situation without impinging on other people and who tried to get the best out of the talent he had.'

J.P.R. Williams

Rugby Union** (Full back)* and ***Tennis
Born 2 March 1949: Cardiff, South Glamorgan
Specialized: Never
Career highlights:
1967 Won Junior Wimbledon Tennis Championships
1969–81 Played international rugby for Wales; captain in 1978, 1979
1971 Played in winning British Lions tour of New Zealand
1974 Played in winning British Lions tour of South Africa
Grand Slam 1976, 1978
Triple Crown 1969, 1971, 1976–79
International Championship 1969–72, 1975, 1976, 1978, 1979

What was his most memorable moment? 'Winning Junior Wimbledon at tennis was a big thing for me. It didn't really hit me until the next day that I'd won the British Junior Championships [Under 18s] and that was a big event. Then next would be winning the Test tours. The two highs on the rugby field were obviously the two British Lions teams, 1971 and 1974, winning in New Zealand and South Africa because no other side had won a Test series abroad. In fact, I think history is important to the game because it shows how rare that was. New Zealand has never won a Test series in South Africa and South Africa has only won once in New Zealand, so you can see how rare it is. You know, they're the big rugby-playing countries, so obviously to have won those two Test series was a highlight. And the other highlight was getting back into the Welsh side in Centenary year, having been out for a year. It's much harder to get back in, and in the game I play it's never easy. That really was a hard test; I felt I came through it really well.'

How did he best cope under stress? 'I'm renowned mostly for taking high balls and that's a very high stress situation. The ball is in the air for five seconds, sometimes longer, and you know that there are eight forwards pounding down on you. It's very easy to take your eye off the ball. I think that is a stress situation, yet I knew I was going to catch the ball. I can't think of any time I actually dropped the high ball. It's a bit masochistic because I was more determined on catching the ball, than afraid of being hit, because you know what it means, it's inevitable! But I did take precautions to defend myself. Even if you are taking the high ball, there are things you can do, like putting your elbow out, half turning as you catch it, and bringing your knee and your elbow up so that if anyone's going to hit you, it will be on a hard part of your body.'

How would he like to be remembered? 'As somebody who gave 100 per cent all the time and even though I competed flat out, at the end of the day if I lost, it wasn't the end of the world . . . As a really competitive opponent who, when the game was over, you could drink with in the bar afterwards.' And as a person? 'As somebody who was good at whatever he took up, whatever he turned his hand to.'

APPENDICES

I
Birth Order in the Family

The following is the percentage distribution of the achievers' birth order.

Only child	7.9%
First child	28.6%
Second child	41.3%
Third child	17.5%
Fourth child	3.2%
Eighth child	1.6%

There is a bias towards the second born. A survey carried out at the Mexico City Olympics in 1968 showed that nearly 60 per cent of the competitors were second born. However, the follow up study at the Munich Olympics in 1972 had a more usual distribution, but no explanation is readily apparent. The breakdown of the exact position of each is as follows.

Only child	5
First of two	9
First of three	2
First of four	5
First of five	1
First of seven	1
Second of two	6
Second of three	12
Second of four	4
Second of five	2
Second of six	2
Third of three	3
Third of four	8
Fourth of four	2
Eighth of eleven	1

Heather McKay is the odd one at the bottom. She talked about the close relationship that she had, in terms of doing things together, with the brother and two sisters who were the three immediately older than herself. She felt like the fourth of four children, within the larger family. With the exception of Heather, only the first or second born are included from families larger than four.

Here is another way of looking at the same data.

First born of two	9
First born of three	2
First born of four	5
First born of five	1
First born of six	0
First born of seven	1
Second of two	6
Second of three	12
Second of four	4
Second of six	2
Third of three	3
Third of four	8
Fourth of four	2

II
Summary of Dates of Birth

Birth sign		No. of athletes born under sign
Capricorn	Dec 22–Jan 19	2
Aquarius	Jan 20–Feb 18	5
Pisces	Feb 19–Mar 20	7
Aries	Mar 21–Apr 19	2
Taurus	Apr 20–May 20	7
Gemini	May 21–Jun 20	5
Cancer	Jun 21–Jul 22	6
Leo	Jul 23–Aug 22	8
Virgo	Aug 23–Sep 22	5
Libra	Sep 23–Oct 22	6
Scorpio	Oct 23–Nov 21	6
Sagittarius	Nov 22–Dec 21	4

III
Review of Questions

(In the order in which they were asked)

CHILDHOOD AND GROWING UP

- At what age did you start any form of competitive sport?
- Were you always good at sport?
- Were you shy or self-conscious off the field of play?
- Would you call yourself more introverted or extroverted?
- How would you describe your childhood? Was it happy or not? Secure or not?
- What class would you put on your social background?
- Do you consider that you were an early, late or average developer, both physically and emotionally?
- Is there any part of your childhood background which you think helped you to reach your level of success?

PARENTS AND SIBLINGS

- What sports did they do?
- Were religious beliefs or values important to them?
- What attributes would you use to describe your parents?
- What was your relationship like with each of them?
- Were they supportive? Encouraging? Pushing? Competitive? Consistent in their behaviour?
- Did they provide a stable home environment and feeling?
- Did they stress fair play and keeping with the rules? Were their standards and values high?
- Was discipline more verbal or physical?
- Did they have high expectations? If so, in what areas?
- What number were you in the family? Out of how many and what were the sexes?
- Was your relationship with them competitive? How was it generally?

TRAINING

- When did you specialize in your main sport?
- How long and how often did you train at that stage, compared with your peak?
- What aspect did you enjoy most?
- Did you give 100 per cent in training? How often?
- How much do you think intensity made a difference to your success?
- Did you always have a will to train hard?
- Do you think that a willingness to initiate and endure pain played any part in your success?

- What were your dietary habits during training?
- Were you creative or experimenting with your training or technique?
- Do you feel that you sacrificed anything in order to pursue your sport?
- Did you do anything special to get an edge on others?
- Did sport force you to lead an imbalanced life in any way?
- How important to you is a sense of humour? What purpose did it have?
- Were you left-handed/right-handed? Which side was the dominant one?

COMPETITIVENESS

- Were you competitive on your own as a child?
- Did you have trouble passing up a challenge?
- Do you consider yourself to be either assertive or aggressive off the field of play?
- Do you consider that either courage or risk-taking played any part in your sport?
- When did you start setting a goal for the top?
- Did you always think that you were going to achieve at a high level?
- What are your thoughts and feelings on the current drug scene in sport, specifically the use of performance-enhancing drugs?
- Have you ever experimented or been encouraged to experiment with them?
- Would you have performed any better if there had been increased financial incentive?

WINNING

- Did you always have the self-confidence that you could produce your best effort when you asked that of yourself?
- Was the desire not to lose the positive stimulant or was the aim to win stronger?
- Did you ever employ gamesmanship in order to get an edge and if so, where would you draw the line?
- What was your most memorable or valued event or win?

SET BACKS

- Was sickness or injury ever a factor during your career? If so, did it increase or decrease your long term determination to achieve?
- How did you respond to losses, mistakes or other set backs?
- Do you think you read your body well?

ATHLETIC INTELLIGENCE

- To what extent was the mind involved in playing your sport?
- Did you use mental rehearsal, imagery, meditation, inner game, etc.?

- In competition, how would you rate your ability to concentrate on a one to ten scale?
- What was your focus of attention while performing?
- Could you pick actions and movements up quickly?

COACH

- Did you have a significant coach–athlete relationship?
- How would you describe his/her coaching style and attributes?
- What was your relationship with him/her?
- Could you have reached the level you did without a coach?

OTHER RELATIONSHIPS

- Was there any significant other person who helped you to achieve?
- How did you get on with others generally?
- Did either physical or emotional relationships ever affect your performance?
- Did you avoid 'involvement' prior to big competition? Did you distance yourself from others or put yourself into a cocoon?

COPING WITH STRESS

- What did you do to cope with pre-competition stress?
- How did you deal with thoughts of your opponents?
- How did you get the best out of yourself in competition?
- How did you spend the day of competition?
- What is your best example of holding together under stress?

DESTINY

- Are your superstitious?
- Do you consider yourself lucky, to have been at the right place at the right time?
- Do you feel that you control your own destiny?
- Did religious values either through church, prayer or meditation ever have any influence on your sporting life?
- Do you feel that sport was a self-expression for you?
- Do you see yourself as being able to adapt to sudden change during or just prior to competition?
- Was it important what others thought of you and did that change?
- Did you want to please others? If so, who?
- How would you want to be remembered, both as an athlete and as a person?
- Is there anything I've missed that you would like to add?

BIBLIOGRAPHY

1 Alderman, R.B., *Psychological Behaviour in Sport*, Saunders, 1974
2 Arnold, Peter, *Meaning in Movement, Sport and Physical Education*, Heinemann, 1979
3 Assagioli, Roberto, *Psychosynthesis*, Hobbs Dorman, 1965
4 Bach, Richard, *Jonathan Livingston Seagull*, Macmillan, 1970; Pan, 1972
5 Balazs, Eva, 'Psycho-Social Study of Outstanding Female Athletes', *Research Quarterly*, Vol. 46, No. 3, 1975
6 Bloom, Benjamin, *Developing Talent in Young People*, Ballantine, 1985
7 Brightwell, Robin, 'Is your child left-handed? Then you may be bringing up a genius', *The Listener*, 7 Feb., 1985
8 Brooke, J.D., Hamley, E.J. and Stone, P.T., 'Review of Physiological and Mental State Variables that Predict Ability at Bicycle Time Trial Racing', *British Journal of Sports Medicine*, Vol. 7, 1973. PROC. 1970 World Congress of Sports Medicine
9 Carron, Albert, and Chelladurai, P., *Psychological Factors and Athletic Success: An Analysis of Coach–Athlete Interpersonal Behaviour* (Unpublished paper, University of Western Ontario, Canada, 1978)
10 Coakley, Jay, *Sport in Society*, C.V. Mosby, 1978
11 Corcoran, D.W.J., 'Personality and the Inverted U Relationship', *British Journal of Psychology*, No. 56, 1965
12 Cousy, Robert, *The Killer Instinct*, Random House, 1975
13 Dass, Ram, *Grist for the Mill*, Unity, 1977; Bantam, 1979
14 DeVore, S., DeVore, G. and Michaelson, M., *Syber Vision*, Chicago Review Press, 1981
15 DeVore, S., 'Neuro Psychology of Achievement', *Syber Vision Systems Ltd*, San Leandro, California, 1982
16 DuBois, Larry, 'Jackie Stewart', *Playboy*, 1972
17 Easterbrook, J.A., 'The Effect of Emotion, Cue Utilization and Organization of Behavior', *Psychology Review*, Vol. 66, 1959
18 Epstein, Joseph, 'Obsessed with Sport', *Harper's*, July, 1976
19 Fox, Edward, *Sports Physiology*, Saunders College/Holt, Rinehart and Winston, 1979
20 Gallon, Arthur, *Coaching Ideas and Ideals*, Houghton Mifflin, 1980
21 Gallwey, Timothy, *The Inner Game of Tennis*, Random House, 1974
22 Goble, Frank, *The Third Force*, Grossman, 1970; Pocket Book, 1971
23 Hemery, David, *Another Hurdle*, Heinemann, 1976; Taplinger, 1976
24 Hemery, David, *Double Achievers*, A study for Odgens Management Consultants, London, 1985
25 Hingley, Peter, and Cooper, Cary, *The Change Makers*, Harper & Row, 1985
26 Jerome, John, *The Sweet Spot in Time*, Summit, 1980
27 Kane, John, 'Personality, Arousal and Performance', *The International Journal of Sports Psychology*, 1972–1975
28 Leonard, George, *The Ultimate Athlete*, Viking Press, 1974; Avon, 1977

29 Lester, Gary, *Australians at the Olympics*, Lester-Townsend, 1984
30 MacKenzie, Jean, 'Biorhythms', *Science Digest*, August, 1973
31 McIntosh, Peter, *Fair Play*, Heinemann, 1979
32 McNab, Tom, *Flanagan's Run*, Hodder and Stoughton, 1982; Coronet, 1983
33 Malina, Robert; Bouchard, Claude; Shoup, Richard; Demirjian, Arto and Larivière, Georges, 'Age at Menarche, Family Size, and Birth or Order in Athletes at the Montreal Olympic Games, 1976', *Medicine and Science in Sports*, Vol. 11, No. 4, 1979
34 Maltz, Maxwell, *Psycho-Cybernetics*, Grosset & Dunlop, 1970; Bantam, 1973
35 Martens, Rainer, *Social Psychology and Physical Activity*, Harper & Row, 1975
36 Maslow, Abraham, *Towards a Psychology of Being*, Litton Educational Press, 1962
37 Maslow, Abraham, *The Further Reaches of Human Nature*, Easlen, 1971; Viking, 1972
38 Mathews, Donald, and Fox, Edward, *The Psychological Basis of Physical Education & Athletics*, W.B. Saunders, 1976
39 May, Rollo, *Man's Search for Himself*, W.W. Norton, 1953; Delta, 1978
40 May, Rollo, *The Courage to Create*, W.W. Norton, 1975; Bantam, 1975
41 May, Rollo, *The Silent Pulse*, W.W. Norton, 1978; Wildwood House, 1979
42 Mourie, Graham, *Captain*, Arthur Barker, 1983
43 Murphy, Michael, *Gold in the Kingdom*, Viking, 1972
44 Murphy, Michael and White, Rhea, *The Psychic Side of Sports*, Addison-Wesley, 1978
45 Nideffer, Robert M., *The Inner Athlete*, Cromwell, 1976
46 Ogilvie, Bruce, 'The Unconscious Fear of Success', *Quest 10*, May, 1968
47 Oxendine, Joseph, *Psychology of Motor Learning*, Prentice-Hall, 1968
48 Palmer, Arnold, *Go for Broke*, Kimber, 1974
49 Patmore, Angela, *Playing on their Nerves*, Stanley Paul, 1979
50 Peters, Thomas and Waterman, Robert, *In Search of Excellence*, Harper & Row, 1982
51 Rhys, Chris, *The Courage Book of Sporting Heroes 1884–1984*, Stanley Paul, 1984
52 Richards, Bob, *Heart of a Champion*, Fleming H. Revell, 1973
53 Ronan, Donald, 'Applied Psycho-Cybernetics, or A Mental Training Program for Swimmers', *Swimming Technique*, Fall, 1977
54 Rushall, Brent, *Psyching in Sport*, Pelham, 1979
55 Ryle, J.C., *The Upper Room*, Banner of Truth, 1978
56 Sagan, Carl, *The Dragons of Eden, Speculations on the Evolution of Human Intelligence*, Random House, 1977
57 Singer, Robert, 'Motivation in Sport', *International Journal of Sports Psychology*, 8, 1977
58 Smith, Adam, 'Sport is a Western Yoga', *Psychology Today*, October, 1975
59 Spielberger, C. 'Trait-State Anxiety and Motor Behavior', *Journal of Motor Behavior*, Vol. 3, 1971

60 Thommen, George, *Is This Your Day?*, Crown, 1973
61 Tutko, Thomas and Tosi, Umberto, *Sports Psyching*, J.P. Tarcher, 1976
62 Vanek, Miroslav and Cratty, Bryant, *Psychology and the Superior Athlete*, Macmillan, 1970
63 Weiner, Bernard, *Achievement Motivation and Attribution Theory*, General Learning Corporation, 1977
64 Weitzberg, Norman and Altman, Kerry, 'Enhancing Sport Performance,' *Convention of the California State Psychological Association*, 1978
65 White, Cyril, 'Success in Sport: A Statement for Discussion', *Olympic Council of Ireland Seminar*, April, 1974
66 Wilson, Colin, *New Pathways in Psychology*, Taplinger, 1972; Signet, 1974
67 Zaichkowsky, Leonard and White, Wesley, *Stress Management for Sport*, The American Alliance for Health, Physical Education, Recreation and Dance, 1982

INDEX

Note: Bold type indicates athlete's personal biography.